当代国际商务文化阅读丛书

Readings for Modern International Business Culture

【英汉对照】

路易斯·波森的朋克摇滚

——『商界精英』篇

The Punk Rock of Louis Posen

Business Elites

吴斐　编著

武汉大学出版社

WUHAN UNIVERSITY PRESS

图书在版编目(CIP)数据

路易斯·波森的朋克摇滚:"商界精英"篇:英汉对照/吴斐编著.—武汉:武汉大学出版社,2016.5
当代国际商务文化阅读丛书
书名原文:The Punk Rock of Louis Posen:Business Elites
ISBN 978-7-307-11773-0

Ⅰ.路… Ⅱ.吴… Ⅲ.企业家—生平事迹—世界—英、汉
Ⅳ.K815.38

中国版本图书馆 CIP 数据核字(2013)第 224204 号

责任编辑:郭园园 金 军 责任校对:汪欣怡 版式设计:韩闻锦

出版发行:**武汉大学出版社** (430072 武昌 珞珈山)
(电子邮件:cbs22@whu.edu.cn 网址:www.wdp.com.cn)
印刷:武汉中远印务有限公司
开本:880×1230 1/32 印张:9.75 字数:213 千字
版次:2016 年 5 月第 1 版 2016 年 5 月第 1 次印刷
ISBN 978-7-307-11773-0 定价:28.00 元

前　言

　　人类社会进入 21 世纪后，国家间的商务往来更加频繁，商务交际手段随着互联网的诞生和电子信息的进步日新月异，国际化企业的文化和理念千差万别，商务话题的表达和沟通能力无疑是人们所遇到的最大障碍。在我们熟知的生活英语、学术英语之外，商务英语不仅是我国目前从事或即将从事涉外商务人员英语实际应用能力不可多得的辅助工具，更是商务工作人员在这个国际化的高科技时代商务竞争能力、外贸业务素质和英语水平的重要体现。《当代国际商务文化阅读》（英汉对照）丛书以从事国际商务活动所必需的语言技能为经、以各种商务活动的具体情景作纬，将商务精神和商务元素巧妙融合，展示时尚而又经典的商务文化世界流行风，为广大读者提供一套语言规范、内容新颖、涉及面广、趣味性强、具有实用价值、富于时代精神的读物，既注意解决人们在国际商务环境中遇到不熟悉的专业词汇无法与外国合作者就工作问题交流沟通的难题，又着力解决人们学外语单纯地学语言而缺乏商务专业知识的弊端。

　　《当代国际商务文化阅读》（英汉对照）丛书由 10 个单行本组成：《拥抱新欢亚马逊（Embracing Amazon Service）——电子商务篇

1

（E-Commerce）》、《华尔街梦魇（Nightmare on Wall Street）——商界风云篇（The Business Circles）》、《路易斯·波森的朋克摇滚（The Punk Rock of Louis Posen）——商界精英篇（Business Elites）》、《希波克拉底誓言（Hippocratic Oath）——商务交际篇（Business Communication）》、《强烈的第一印象（A Powerful First Impression）——商务礼仪篇（Business Etiquette）》、《企业帝国继承权之争（Corporate Empires' Grappling with Succession）——商务文化篇（Business Culture）》、《紫色血液（The Purple Blood）——商务心理篇（Business Psychology）》、《多米诺骨牌效应（The Domino Effects）——商务知识篇（Business Knowledge）》、《公开的赌注（Public Stakes）——商务演讲篇（Business Speeches）》、《伊斯特林悖论（The Easterlin Paradox）——感悟财富篇（Comprehension of Wealth）》。　这套丛书的编写旨在帮助读者在国际商务环境下，能够读懂英文的商务信息和商务新闻，并能对某一商务话题的知识有全面透彻的了解，领悟当代时尚商务文化成长的环境和思维方式，提高在全球化高科技时代的商务竞争能力、外贸业务素质和英语交际水平。　丛书中的阅读材料力求做到题材广泛，内容精辟，语言规范，遵循趣味性、知识性和时效性原则，培养读者在商务环境下的英语竞争能力和综合应用能力。　丛书融时代性与经典性为一体，内容经得起时间考验，文字经得起反复咀嚼，保证其可读性。　读者在阅读过程中接收大量的语言输入，为合理组织和娴熟运用英语语言表达自己的思想打下牢固的基础。　丛书的单行本包括以一个主题为中心的 30 篇文章，每篇文章包括题记、英语原文、汉语译文、生词脚注和知识链接。"题记"用丰富生动的语言点评文章的精髓，对文章的内容起到提炼和画龙点睛的作用。"英语原文"主要摘自当代国际主流报纸杂志，具有语言规范、内容新颖、涉及面广、趣味性和时代感等特点。"汉语译文"力求准确流畅，既关注译文的文化语境及其内涵，也重视译文的外延和现当代标志性语言符号。"生词脚注"的难度把握在大学英语六级和研究生英语词汇程度，以帮助读者及时扫清阅读障碍。"知识链接"根据文章内容，或精解一个专业术语，或阐释一种新的商务理念，或介绍叱咤商界的企业或公司，以帮助读者培养游弋商海、运筹帷幄的能力，具备洞悉中西文化的国际视野。

《路易斯·波森的朋克摇滚（The Punk Rock of Louis Posen）——"商界精英"篇（Business Elites）》为读者揭示了商界精英跌宕起伏的人生经历和风云世界的财富传奇。精英是商界的宝贵资源。凯特·鲁德曼和埃迪·厄兰森曾总结出商界精英的四种类型：商界指挥官——魅力超凡、才干出众的领头羊；商界梦想家——高瞻远瞩的追梦人；商界战略家——固执地自以为无所不知的分析天才；商界实干家——能把人逼到墙角的推动者。他们在翻手为云覆手雨的商界群雄逐鹿，寻找各自的发展空间，就好像面对一场孤岛生存的游戏，市场的精英可以一夜之间创造亿万财富的神话，更可以让多年基业荡然无存。商界精英们张扬的个性使他们出类拔萃、绩效非凡，为企业创造着巨大的财富价值。股神巴菲特的投资策略让所有人对他肃然起敬；"华尔街的拿破仑"约翰·皮尔庞特·摩根曾两度使美国经济起死回生；鲍勃·戴蒙德对投资银行业务运筹帷幄的特质铸就了刻意不赶时髦的巴克莱资本的典型风格；孤注一掷的杰夫·贝佐斯将亚马逊网络购物中心缔造成世界上最神秘的网上生命

3

王国；迈克尔·戴尔亲手打造的企业文化创造了新经济时代赚钱最快的纪录；"产业独夫"比尔·盖茨一手缔造了世界信息产业的霸主——微软公司，推动了人类计算机工业的革命；拥有梦幻般传奇经历的苹果电脑公司创始人史蒂夫·保罗·乔布斯的成就和人格魅力影响了一代人和世界，改变了整个计算机硬件和软件产业。本书在遍地精英人士的商海中撷取了几朵浪花，讲述不同领域企业家的辉煌成就、人生经历、精神世界、财富传奇、奋斗历程、价值观念和家庭事业。今天，健康的精英文化正激励着人们在工作中发挥精英优势，与精英共生共荣。阅读全球化经济中的商界精英，让我们跟随时代潮流，追赶掌握市场脉搏、洞悉宏观大势、运筹方寸之间、决胜千里之外的商界领袖的脚步，享受世界流行文化创造的快乐、荣誉、价值和成就感！

作　者

2016 年 1 月

目　　录

目 录

2

目 录

题 记

朋克用简陋的音乐把露骨的叛逆行为提升到了哲学层次，在主观能动性和否定之否定理论的指导下创造了一种扭曲的责任感和边缘文化。美国诗篇式的朋克摇滚已经变身成一种行为艺术，一种思想，甚至是一种人生。"绝望唱片公司"的创始人路易斯·波森就是其中的杰出代表。他在朋克摇滚独立自主的精神和朴实的声音中获得灵感，成功地利用大公司操纵商业运作背景，用"健康向上"的商业流行因素取代朋克摇滚"愤世嫉俗"的本色，运作一个又一个乐队的盈利神话，再将利润投入慈善事业，并加入"社会企业家"的新潮流。

The Punk Rock of Louis Posen

After Hopeless Records started bringing in cash, founder Louis Posen began spinning profits into charity and joined a new trend in "social entrepreneurship".

Louis Posen's dream of becoming a movie director was coming to an end. The 19-year-old was studying film at California State University at Northridge in 1991 when he was diagnosed with retinitis pigmentosa, a degenerative① eye disease that leads to blindness. Looking for another creative endeavor, he bought a book called *How to Run an Independent Record Label* and launched Hopeless Records from his garage. Today, Hopeless is profitable, employs nine people, and will gross. $ 5 million annually. Boosting revenues and earnings every year in an industry barraged② by digital piracy and slumping sales is an accomplishment. But Posen has another hit on his hands: He figured out a way to spin a sizable chunk of the money his company generates into philanthropy. "Although we didn't really plan it," Posen says. "We're part of this whole movement of social entrepreneurship."

The notes of inspiration came seven years ago, after a compilation of the label's artists called Hopelessly Devoted to You Too sold more than

---

① degenerative [di'dʒenərətiv] *adj.* 退化的
② barrage ['bærɑːʒ] *vt.* 以密集火力攻击

路易斯·波森的
朋克摇滚

"绝望唱片公司"刚刚开始赚钱之时，其创始人路易斯·波森随即就将利润投入慈善事业，加入"社会企业家"的新潮流。

路易斯·波森成为电影导演的梦想已经宣布结束了。 这位19岁的年轻人1991年在诺森瑞吉的加利福尼亚州立大学攻读电影专业时被诊断患有色素性视网膜炎，这是一种将导致失明的退化性眼疾。 他在寻找另一种创造性奋斗时，买了一本名为《如何运行独立唱片公司》的书，于是他在车库里创建了"绝望唱片公司"。 如今，公司已经盈利，拥有9名雇员，年利润高达500万美元。 在数字盗版猖獗和销售低迷的行业，能够做到每年大幅度增加税收和收入是一种成就。 不过，目前波森正在做另一件大事：他打算从公司拿出一大笔钱投资慈善事业。 波森说："虽然我们还没有对此做出真正的计划，但我们属于社会企业家整体运作的一部分。"

这种想法的灵感来自7年前标签艺人汇编的专辑"对你专情也绝望"，当年该专辑销售量达100 000多张。 波森领悟到了数字的力量。 他创造了另一个标签"边缘城市"，这个标签是单词"津贴"的辞藻游戏，也是对公司所专长的朋克摇滚乐的亚文化戏谑。

100,000 copies. Posen realized there was strength in numbers. He created another label called Sub City, a play on the word subsidy and on the punk rock subculture in which the company specializes. Then he offered his artists the option of releasing their records on Hopeless or Sub City. If they choose Sub City, 5% of the gross goes to charity. On a $14 compact disk that's about 70 cents, but those dimes add up. Posen recently celebrated what he calls a "million-dollar milestone," having given more than $1 million to charity. Half of the money comes from the artists. royalties, the other from Posen's profits. Sub City also sponsors tours from which 10% of ticket sales go to various causes. The label works with more than 50 charities, including causes such as fighting blindness and music education in schools. Not every band chooses to participate. Posen figures about 3 of the 10 releases his company puts out each year are on the Sub City label. "Some artists prefer to give on their own," he says. "Some can't afford it."

Posen learned to be creative from a business standpoint early on. Punk rock isn't a huge market. His top selling album — from a band called Avenged Sevenfold — has sold 400,000 copies in the U.S. That's 100,000 shy of what's needed to qualify as a gold record. Posen generates extra revenue for his company by keeping the rights to sell a couple of merchandise designs from each of his bands, such as a T-shirt or a poster. He also takes a fee for licensing their music to television shows and movies. It's a business model many major labels are now pursuing. "Louis has the spirit of an entrepreneur and a heart of gold," says Mitchell Wolk, an executive at Warner Music Group (WMG), which helps distribute Posen's albums. "He is truly an inspiration to us all."

Marketing punk rock is difficult. The segmentisn't① driven by hit

---

① segment ['segmənt] n. 部分

然后，他让旗下艺人自己选择唱片专辑放在"绝望"或"边缘城市"的网站上。 如果他们选择"边缘城市"，5% 的收益划归慈善机构。 一张 14 美元的光盘大约 70 美分，但这些硬币也会积少成多。波森最近举行了他称之为"百万美元里程碑"的庆祝活动，给慈善机构捐献了 100 多万美元。 资金一半来自艺术家版税，另一半来自波森的盈利。"边缘城市"还赞助了旅游业，10% 的门票折扣收入用于各种事业的发展。 该标签与 50 多家慈善机构合作共事，包括治疗失明和学校的音乐教育。 并不是每支乐队都选择参与这项事业。波森认为，公司每年十分之三的发行量都放在"边缘城市"的标签下。 他认为，"有些艺人更喜欢独立行事，有些艺人则负担不起"。

波森很早以前就学会了从商业的角度寻求创新。 朋克摇滚乐并不是一个巨大的市场。 他最畅销的签售专辑来自 A7X 乐队，已在美国售出 40 万张。 这个事实足以使那些销售 10 万张、取得金唱片资格的光碟蒙羞。 波森为每支乐队保留了数个商品设计的销售权，如T 恤衫或海报，从而为公司创造了额外的收入。 他还采取收费方式，为他们的音乐制作电视节目和电影发放许可证。 这是现在许多主要的唱片公司正在推行的商业模式。 帮助波森发放密纹唱片的华纳音乐集团（WMG）现任执行总裁米切尔·沃尔克认为，"路易斯具有企业家的精神和金子般的心，他是我们所有人真正的精神领袖"。

营销朋克摇滚乐非常困难。 这种音乐并不像畅销单曲或广播唱片等大多数音乐业务一样受到热捧。 波森和他的团队必须相应地提

singles or radio airplay like most of the music business. Instead, Posen and his team must build awareness for their artists through appearances in record stores, on social networking sites such as MySpace and PureVolume, and through relationships with other companies looking to stay in tune with youth culture such as the Hot Topic (HOTT) retail chain. For example, Hopeless is releasing the new album from All Time Low, a pop-punk quartet from suburban Baltimore. The company has a marketing alliance with Hollister, an Abercrombie & Fitch (ANF) spin-off that will sell the CD in its stores and stream All Time Low's music on its Web site. "We call ourselves a record label but we've never looked at ourselves as being in the record business, " says Posen, dressed casually in jeans and Vans sneakers. "It's a lifestyle."

Left with only the ability to see light and dark in one eye, Posen takes a cab to work most mornings. His wife picks him up at the end of the day. At the office, he uses a software program called Jaws that reads his e-mails and Excel spreadsheets aloud. With profits from the business, Posen recently bought a 5,500-square-foot warehouse in the Los Angeles suburb of Van Nuys. On a morning, he was bumping into walls and furniture. "We moved in two weeks ago, and I'm still getting used to the place, " he says. Scientific studies have shown that the blind can become suburb musicians, their ears compensating for the loss of sight, à la Stevie Wonder and Ray Charles. "Not me, " Posen says. "I've tried to play guitar, drums, everything." Posen has more than made up for his lack of musical ability, finding other ways to make music and give back to others at the same time. "Losing your sight is not something anyone would choose, " he says. "But there are worse things that can happen to you."

(833 words)

高艺人的曝光率，让他们的专辑频繁地出现在唱片商店、MySpace 和 PureVolume 之类的社交网站上，与其他寻求青春文化的公司如热门话题（HOTT）零售连锁店等保持一致。 例如，"绝望唱片公司"正在发行来自巴尔的摩市郊的流行朋克四重唱组合"All Time Low"创作的新专辑。 公司已经与"阿贝克隆比 & 费奇"旗下的子公司"霍利斯特"组成营销联盟，在其商店销售光盘，在其网站上源源不断地推出"All Time Low"的音乐。 身着休闲牛仔裤和万斯运动鞋的波森说，"我们自称为唱片公司，但我们从来没有认为自己存在于唱片的商业领域。 这就是一种生活方式"。

波森的一只眼睛仅能看见光线，另一只眼睛什么也看不见，他大多在早上乘坐出租车上班。 妻子在一天结束时来接他回家。 他在办公室使用一种叫做"大白鲨"的发声软件程序，帮助他阅读电子邮件和 Excel 电子数据表。 波森最近用经商收入在洛杉矶郊区的梵奈斯买下了一个 5 500 平方英尺的大货栈。 一天早上，他撞到了墙壁和家具上。 他说，"我们两周前刚搬来，我还在熟悉这里的环境"。 科学研究已经表明，盲人可以成为边缘音乐家，他们的耳朵能补偿损失的视力，史提夫·汪达和雷·查尔斯就是范例。 波森说，"那可不是我。 我已经尝试着演奏吉他、击鼓以及做所有力所能及的事情"。 波森更加努力地提高自己的音乐才能，寻求其他方式创作音乐，同时回报他人。 他说，"失去视力不是谁都愿意做出的选择，但更糟糕的事情有可能就发生在你身上"。

知识链接

MySpace 聚友网（MySpace. com）成立于 2003 年 9 月，是一个精彩纷呈的在线社区，全球第二大社交网站。它为全球用户提供了一个集交友、个人信息分享、即时通讯等多种功能于一体的互动平台。聚友网现已拥有超过 2 亿名注册用户，并正在以每天新增 23 万注册用户的速度继续增长，开通了加拿大、澳大利亚、新西兰、法国、英国、德国、意大利、西班牙、日本、印度、中国等 20 个国家或地区的分站点。

PureVolume 是一个发现和推广新音乐和艺术家的网站，2003 年推出。网站上每一位艺术家的配置文件通常包含基本信息、更新、照片、音乐节目和流量。艺术家们的选择使各自的歌曲可以免费下载。听众和歌迷也可以建立个人档案，与艺术家互动，以及跟踪和共享他们喜欢的音乐。

All Time Low 是一支来自美国马里兰州的流行朋克乐队，成立于 2003 年。乐队成员包括主唱亚历山大·加斯卡斯，吉他手杰克·巴拉卡特，贝司手扎克·梅里克，鼓手瑞恩·道森，乐队的名字源自新兴荣耀乐队"头对头碰撞"这首歌的歌词，在 Myspace 他们拥有超高的人气。

A&F（***Abercrombie & Fitch***） 阿贝克隆比 & 费奇是美国的休闲服饰品牌，但大家更喜欢直接简称：A&F，或昵称小麋鹿。它是一个在美国青少年心目中极富影响力的超流行服饰品牌，旗下共有 Abercrombie & Fitch、Abercrombie Kids、Hollister、Ruehl、Ezra Fitch 五个子品牌。A&F 衣服的有趣之处在于创意几乎每季都在改变。A&F 广告全是采用年轻人喜欢的音乐、体育运动等形式，表现 A&F 服饰的内涵。

题 记

　　卡洛斯·斯利姆·埃卢生于 1941 年，1962 年毕业于墨西哥国立自治大学土木工程系。20 世纪 80 年代，他着手收购了一些濒临破产的烟草企业和餐饮连锁公司，并逐步使其扭亏为盈，成为那个时期最成功的商人之一。20 世纪 90 年代，在墨西哥国有企业私有化的浪潮中，身为黎巴嫩移民之子的埃卢买下了墨西哥的电话公司，并成功地把这个负债累累的国企打造成为摇钱树。尽管有人把埃卢视为墨西哥的民族骄傲，但更多人仍然在指责他通过垄断聚敛财富，阻碍国家经济正常发展，侵害消费者利益。他们认为，埃卢是墨西哥贫富差距悬殊、缺乏竞争机制的社会矛盾的最好体现。

A latter-day Latin American J.P. Morgan

Portly① and often puffing a cigar, Slim could pass for a latter-day Latin American J.P. Morgan. But with his dominant stakes in everything from phones to finance, his business profile more closely resembles that of John D. Rockefeller, who likewise thrived in a loosely regulated environment. Though even in current dollars Rockefeller's wealth pales in comparison to Slim's: At his death in 1937, Rockefeller was worth $ 20.3 billion, representing one fifty-second of 1937 U.S. GDP. By the late 1980s Slim was one of Mexico's most successful businessmen. When the government put the state-owned telephone company up for sale, Slim jumped. He partnered with now AT&T to buy 20% of the company in late 1990 for about $ 2 billion — a fair price, based on other phone companies, market values at the time. What rankled would-be competitors of TelMex, including U.S. long-distance companies, were the terms of the privatization: Slim and company got what amounted to a seven-year guarantee of monopoly status at a time when phone companies around the world had the money to expand into new markets.

"I remember there was a time when the value of his enterprises was

---

① portly ['pɔːtli] *adj.* 肥胖的

现代拉丁美洲的
摩根大通

　　大腹便便、常常叼支雪茄的斯利姆被认为是现代拉丁美洲的摩根大通。 但他的商业形象更接近约翰·D. 洛克菲勒，因为他同样拥有上至电话、下至金融等一切占主导地位的股份。 洛克菲勒也是在松散的管理环境中茁壮成长起来的公司。 但即使以目前的美元计算，洛克菲勒的财富与斯利姆相比仍然相形见绌：洛克菲勒 1937 年去世时，财富总值 203 亿美元，相当于 1937 年美国国内生产总值的五十二分之一。 20 世纪 80 年代末，斯利姆成为墨西哥最成功的商人之一。 当政府要出售国有电话公司时，斯利姆站了出来。 他与现在的美国电话电报公司联手，在 20 世纪 90 年代末以 20 亿美元购买了公司 20% 的股份，相对于当时其他电话公司的市场价值，这是个公平的价格。 包括美国长途电话公司在内的墨西哥全球电信公司的竞争对手最终耿耿于怀的是私有化的条件：斯利姆和公司一次性得到长达 7 年的垄断地位，总额相当于全世界电话公司用来开发新市场的资金。

　　卡洛斯·斯利姆·埃卢最小的儿子帕特里克回忆说："我记得有段时间企业价值非常低。" 时值 20 世纪 80 年代初，墨西哥陷入大规模金融危机的深渊。 老斯利姆定期召集三个未成年的儿子，给他们

very low, " recalls Patrick, the youngest son of Carlos Slim Heluu. It was the early 1980s, and Mexico was in the depths of a massive financial crisis. Periodically the elder Slim would round up his three teenage sons for an economics lesson. Sitting them down in the living room of the family home, Slim would produce a single handwritten list. One line would show, for instance, how a Mexican insurance company was selling for far less than a similar American insurer. Another would show that compared with European candy or cigarette makers, Mexican manufacturers were drastically undervalued. "It was a very, very long time ago, " says Patrick, "but I absolutely remember him teaching us at an early age." For Slim, a onetime math instructor, this was no mere academic exercise. Yes, he wanted to instill in his sons the same lesson his father — a Lebanese immigrant who started acquiring real estate in Mexico City during the Revolution of 1910 — taught him: Though Mexico will have its ups and downs, don't ever count the country out. But Slim wasn't just teaching, he was buying. He spent $ 55 million on an insurance company. He took a stake in retailer Sanborns, and invested in a hotel chain.

Now those early investments are paying off big time. His three heirs — Carlos Jr., 40; Marco Antonio, 39; and Patrick, 38, run day-to-day operations at various Slim businesses and are increasingly making strategic decisions, while their father, Slim has amassed a $ 59 billion fortune. This number puts him just ahead of perennial No. 1, Microsoft founder Bill Gates, whose net worth is estimated to be at least $ 58 billion. But Gates is selling off his single greatest source of wealth, Microsoft stock, to fund his foundation, while Slim's fortune is growing

讲解经济学的知识。 斯利姆经常让他们坐在家中的客厅，拿出一个手写的清单。 例如，一行记录可能表明，墨西哥保险公司的销售如何远低于类似的美国保险公司；另一行记录则显示，与欧洲糖果或香烟制造商相比，墨西哥制造商被大大低估了。 帕特里克说，"那是很久很久以前的事了，但我绝对记得他很早就开始教导我们"。斯利姆曾是个数学教师，这可不只是学术经历。 是的，他想把父亲曾教给他的理念灌输给儿子。 他父亲是个黎巴嫩移民，早在 1910年墨西哥城革命时期就开始收购房地产。 他父亲教导他说：虽然墨西哥也会经历兴衰沉浮，但它仍然是一个充满希望的国家。 斯利姆不仅仅只是教导，他也在付诸行动购买。 他在一家保险公司花了5 500万美元。 他购买了桑伯恩零售商的股份，投资了一家连锁酒店。

如今是这些早期投资获取丰厚回报的大好时机。 他的三个继承人——40 岁的小卡洛斯、39 岁的马科·安东尼奥、38 岁的帕特里克，打理着斯利姆事业的各种日常业务，越来越多地制定战略决策。 而他们的父亲斯利姆已经积累了 590 亿美元的财富。 这一数字使他正好领先于曾经的第一名——微软创始人比尔·盖茨，其净资产估计至少有 580 亿美元。 但盖茨廉价卖清了他单一的最大财富来源——微软股票，以资助他的基金会，而斯利姆的财富却以惊人的速度增长。 他的净资产年均上扬 120 亿美元，家人的财产占墨西哥年度国内生产总值的 5% 以上，斯利姆控股的公司占墨西哥博尔萨或证券交易所 4 220 亿美元中的三分之一。

现代拉丁美洲的摩根大通不是一个值得尊敬的名称。 这个称呼最早出现于 20 世纪 90 年代初，当时很多墨西哥人希望私有化创造

at a stunning clip. His net worth jumped $ 12 billion annually, his family's holdings represent more than 5% of Mexico's gross domestic product, and Slim-controlled companies make up one-third of the $ 422 billion Mexican Bolsa①, or stock exchange.

A latter-day Latin American J.P. Morgan is not a reverential② term. Many Mexicans hoped privatization, which began in the early 1990s, would create competition and drive prices down drastically. That hasn't happened. "Slim is one of a dozen fat cats in Mexico who impede③ that country's growth because they run monopolies or oligopolies," says Grayson. "The Mexican economy is highly inefficient, and it is losing its competitive standing vis-a-vis other countries because of people like Slim." "The accusations are not well. founded," Carlos Jr. fires back during an interview. He then pulls out an analyst's report showing how the average price of long-distance phone service in Mexico compares with that in other countries. Mexico is third cheapest, according to the report, behind the U.S. and Finland. Wooing the public isn't exactly a favorite activity for the Slims. "I think sometimes when you are successful in business," says Slim in heavily accented English, "you have others trying to turn public opinion against you because they are trying to compete with you." Slim, however, is beginning to court public opinion, pledging earlier to increase the size of his charitable foundations. Meanwhile, his sons are doing what the Slims do best: making more money.

---

① Mexican Bolsa 墨西哥股票交易所
② reverential [ˌrevəˈrenʃəl] *adj.* 表示尊敬的
③ impede [imˈpiːd] *vt.* 阻碍

14

竞争、并推动价格大幅下跌。 但这并没有发生。 格雷森认为，"斯利姆是墨西哥十几个肥猫中的一只，他们阻碍了国家的经济发展，因为他们实行了垄断或寡头卖主垄断。 墨西哥的经济效率极低，就因为斯利姆之流，墨西哥与其他国家相比正在失去竞争地位"。 而小卡洛斯在接受采访时还击道："指控是没有足够依据的。"他接着拿出一份分析师报告，说明墨西哥长途电话的平均价格与其他国家的比较。 根据这份报告，墨西哥低廉的费用位列第三，仅次于美国和芬兰。 争取公众的支持并不是斯利姆喜欢的事情。 斯利姆用浓重的英国口音申辩说，"我认为，有时你做买卖赚钱了，就有人设法主导公众舆论反对你，因为他们试图与你竞争"。 不管怎样，斯利姆开始博取公众的舆论支持，承诺尽快扩大他的慈善基金会。 与此同时，他的儿子正在为斯利姆做到最好：赚更多的钱。

任何期望在墨西哥城找到斯利姆金融帝国纪念碑的人总会失望地离开，这座纪念碑就是矗立在空中隐约闪烁的墨西哥电信塔。 事实上，拉丁美洲最大的无线服务供应商坐落在一个经过改装的轮胎厂里面。 节俭和财富的毗邻真是出人意料。 大厅之外是一个临时代用的艺术画廊，从苏玛雅博物馆循环挑选借来的绘画占据显著地位，苏玛雅博物馆是斯利姆融资、并以他妻子的名字命名的艺术博物馆，他的妻子于 1999 年去世。 房间有点破旧。 这里光线暗淡，混杂着淡淡的烟味，几个大板条箱靠在一面墙壁上，房间中央有一张可折叠的桌子。 斯利姆的女婿兼发言人阿图·埃利亚斯·阿尤布实事求是地说，"斯利姆先生有时喜欢在这里吃午餐"。 这就是斯利姆著名的节俭风格：他过去经常戴一块廉价的计算器手表出席商务会议，这一风气在全公司蔓延开来。 多年前，他为自己的联合大企

Anyone expecting to find monuments to the Slim financial empire in Mexico City—a gleaming TelMex tower jutting out of the skyline— would leave disappointed. In fact, Latin America's largest provider of wireless services, is housed in a converted tire factory. The juxtaposition of austerity① and wealth can be quite odd. Just beyond the lobby is a makeshift② art gallery that features a rotating selection of paintings on loan from the Museo Soumaya, a Slim-financed fine-arts museum named after his wife, who died in 1999. The room is a bit shabby. It is poorly lit and smells faintly of cigarettes; several large crates are propped against one of the walls, and there's also a folding table in the center of the room. Arturo Elias Ayub, Slim's son-in-law and spokesman, says matter-of-factly, "Mr. Slim sometimes likes to eat his lunch here." The famous Slim thrift — he used to show up for business meetings wearing a cheap calculator watch — extends across the entire company. Years ago he wrote "official principles" for Grupo Carso, his industrial conglomerate, which are distributed annually to all employees. One tenet③ translates into English as follows: "Maintain austerity in prosperous times (in times when the cow is fat with milk); it accelerates corporate development and avoids the need for drastic change in times of crisis."

(937 words)

---

① austerity [ɔs'teriti] *n.* 节俭
② makeshift ['meikʃift] *adj.* 临时的
③ tenet ['tenit] *n.* 宗旨

业卡苏集团写下了每年颁布给每位雇员的"正式原则"。 其中一条原则翻译成英文如下："繁荣时（奶牛肥壮有奶时）厉行节约。 节俭加速了企业的发展，避免危机袭来时的不测之风云。"

知识链接

J. P. Morgan 约翰·皮尔庞特·摩根（John Pierpont Morgan）是"华尔街的拿破仑"，他曾两度使美国经济起死回生。他有一句至理名言："有攀升，就有下跌；有过热，就有疲软。"历史上的摩根财团是世界上最可畏的金融机构之一，它由美国银行家乔治·皮博迪于 1838 年创办于伦敦，后由摩根家族继承过来，迁至纽约后声名鹊起。现时的摩根大通集团（JPMorgan Chase & Amp；Co.，NYSE）于 2000 年由大通曼哈顿银行及 J. P. 摩根公司合并而成，并于 2004 年与 2008 年分别收购芝加哥第一银行和美国著名投资银行贝尔斯登和华盛顿互惠银行，成为仅次于美国银行的美国第二大金融服务机构，业务遍及 50 多个国家，包括投资银行、金融交易处理、投资管理、商业金融服务、个人银行等。

John D. Rockefeller 约翰·D. 洛克菲勒（1839.7.8 — 1937.5.23）美国实业家、超级资本家，美孚石油公司（标准石油）的创办人。

TelMex 墨西哥 Carso 全球电信公司（Carso Global Telecom）设于墨西哥城，是一家国际水平的电信公司，针对其客户提供各种电信解决方案，包括：地方和长途通信服务、无线通信，用于录影、音像和资料的多媒体网路、网路工程、数字式无线网路接入和网际网路，主要业务范围涵盖墨西哥、美国、波多黎各和巴西。

题　记

　　巴菲特被誉为有史以来最伟大的投资家，他依靠股票、外汇市场的投资，成为世界顶级富翁。友人认为他今生从来没正正经经地工作过一天，每天在办公室的时间就是在度假，在继续跳着踢踏舞永葆青春。然而，他的投资策略让所有人对他肃然起敬：他在 20 年前就洞察到哪只股票将要创造奇迹。他认为市场既是一部短期的投票计算器，又是一台长期的称重器，他在这里赚得盆满钵满，当仁不让地传递着"当别人疯狂的时候我恐惧"、"市场总是与大多数人的想法相反"的经营理念。巴菲特职业生涯中持之以恒的品质、简朴的个人生活和慷慨的慈善捐赠给世人留下了一笔丰厚宝贵的遗产。

A Bread-and-butter Realist
— Warren Buffett

Warren Buffett, the newly anointed① "world's richest man", claims he has never been to bed with an ugly woman, but admits: "I've sure woken up with a few." In truth, the famously conservative Buffett was quoting a favorite country and western song at the time and, as usual, he was talking about his investments, not the women in his life. His personal fortune swelled by $10bn in a year to more than $62bn, he has dwelt among the world's richest for decades. What is remarkable about Buffett and his wealth, though, is his steadfastness in its accumulation. He is a plodding tortoise in a world of racing hares, whose slow and steady tactics have beaten every boom and bust Wall Street has endured in 30 years. He claims not to have one. And, yes, you or I should be able to do what he has spent his lifetime doing — that is, making a lot of money by making a lot of very sound investments. He is an entirely self-made man about whom nobody ever seems to have a bad word to say. It's a bit sickening, really.

The middle child of three, Buffett was born on 30 August 1930. His

---

① anoint [ə'nɔint] vt. 冠以……称呼

实用现实主义者——
沃伦·巴菲特

新晋世界首富沃伦·巴菲特声称,他从不和丑陋的女人上床,但他承认:"有少数人却让我保持清醒。"事实上,以保守著称的巴菲特引用的是当时一首非常受欢迎的西部乡村歌曲中的一句歌词,像往常一样,他谈论的是投资而不是他生命中的女人。 他的个人财富在一年中从 100 亿美元增加到 620 亿美元,几十年来一直位居世界最富有者的行列。 然而,有关巴菲特及其财富最引人注目的是他在人生积累中持之以恒的态度。 在这个竞争激烈的世界中,他是一只缓慢爬行的"乌龟",三十年来,他缓慢而稳健的策略使他在华尔街经济繁荣和萧条的交替中稳操胜券。 他声称成功没有秘密。 当然,我或你也能够做他一生所从事的工作,即通过许许多多的理性投资赚钱。 他完全是自学成才,任何人似乎都不会贬低这一点。这真是令人不可思议。

巴菲特出生于 1930 年 8 月 30 日,三个孩子中的老二。 他的父亲霍华德出身于杂货商家庭,他通过开创自己的事业成为内布拉斯加州的一个小镇股票经纪人。 沃伦 11 岁时已经开始在外赚钱,他和一个朋友挨家挨户推销冰镇饮料。 他俩开发了一项挑选赛马胜者的计算系统,用推销饮料赚来的利润编制了一种叫做"马童精英"

father, Howard, came from a family of grocers but set himself up in business as a small-town stockbroker in Nebraska. At the age of 11, Warren was already out to make a profit, selling fizzy drinks door-to-door with a friend. The pair developed an arithmetical system for picking winning race horses and set up a tip sheet called Stable Boy Selections with their drinks profits. Warren was an earnest child. He filed his first tax return aged just 13 in 1943, listing his bicycle — used on the drinks delivery round — as a deductible expense.

The family moved to Washington, D.C., a few years later, as Buffett's father was elected to the US Congress, but young Warren did not rest on his laurels①. Like a lot of kids of his age, he donned the customary newsboy cap and took to hawking papers in the wealthy Washington suburbs. Buffett added magazines and comics to his bag on those days so he could offer something extra to the servants or the lady of the house. Again, he didn't fritter② away his earnings, but invested what he made in pinball machines that he leased to local barbers' shops. Most people in D. C. took the Washington Post, still the American capital's favoured journal, and Buffett grew to love the paper. Even though he was only one of hundreds of delivery boys, he managed to strike up relationships with the paper's management and many years later its owner Katharine Graham.

In 1973, Buffett bought a large shareholding in the Washington

---

① laurels [ˈlɔːrəlz] n. 荣耀
② fritter [ˈfritə] vi. 挥霍

的内情报告。 沃伦是一个非常认真的孩子。 1943 年，年仅 13 岁的巴菲特第一次填写了纳税申报单，将用于推销饮料的自行车列为可减免的开支。

几年后，由于巴菲特的父亲当选为美国国会议员，全家搬到华盛顿特区，但小巴菲特并没有啃老本。 像许多他这个年纪的孩子一样，他穿着报童的衣服，在富裕的华盛顿郊区沿街叫卖报纸。 他还增购了当时的杂志和漫画，向佣人或主妇提供额外服务。 此外，他没有挥霍自己的收入，而是把钱投在弹球游戏机上，然后租给当地理发店。 华盛顿特区的大部分人都购买《华盛顿邮报》，它仍然是美国首都最畅销的报纸，巴菲特逐渐喜欢上这份报纸。 虽然他只是许许多多报童中的一个，但他设法与报纸的管理者、多年后成为业主的卡瑟林·格拉汉姆建立了联系。

1973 年，巴菲特购买了《华盛顿邮报》的大部分股权，时至今日他仍持有这些股权，并是伯克希尔·哈撒韦控股公司的主要投资之一。 这只股票已经增值 100 多倍，是巴菲特具有代表性的投资策略。《巴菲特：一个美国资本家的成功之道》的作者罗杰·莱温斯坦认为，"《华盛顿邮报》的股票是巴菲特持有时间最长的一支，真正代表了他的持之以恒，就其个人品格而言，理解他的关键是做任何事情都要坚持不懈"。 90 年代网络繁荣时期，人们认为巴菲特错过了从中获利的机会。 他拒绝与成千上万家不可靠的网络公司中的任何一家接触，这些公司设法说服投资者投入上亿的美元，然后却迅速倒闭。 巴菲特不理解竟然有人将他的做法归类于"遗漏"。 其实投资前他就已经洞晓一切。 在"戈戈舞"流行的 60 年代，他喜欢称之为时代，尽管他周围的人都在投资最新的高科技新发明和流行

Post, which he still holds today, as one of the central investments in his Berkshire Hathaway holding company. It has increased in value more than 100 times and is typical of a Buffett tip. "The Washington Post is the stock he has held the longest," says Roger Lowenstein, author of Buffett: The Making of an American Capitalist. "And really it typifies his constancy. The key to understanding him as a man is that he is so constant in everything he does." Buffett was written off in the Nineties for missing out on the dotcom boom. He didn't touch any of the thousands of fly-by-night internet companies that managed to convince investors to part with billions of dollars before promptly going bust. That anyone can class that as "missing out" is beyond Buffett's comprehension. He had seen it all before. He came of age in the "go-go" Sixties, as he likes to call the era. While all around him were investing in the latest hi-tech gadgets and faddish corporations, Buffett was following the teachings of Benjamin Graham, the economist and investor who became his tutor and some would say guru, at Columbia Business School in New York. Graham and his colleague David Dodd were champions of a method known as "value investing". Simply put, value investing relies upon studying a company's fundamental underlying value and then deciding if that value is reflected in its share price. Following this relatively simple method is how Buffett managed to make another $ 10bn in a year when Wall Street lost hundreds of billions in the sub-prime crisis.

As consistent as Buffett is in his professional life, so, too, is he in many aspects of his personal life. He does not live the life of a billionaire. He bought his current home in humble Omaha, Nebraska, for $ 31,000

时尚公司，但巴菲特却听从了纽约哥伦比亚商学院的经济学家兼投资家杰明·格雷厄姆的教诲，杰明·格雷厄姆成为巴菲特的导师，也有人称其为大师。格雷厄姆和他的同事大卫·多德是著名的"价值投资"方法的拥护者。简单地说，价值投资依赖于研究一个公司的基本潜在价值，然后判断价值是否反映在股票价格上。当华尔街在次贷危机中损失上千亿美元的时候，巴菲特却根据这一相对简单的道理，设法在一年之中又赚了100亿美元。

巴菲特职业生涯中持之以恒的品质显示在他个人生活的很多方面。他过的不是亿万富翁的生活。他现在的住宅位于内布拉斯加州简陋的奥马哈地区，1958年购买时价值31 000美元，现在价值70万美元，这是中上等收入的家庭一个很普通的价格。他开的车是中等价位的凯迪拉克，穿着夹克外套或皱巴巴的西装，他没有移动电话，不喜欢电脑。他一天喝五罐樱桃可乐，喜欢吃他住的那条街上的科拉特牛排店做的半熟丁骨牛排，还要加上两份油炸马铃薯饼。他有一帮赞美他无拘无束魅力的狂热追随者，每年都会成群结队地赶往奥马哈参加他的年会，享受丰盛的奶品皇后冰淇淋和樱桃可乐。

2006年6月，巴菲特向比尔·盖茨和梅琳达·盖茨基金会捐赠了1 000万伯克希尔·哈撒韦的股份（时值307亿美元左右），这是历史上最大的慈善捐赠，那些谴责巴菲特吝啬的声音随之销声匿迹。他的全部财富今后都将以这种方式捐赠，但不用他的名义。移交他倾注一生心血的金融产品是巴菲特迈出的重要一步，他已经在公司内部培养了一批潜在的接班人，待他去世之后管理公司。他在最近写给股东的信中，仍像往常那样顽皮地开着标志性的玩笑：

in 1958. It is worth about $ 700,000 today, a very average price for an upper-middle-income family home. He drives around in a modest Cadillac, he wears jumpers and rumpled suits, he doesn't own a mobile phone and doesn't like computers. He drinks Cherry Coke — up to five cans a day — and likes to eat a T-bone steak, cooked rare, with a double order of hash browns from Gorat's Steak House down the street from his house. His followers are a cultish bunch who celebrate his folksy charm and flock to his annual meeting every year in Omaha to enjoy Dairy Queen ice cream and Cherry Cokes galore.

But the accusations of stinginess stopped when, in June 2006, Buffett gave 10 million Berkshire Hathaway shares (worth some $ 30.7bn at the time) to the Bill and Melinda Gates Foundation, the largest charitable donation in history. Over the years, his entire wealth will be disbursed in this way, but none of it in his name. Handing over the financial product of his life's work was a big step for Buffett, who has lined up a number of potential successors inside Berkshire Hathaway to run the company after he dies. In his most recent letter to shareholders, he revealed as much with another of his trademark bad jokes. "I've reluctantly discarded the notion of my continuing to manage the portfolio after my death, abandoning my hope to give new meaning to the term 'thinking outside the box'."

(999 words)

"我不情愿地放弃了死后继续管理投资组合的想法，放弃我的希望，赋予'站在局外思考'这一措辞新的含义。"

知识链接

The Bill and Melinda Gates Foundation 比尔·盖茨和梅琳达·盖茨基金会是比尔·盖茨和夫人梅林达名字的结合。它由比尔·盖茨之前创立的两个基金会合并而来：1994 年盖茨创立了威廉·盖茨基金会，目标是在世界范围内推进人类健康。1997 年盖茨和夫人又成立了一个新的基金会——盖茨图书馆基金会，目标是帮助美国的公共图书馆接上互联网。1999 年，后者更名为盖茨学习基金会，由资助公共图书馆转变为资助家庭困难和少数族裔的学生。2000 年 1 月，两大基金会正式合并成比尔·盖茨和梅琳达·盖茨基金会，其工作重点除了帮助美国公共教育改革、健康隐患、国内的穷人外，每年还拿出 8 亿美元研究艾滋病的治疗方法。

题 记

　　巴克莱资本的首席执行官鲍勃·戴蒙德大胆收购了雷曼兄弟，这项"伟大但走运"的神来之笔标志着戴蒙德在快速扩张的 10 年中展示出的自负达到巅峰。在他的职业生涯中，戴蒙德一直希望通过有计划、迂回的途径实现自己的愿望。他对投资银行业务运筹帷幄的特质：至高无上的自信、诚实坚定的果断、激励大众和敢于冒险的能力铸就了刻意不赶时髦的巴克莱资本的典型风格。能否重塑华尔街投行的巨擘？位于纽约第 7 大道的巴克莱资本美国总部，两米高的老鹰形状的霓虹灯投射出耀眼的青色光芒正怪异地象征着其傲视周围一切的自信。

The Bond Empire of Bob Diamond

Mr Diamond and his team at Barclays Capital had worked frantically① on a rescue takeover of Lehman, but it fell apart when the US government refused financial support. After sleepless nights, Mr Diamond agreed to consider buying Lehman's businesses out of bankruptcy. Arriving at the office as usual one morning, he began finessing a deal to keep Lehman's US operations intact. In the afternoon, Mr Diamond walked on to the trading floor of Lehman's head office near Times Square. To raucous② applause, he declared: "You have a new partner, Barclays Capital."

By snapping③ up one of Wall Street's most venerable④ names, the 57-year-old Mr Diamond has demonstrated the traits that have characterised his investment banking career: supreme self-confidence, single-minded determination, an ability to motivate people and take risks. Three decades after he started in a lowly position at Morgan Stanley, the

---

① frantically ['fræntikəli] *adv.* 疯狂似地
② raucous ['rɔːkəs] *adj.* 刺耳的
③ snapping ['snæpiŋ] *adj.* 显著的
④ venerable ['venərəbl] *adj.* 值得尊敬的

鲍勃·戴蒙德的
债券帝国

　　戴蒙德先生和他的巴克莱资本团队曾为接管雷曼公司做出过疯狂的营救工作，但这一切努力在美国政府拒绝金融援助时宣告失败。经过数个无眠之夜，戴蒙德先生同意考虑收购雷曼公司破产的业务。一天早上，他和平常一样到达办公室，开始为保持雷曼公司的美国业务运营不受损害制订周密的交易计划。下午，戴蒙德步行到位于时代广场附近的雷曼公司总部的交易场地。他在嘈杂无序的掌声中宣布："你们有了一个新的合作伙伴——巴克莱银行。"

　　戴蒙德在华尔街是最值得尊敬的名字之一，57岁的他已经显示了对投资银行业务运筹帷幄的特质：至高无上的自信、诚实坚定的果断、激励大众和敢于冒险的能力。他从摩根士丹利的低层做起，30年后的一次交易让他迅速跻身于华尔街的精英之群。从事银行业对戴蒙德来说可不是命中注定的。他于1951年出生在马萨诸塞州的斯普林菲尔德，父亲是位大学讲师，他称其为"心目中的英雄"。父亲教导他说："不要追求地位，不要寻求荣誉……如果你不能实现梦想，就最大限度地利用你所拥有的东西。"在他的职业生涯中，他一直希望通过有计划、迂回的途径实现自己的愿望。完成康涅狄格州大学的MBA学业并经历了短暂的节衣缩食的教学工作之后，他加

deal elevates him instantly into Wall Street's elite. Mr Diamond was not destined for a banking career. Born in Springfield, Massachusetts in 1951, his father was a university lecturer, a man he calls "his hero", who taught him: "Don't look for status. Don't look for glory ... if you couldn't have your dream, you made the most of what you had." In his career he has been willing to take calculated, circuitous routes to get where he wants. After an MBA at the University of Connecticut and a brief stint teaching, he joined a small medical technology company to soak up experience faster. Then he worked towards his desire to be a bond trader, finally reaching Morgan Stanley's trading floor. After 13 years, he defected to Credit Suisse First Boston. He described the four years at the Swiss bank as "really miserable". He said, "Without those four years, I wouldn't have known that the most important thing in successfully building an organisation or building a business is talent and culture."

He left CSFB after a row over bonuses— his team thought it deserved bigger ones — moving to London as head of fixed income at BZW, then Barclays, investment banking arm. As his timing was poor, within a year, Barclays ditched its investment banking ambitions. Mr Diamond took charge of the remaining business, "the rump", and built up its fixed-income operations. A year later, Barclays Capital suffered heavy losses following Russia's default. Despite pressure to close the business, Barclays stuck by him. "At the time, no one gave the organisation any credibility, " says Jerry del Missier, president of Barclays Capital and one of Mr Diamond's longest-serving associates. "The positive thing was that the board really had to commit to be in investment banking." For the next nine years, Barclays Capital rode the debt markets boom fuelled by low

入了一家小型医药技术公司，以便更快地积累经验。然后，他朝着成为债券商人的目标努力，最终进入摩根士丹利的交易所。13 年后，他投奔了瑞士信贷第一波士顿银行。他把在瑞士银行的这四年描述为"真的很悲惨"。他认为，"没有这四年，我不会知道成功地构建一个组织或发展一项业务最重要的是才能和文化"。

拿到一系列的奖金之后，他离开瑞士信贷第一波士顿银行（他的团队认为他们本该得到更大的奖赏）移师伦敦，担任有固定收入的巴克莱银行的首脑，后来成为巴克莱投资银行的操盘手。由于不善于掌握时机，巴克莱在一年之内就放弃了投资银行的野心。戴蒙德接管了残留的业务——"一个烂摊子"，建立了固定收入机制。一年之后，巴克莱资本在俄罗斯的违约使之蒙受了巨大的损失。尽管承受着关闭这项业务的压力，巴克莱仍然坚持己见。巴克莱资本总裁、戴蒙德服务时间最长的合作人杰里·戴尔·密斯耶说："那时候，没有人信任这个机构。值得肯定的是，董事会不得不表态承诺投资银行业。"接下来的九年间，巴克莱资本驾驭着低利率和欧元的到来，驱动着债券市场的繁荣。

戴蒙德先生通过严格的面试程序打造了一个具有竞争文化的偷猎团队。潜在的新雇员必须承受四个小时的面试，展示他们真实的性格，并淘汰不具备团队精神的求职者。戴蒙德先生称之为"中性规则"。戴蒙德既风趣又魅力四溢，总是人们瞩目的中心。尽管他对那些不符合他标准的人冷淡无情，但同事们还是赞扬他愿意听取忠告或批评。即使这样，他仍然博得了大家的衷心信任，而他更喜欢见机行事，在巴克莱资本交易所落地窗前的操作使他获得了市场的即时反馈。他的办公室里装饰着运动大事记、高尔夫球（他虽身

interest rates and the arrival of the euro.

Mr Diamond forged a competitive culture, poaching teams after a rigorous interviewing process. Potential recruits are subjected to four-hour interviews to reveal their true characters and to weed out those who are not team players. Mr Diamond calls this the "no-jerk rule". He can be funny and charming and enjoys being the centre of attention. Colleagues praise his willingness to listen to advice or criticism, though he can be ruthless with those who do not meet his standards. Even so, he inspires immense loyalty and prefers to be close to the action — operating from a glass-fronted office on Barclays Capital's trading floor, which gives him instant feedback on the markets. It is decorated with sports memorabilia, golf balls (he has a respectable handicap), and family photos. "He has his ear on the trading floor and knows what is going on. That is a key element," says Hans-Jorg Rudloff, chairman of Barclays Capital.

As his bond empire expanded, Mr Diamond's influence within Barclays also increased. He was a contender for chief executive, but was passed over for John Varley, the cerebral Englishman. Mr Varley promoted him to president and he joined the board — a move that forced the disclosure of his enormous pay. He made £21m annually, making him one of the UK's best paid bosses. He found the tabloid backlash intrusive, but also sees his elevation as a sign that the 300-year-old British bank is beginning the embrace the meritocratic ethos that has inculcated① at Barclays Capital. Barclays, head office struggles to exert its influence over his Mr Diamond's empire, which at times operates as an independent

---

① inculcate [in'kʌlkeit] *vt.* 灌输

34

患残疾，但令人敬佩）和家人的照片。 巴克莱银行主席汉斯·约格·鲁德洛夫说："他在交易场眼观六路、耳听八方，了解正在进行的交易。 这就是他成功的关键因素。"

戴蒙德在巴克莱内部的影响力随着他的债券帝国的扩大而增强。 他是首席行政官的竞争者，但却错失晋升机会，理智的英国人约翰·瓦利赢得了这一地位。 瓦利先生提拔他为总裁，他加入了董事会，这个变动暴露了他的巨额薪酬。 凭借 2 100 万英镑的年收入，他成为英国薪酬最高的老板之一。 他对小报侵犯隐私的行为产生了一种对抗情绪，但也明白他的提升标志着有 300 年历史的英国银行开始接受巴克莱资本灌输的精英精神。 巴克莱的总公司竭尽全力施加其对戴蒙德帝国的影响，可有时它仍像一个独立的运营机构。 尽管两人坚称相处得很好，但一位前同事描述他们的关系实际处于"热忱与紧张的边缘"。

现在，戴蒙德转而加强美国的业务运作，并宣布他将把更多的注意力放在纽约，部分原因是为了更靠近他在美国的三个孩子。 尽管他在伦敦生活十年有余，并有双重国籍，但戴蒙德先生仍然毫不掩饰地认为自己是个美国人。 他之所以在伦敦生活主要是因为他一直是老维克剧团的主席，他对切尔西足球俱乐部的热爱，这种热情如同他对波士顿红袜队和新英格兰爱国者队的支持。 德意志银行的全球银行业首脑迈克尔·克尔斯说："如果想想我那些在伦敦生活了很长一段时间的美国朋友，戴蒙德是变化最小的人。"迈克尔·克尔斯在切尔西的斯坦福桥体育馆有一个总裁包厢，而戴蒙德先生的包厢就在隔壁。

巴克莱资本不可避免地担心自己的资产负债表。 虽然它的复杂

institution. Though the two men insist they get on well, a former colleague describes relations as "verging between cordial and strained".

Now he moved to beef up his US operations and declared his intention to spend more time in New York, in part to be near his three children, who are all now in the US. Even though London has been his home for more than a decade, and he has dual nationality, Mr Diamond remains unabashedly American. His key concessions to life in London are as chairman of the Old Vic theatre and a love of Chelsea football club, which he supports with the same fervour as the Boston Red Sox and New England Patriots. "If I think about my fellow American expatriates who have been in London a long time, he's the person that has changed the least," says Michael Cohrs, head of global banking at Deutsche Bank, who occupies the executive box next to Mr Diamond's at Chelsea's Stamford Bridge stadium.

Barclays Capital has not been immune to fears about its own balance sheet. Its losses from complex debt securities have been less severe than rivals, but analysts have questioned its policy of not using market prices to value its portfolio of private equity loans. Rivals admit the Lehman deal — at $ 1.75bn for the bank's US operations, head office and data centres— is a coup, even as questions remain about whether his team can absorb 10,000 new staff. Mr Diamond is unapologetic. "We're in a consolidating world where there will be three or four or five bulge bracket firms. If we were sitting here watching Bank of America and Merrill Lynch and others merge, you'd have to question whether it was OK to sit on your hands."

(1,007 words)

债权证券损失没有竞争对手严重，但分析家仍在质疑它不采用市场价评估个人权益贷款的证券投资组合政策。尽管对手承认雷曼交易是个妙招，据总公司和数据中心的资料显示，巴克莱投资银行在美国操作了 17.5 亿美元，他的团队是否能吸纳 1 万名新员工仍然是个问题。戴蒙德先生没有道歉。"我们处于一个有着三个、四个或五个稳定的华尔街投资银行领导集团之中。如果我们坐在这儿看着美国银行、美林证券和其他机构合并，你不得不质疑坐视不理是否为良策。"

知识链接

Morgan Stanley 摩根士丹利（Morgan Stanley），财经界俗称"大摩"，是一家成立于美国纽约的国际金融服务公司，提供包括证券包销、资产管理、企业合并重组、企业金融咨询、机构性企业营销、房地产等多种金融服务，目前在全球 37 个国家设有超过 1 200 家办事处。

Barclays Capital 巴克莱资本（Barclays Capital）是巴克莱银行内部的一个投资银行部门，专门负责交易市场风险。它通过不断深化利率市场化和汇率形成的机制，利率衍生产品的推出以及金融衍生产品交易的建立为巴克莱银行业提供了快速发展的良好环境平台。巴克莱银行近年的快速成长离不开巴克莱资本业务的快速稳健拓展。

Credit Suisse First Boston 瑞士信贷第一波士顿银行（Credit Suisse First Boston）是一个全球领导级的银行投顾公司，提供各式金融产品、综合性的财经顾问、资本筹募、行销与贸易等项服务，在全球 37 个国家设有办事处，并拥有 15 000 多名员工。

题 记

　　亚马逊公司首席执行官希望借助高科技在他的网站上经营业务，但华尔街的投资者希望人们留意实体商铺。杰夫·贝佐斯，全球最大的互联网书店——亚马逊网络购物中心缔造者，从不安分守己，持续缔造着他的亚马逊神话。他孤注一掷，雄心勃勃，目标是将亚马逊转变成21世纪的数字万能器："弹性计算云"提供低价、自然状态的计算服务；微软公司使用存储服务加快软件下载速度；搜索引擎营销公司"效率限界"使用"机械特克"驱动搜索站点……人们相信，流淌着贝佐斯执着、自信和聪明才智的亚马逊网站犹如亚马逊河一样，必将成为世界上最神秘的网上生命王国。

Jeff Bezos' Risky Bet

It was one of the Web's typical flash frenzies, a gaggle of geeks seeking the new, new thing. At 2 a.m., a new venture called Elastic Compute Cloud quietly launched in test mode. Its service: cheap, raw computing power that could be tapped on demand over the Internet just like electricity. In less than five hours, hundreds of programmers, hoping to use the service to power their MySpace (NWS) and Google (GOOG) wannabes, snapped up all the test slots. One desperate latecomer instant-messaged a $10,000 offer for a slot to a lucky winner, who declined to give it up. "It's really cool," enthuses① entrepreneur Luke Matkins, who will run his soon-to-launch music site on the service. The creator of this très cool service: Amazon.com Inc. (AMZN)

Yes, Amazon founder and Chief Executive Jeffrey P. Bezos, the onetime Internet poster boy who quickly became a post-dot-com pinata, is back with yet another new idea. Many people continue to wonder if the world's largest online store will ever fulfill its original promise to revolutionize retailing. Bezos wants Amazon to run clients, business, at least the messy technical and logistical parts of it, using those same

---

① enthuse [in'θjuːz] vt. 使热心

杰夫·贝佐斯孤注一掷

    一群吵吵嚷嚷、行为怪诞的人不断寻求新新事物，这是对网络典型动画编辑工具的疯狂写照之一。 凌晨两点，一个名为"弹性计算云"的新风险实验悄然进入测试模式。 它提供低价、自然状态的计算服务，可以使互联网像通电一样，需要时一摁即可连通。 数以百计的程序员希望使用这项服务为聚友网（NWS）、谷歌（GOOG）的赶超崇拜者提供动力，不到 5 个小时就抢购了所有的测试槽。 一位绝望的姗姗来迟者发出即时信息，出价 1 万美元从一位拒绝放弃的幸运赢家那里购买了一个插槽。 企业家卢克·马特金表现出很大的热情："真是太酷了"，他将使用这项服务来运营即将投产的音乐网站。 这项超酷服务的缔造者就是亚马逊公司。

    是的，摇身变为后网络时代皮纳塔的曾经的互联网招贴男孩、亚马逊的创建者兼首席执行官杰夫·贝佐斯，又在筹划另一个新的概念。 许多人一直感到诧异，这个世界上最大的网上销售商是否履行其最初的彻底改革零售业的承诺。 贝佐斯希望亚马逊帮助客户经营业务，借助网上商店提供的价值 100 亿美元的相同技术和操作手段，至少能处理棘手的技术和计算部分。 在这个过程中，贝佐斯的目标是将亚马逊转变成 21 世纪的数字万能器。 他决定像沃尔玛一

technologies and operations that power his $ 10 billion online store. In the process, Bezos aims to transform Amazon into a kind of 21st century digital utility. It's as if Wal-Mart Stores Inc. (WMT) had decided to turn itself inside out, offering its industry-leading supply chain and logistics[1] systems to all outsiders, even rival retailers. Except Amazon is starting to rent out just about everything it uses to run its own business, from rack space in its 10 million square feet of warehouses worldwide to spare computing capacity on its thousands of servers, data storage on its disk drives, and even some of the millions of lines of software code it has written to coordinate all that. It's fine with him. Even after all these years spent battling back claims that his company would be "Amazon. toast, " he's still bounding up and down stairs two at a time to exhort his band of nerds on to the Next Big Thing. And now, more than ever, he's determined to keep going for the big score, even if people think he's crazy.

But if techies are wowed by Bezos, grand plan, it's not likely to win many converts on Wall Street. To many observers, it conjures up[2] the ghost of Amazon past. During the dot-com boom, Bezos spent hundreds of millions of dollars to build distribution centers and computer systems in the promise that they eventually would pay off with outsize returns. That helped set the stage for the world's biggest Web retail operation, with expected sales of $ 10.5 billion annually. All that has investors restless and many analysts throwing up their hands wondering if Bezos is merely

---

① logistics [ləˈdʒistiks] *n.* 计算
② conjure up 召唤

样采取返销手段，向所有的外部人员、甚至零售业的竞争对手提供业界领先的供应链和物流系统。 亚马逊除了开始出租用来经营自身业务的一切之外，还包括世界各地共 1 000 万平方英尺的仓库中的货架、数以千计的空余计算能力服务器、磁盘驱动器中的数据存储，甚至包括一些为协调所有程序而编写的数百万行软件代码。 这一切对他来说很美妙。 即使多年来他一直支持这些做法，声称公司陷入"亚马逊困境"，他仍然一度上蹿下跳，鼓动他那令人厌恶的团队关注"下一个重大热点"。 他现在比以前更狂，决心继续争取高绩效，即使人们认为他已经疯了。

但是，如果技术专家为贝佐斯的宏伟计划叫绝，就不太可能赢得华尔街的皈依者。 对许多观察者而言，他用魔法召来了亚马逊过去的幽灵。 在网络繁荣的热潮中，贝佐斯花费成百上千万的美元建立配送中心和计算机系统，承诺这些开支最终因巨额回报而得以清偿。 此举为建立世界上最大的网上零售交易系统打下基础，预期年零售额达 105 亿美元。 所有这些令投资者忐忑不安，很多分析师感到手足无措，担心贝佐斯只是旁敲侧击地为零售业寻找替代品。 27 个跟踪公司的分析师中的 11 人给出了低于或卖出该公司股票的评级，如此不信任的投票让人感到震惊。 根据股票明星公司投资顾问的分析，推荐卖出的人数之多，在大公司中只有奎斯特国际通讯公司能与之相比。

更有甚者，就在贝佐斯思考大计划之时，亚马逊的零售业务面临新的威胁。 它的 25% 增长轨迹只略高于整个电子商务的增长速度，它本应该在很久以前就达到目前增长速度的两倍左右。 不过其他网站正在快速进入互联网首选站点。 谷歌就是其中之一，它已替

flailing around for an alternative to his retail operation. Eleven of 27 analysts who follow the company have underperform or sell ratings on the stock— a stunning vote of no confidence. That number of sell recommendations is matched among large companies only by Qwest Communications International Inc., according to investment consultant StarMine Corp.

What's more, at the same time Bezos is thinking big thoughts, Amazon's retail business faces new threats. Its 25% sales growth tracks a little above the pace of overall e-commerce expansion and nearly double its own pace way back. But other sites are fast becoming preferred first stops on the Web. Google, for one, has replaced retail sites such as Amazon as the place where many people start their shopping. And more personalized and social upstarts such as News Corp.'s (NWS), MySpace and YouTube, which Google is buying, have become the prime places for many people to gather online— and eventually shop. It's a trend Amazon could have trouble catching up to. Says consultant Andreas Weigend, Amazon's chief scientist: "The world has shifted from e-business to me-business." With all those problems, some might view Bezos. latest tech toys as an attempt to take their eye off the ball. But spend some time with Bezos, and it becomes clear there may well be a method to his madness. Amazon has spent 12 years and $ 2 billion perfecting many of the pieces behind its online store. By most accounts, those operations are now among the biggest and most reliable in the world. "All the kinds of things you need to build great Web-scale applications are already in the guts of Amazon, " says Bezos. "The only difference is, we're now exposing the guts, making them available to others."

代亚马逊之类的在线零售网站，成为许多人开始网上购物的地方。谷歌收购的新闻集团网、聚友网和 YouTube 等更多个性化、或者社会暴发户式的网站，已经成为很多人在线收集和最终购买的首选。这种趋势让亚马逊追赶起来可能存在困难。 亚马逊的首席科学家安德里德·魏根认为："世界已从电子商务转变为自我商务。" 有些人可能会将所有这些问题视为贝佐斯企图转移他们视线的最新科技玩具。 但是与贝佐斯待上一段时间，就会明白他的疯狂背后很可能存在一定的道理。 亚马逊花费 12 年时间和 20 亿美元完善了网上商店的许多幕后工作。 大多数人认为，这些操作系统是世界上目前最大和最可靠的。 贝佐斯说，"构建大规模网络应用软件所需要的一切都已存在于亚马逊的精髓之中。 唯一不同的是，我们正在揭示这一精髓，使其惠及他人。"

贝佐斯最初致力于为具有科技头脑的创业者和其他小公司提供服务。 但很显然，将各种类型的企业囊括在其旗下才是最终的目标市场。 亚马逊已经吸引了一些高端客户。 例如，美国微软公司（MSFT）正在使用存储服务加快软件下载速度，该服务帮助林登实验室处理软件下载挤压，协调快速增长的第二人生网络虚拟世界。尽管亚马逊的计算服务仍处于测试阶段，搜索暴发户动力之源公司还是对其寄予了高度期待，计划一旦系统开发成功就用其扶助自己的计算机。 搜索引擎营销公司"效率限界"使用"机械特克"确定最有效率的关键词，以驱动搜索站点。 贝佐斯希望赚钱。 亚马逊使用简单的存储服务，对在其庞大的硬盘驱动上存储数据和方案的商业活动，每十亿字节每月收取 15 美分的费用。 它还对其他店主占用其存储库中的真实空间按照每平方英尺每月收取 45 美分的标准

Bezos is initially aiming these services at startups and other small companies with a little tech savvy. But it's clear that businesses of all kinds are the ultimate target market. Already, Amazon has attracted some high-powered customers. Microsoft Corp. (MSFT) is using the storage service to help speed software downloads, for instance, and the service is helping Linden Lab handle the crush of software downloads for its fast-growing Second Life online virtual world. Highly anticipated search upstart Powerset Inc. plans to use the Amazon computing service, even though it's still in test mode, to supplement its own computers when it launches its service sometime. And the search engine marketing firm Efficient Frontier uses Mechanical Turk to determine the most effective keywords that drive traffic to Web sites.

Bezos hopes making money. With its Simple Storage Service, Amazon charges 15 cents per gigabyte per month for businesses to store data and programs on Amazon's vast array of disk drives. It's also charging other merchants about 45 cents a square foot per month for real space in its warehouses. Through its Elastic Compute Cloud service, it's renting out computing power, starting at 10 cents an hour for the equivalent of a basic server computer. And it has set up a semi-automated global marketplace for online piecework, such as transcribing snippets of podcasts①, called Amazon Mechanical Turk, and Amazon takes a 10% commission on those jobs.

(988 words)

---

① transcribing snippets of podcasts 转录播客片段

收费。 通过弹性计算云服务，它对外出租计算能力，同等标准服务器计算机起始价为每小时 10 美分。 它俨然已经形成一个半自动化的网络计件工作的全球市场，如称之为亚马逊机械特克的转录播客片段，亚马逊对这些资源使用抽取 10% 的佣金。

知识链接 🔍

piata 一种纸做的容器，造型千变万化，从圣诞老人到飞机、小丑，各种形状应有尽有。同时 Pinata 也是在过节，尤其是圣诞节的时候，最受拉美儿童欢迎的一种游戏。游戏的方法是先把 Pinata 用细绳绑在天花板上，然后所有的小朋友围成一圈，大家轮流出来，蒙着眼睛，手上拿着一根棍子，设法把挂着的 Pinata 打下来，从容器中散落的礼物，就代表了上帝给予人类战胜邪恶的恩赐。

StarMine Corp. StarMine 公司在北美、欧洲和亚太地区提供股票研究分析、预测股票的数量组合和资产净值管理工具，客观评价有价证券的绩效，帮助机构投资者、分析师和专业投资者作出投资决定，研究解决方案，包括定量分析和生产力增强功能，提高洞察力和效率。

Qwest Communications International Inc. 奎斯特通讯国际公司是美国传统的电信运营商。公司是著名的宽带国际互联网通讯公司，在与地方电话公司美国西部通信(USwest) 完成合并后，逐渐从最初的光纤网络铺设者转型为全方位的电信服务巨头。公司目前提供的光纤宽频网路已达255 500里，服务范围遍及全球 160 多个城市。公司同时以批发的形式向其他电讯公司提供产品和服务。主要业务包括长途服务、宽频数据和语音业务、无线业务、本地通话业务等。

题 记

　　欧文公司的总裁唐纳德·布伦作为总体规划师、营造商和长期的投资者，一直精心打理他在加利福尼亚州的房地产业。作为房地产行业的领军人物和创新标兵，布伦先生是率先将公园、大量的开放空间、一流的学校、就业中心和购物中心等设施融入设计精美的住宅区，创造和谐的总体规划社区的建造者之一。布伦不仅为人低调、投资眼光敏锐，而且在政治领域的投资眼光也一样独到，这一点在他对教育和研究事业的慷慨赞助上得到了最好的验证。尽管他谦逊地认为欧文公司面对的是任何一位房地产从业者所遇到的典型的机遇和挑战，稳坐美国房地产商首富位置还是令人刮目相看。

A Master Builder of Balanced Communities — Donald Bren

For several decades, Donald Bren, chairman of The Irvine Company, has been deeply involved in California real estate as a master planner, master builder and a long-term investor. A leader and innovator within the real estate industry, Mr. Bren was one of the first to combine well-designed homes with such amenities① as parks and substantial② open space, excellent schools, employment centers and shopping centers to create balanced master-planned communities. Through his accomplishments, he has earned a national reputation as an expert in the interrelated fields of planning, design, architecture, construction, marketing and finance. Under Mr. Bren's leadership, The Irvine Company has been evolving from an internationally recognized community developer to one of the nation's premier real estate investment companies. Most of The Irvine Company's land and real estate assets are in Orange County, but the company also owns high-quality investment properties in Los Angeles, San Diego and Silicon Valley. The company's portfolio includes approximately 400 office buildings, 40 retail centers, 90 apartment

---

① amenity [əˈmiːniti] *n.* 便利设施
② substantial [səbˈstænʃəl] *adj.* 大量的

和谐社区的营造商
——唐纳德·布伦

作为总体规划师、营造商和长期的投资者，欧文公司的总裁唐纳德·布伦几十年来一直精心打理他在加利福尼亚州的房地产业。作为房地产行业的领军人物和创新标兵，布伦先生是率先将公园、大量的开放空间、一流的学校、就业中心和购物中心等设施融入设计精美的住宅区，创造和谐的总体规划社区的建造者之一。他凭借这些成就，在规划、设计、建筑、建造、市场和金融等相关领域赢得了国家级专家称号的荣誉。欧文公司在布伦先生的领导下，已经从国际认可的社区开发商转变为美国主要的高级房地产投资公司。欧文公司的大部分土地储备和房地产资产虽然在奥兰治县，但公司在洛杉矶、圣地亚哥、硅谷也拥有高质量的投资资产。公司的投资组合包含约 400 栋写字楼、40 家零售中心、90 个公寓社区、2 座酒店、5 座船坞和 3 所高尔夫俱乐部。

唐纳德·布伦也是美国最慷慨的慈善家之一，他在教育和研究领域的集中捐赠以及对敏感开放空间和物种保护实施的创新方法产生了重要的影响力。自 2003 年以来，他捐赠或承诺的捐赠约计 9.15 亿美元。为表彰他对加利福尼亚大学体制的多方支持，加利福尼亚

communities, two hotels, five marinas and three golf clubs.

Mr.Bren also is one of the state's most generous philanthropists①, focusing his contributions to significantly impact education and research, as well as to implement innovative approaches to the conservation of sensitive open spaces and species. He has given or pledged an estimated $ 915 million since 2003. In recognition of his wide-ranging support for the University of California system, Mr. Bren was awarded its highest honor, the University of California Presidential Medal. The Los Angeles Times placed him atop its list of the 100 most influential people in Southern California, And Mr. Bren was elected a Fellow of the prestigious American Academy of Arts & Sciences. Fellows are elected from throughout the world through a highly competitive process, and are chosen for their major and lasting contributions to their disciplines and society. Mr. Bren was elected in the category of Business, Corporate and Philanthropic Leadership— Private Sector. Mr. Bren has made education and research his other philanthropic priorities. The Irvine Company and the Donald Bren Foundation have contributed more than $ 200 million to public schools on The Irvine Ranch and to institutions of higher education. Mr. Bren's educational philanthropy ranges from major contributions to local schools for enrichment programs, after-school programs for low-income children, and scholarship awards, to funding more than 50 endowed chairs for distinguished faculty at institutions for higher learning. At the University of California, Mr. Bren has contributed more to support endowed chairs than any other single donor in the University of

① philanthropist [fi'lænθrəpist] *n.* 慈善家

52

大学授予他校级最高荣誉：加利福尼亚大学校长勋章。 洛杉矶时报评选的南加利福尼亚最具影响力的 100 人中，唐纳德·布伦名列榜首。 唐纳德·布伦还当选为享有很高声望的美国科学与艺术学院院士。 这些院士是经过激烈竞争在全球范围内遴选出来的，他们对各自的领域和社会都做出了主要和持续的贡献。 布伦先生当选的学科属于私营部门：商业、公司和慈善领导。 布伦先生将教育和研究作为慈善事业的首选。 欧文公司和唐纳德·布伦基金给欧文农场的公立学校和高等教育机构的捐赠已经超过 2 亿美元。 布伦先生教育慈善事业的主要捐赠对象涵盖致富项目中的地方中小学学校、低收入家庭的儿童课后教育和奖学金项目、为高等教育机构中的杰出教师设立了 50 多个资深教授职位。 在加利福尼亚州立大学，布伦先生对资深教授的赞助多于加州大学历史上其他的任何个人资助者。 他私下通过多纳德·勃仁基金、欧文公司和相关实体，定向捐赠 6 000 多万美元，资助加州大学的教师和卓越研究项目。

布伦先生在南加利福尼亚一直努力走在保护敏感生态环境的前列，这项承诺得到美国内政部长的认可，并指定欧文农场保护的公园和露天空地为国家自然地标。 布伦先生宣布与自然资源保护机构共同创办"罕见物种保护联盟"，管理公司的野生土地，研究和改善大量敏感物种栖息地的生态环境。 欧文公司与联邦、州和县政府达成了一项创造性的自愿协议，同意拨出一块不少于 21 000 英亩的宝贵空地，作为濒危动植物物种的栖息地。 公司捐出位于欧文农场北部的 11 000 英亩的多样性生态土地，作为永久性空地接受长期保

California's history. Privately and through the Donald Bren Foundation,
The Irvine Company and related entities, he has directed more than $ 60
million to support faculty and programmatic excellence at the University of
California.

Mr. Bren has been at the forefront of efforts to preserve
environmentally sensitive land in Southern California, a commitment that
was recognized with the designation of The Irvine Ranch's protected parks
and open spaces as a National Natural Landmark by the U.S. Secretary of
the Interior. Mr. Bren announced the creation of an "uncommon
alliance" with The Nature Conservancy to manage the company's
wilderness land, and study and improve habitat for a variety of sensitive
species. Under a creative, voluntary agreement with the federal, state and
county governments, The Irvine Company agreed to set aside more than
21,000 acres of precious open space habitat for endangered and threatened
plant and animal species. The company donated 11,000 acres of
environmentally diverse land in the north portion of The Irvine Ranch to be
protected forever as permanent open space. That donation brought to
50,000 acres the amount of land permanently protected for open space and
recreation on The Irvine Ranch— more than half of the entire 93,000-acre
ranch. Mr. Bren also has committed $ 50 million for the long-term
management, preservation and restoration of the natural resources on The
Irvine Ranch, now being carried out by the Irvine Ranch Conservancy,
which Mr. Bren created. Its mission also is to increase public access to the
lands.

Born in Los Angeles, Mr. Bren was raised in Los Angeles and Newport
Beach, California. He earned a degree in business administration and

护。 这次捐献将欧文农场 5 万英亩的土地留作永久性保护空地和休闲娱乐区，占农场总面积 93 000 英亩的一半以上。 布伦先生还承诺出资 5 000 万美元，作为长期管理、保护和恢复欧文农场自然资源的费用，这项计划目前由布伦先生创立的欧文农场自然物源保护组织执行。 该组织的任务也是增加公众土地使用权。

生于洛杉矶的布伦先生在加利福尼亚州的洛杉矶和纽波特海湾市长大。 他在华盛顿大学取得管理和经济学学位，并在这所大学完成了商学院研究生的学习。 他毕业后作为文职人员在美国海军陆战队服役 3 年。 布伦先生于 1958 年注册"布伦公司"开始了自己的职业生涯，公司的主要业务是在奥兰治县建造房屋。 他后来成立韦霍使命公司，并担任总裁，开始在奥兰治县实施整体规划，开发面积为 11 000 英亩的韦霍使命新社区。 随后，布伦先生把自己的所得利益卖给韦霍使命公司，集中精力经营布伦公司，后来更名为加利福尼亚太平洋房屋公司，在奥兰治县、洛杉矶、圣迭戈和北加利福尼亚州建造住宅社区。 布伦先生加入投资人组织，试图从欧文基金会入手购买欧文公司。 他持有公司 34% 的股份，成为公司最大的股东。 他后来担任公司执行委员会成员和副总裁。 布伦先生从股东手中购买了额外的流通股，获得公司 92% 的股份，并当选为董事长。 他现在是公司的唯一股东。

布伦先生描述自己在欧文公司的使命时说："作为营造商，我们正在融合建筑和规划技巧，加之商业和金融规则，从而建造优质的和谐社区。 我认为，欧文公司面对的是任何一位房地产从业者所遇

economics from the University of Washington where he also pursued business school graduate studies. Following school, he served for three years as an officer in the U.S. Marine Corps. Mr. Bren began his business career in 1958 by founding the Bren Company, which built homes in Orange County. Then, he formed the Mission Viejo Company and, as president, began the master planning and development of the 11,000-acre new community of Mission Viejo in Orange County. Following that, Mr. Bren sold his interest in the Mission Viejo Company to focus his attention on the Bren Company, subsequently renamed California Pacific Homes, which has built residential communities in Orange County, Los Angeles, Ventura County, San Diego and Northern California. Mr. Bren joined a group of investors to purchase The Irvine Company from the Irvine Foundation. His 34 percent share of the company made him the largest shareholder. He became a member of the company's executive committee and vice chairman. Mr. Bren purchased additional outstanding shares from shareholders to secure ownership of 92 percent of the company and was elected chairman of the board. He is now the company's sole shareholder.

Describing his mission for The Irvine Company, he says, "As master builders, we are blending architectural and planning skills, plus business and financial disciplines, to produce superbly balanced communities. I consider The Irvine Company land a quintessential① opportunity and challenge for anyone in real estate."

(925 words)

---

① quintessential [kwinte'sənʃəl] *adj.* 典型的

到的典型的机遇和挑战。"

知识链接 🔍

The Irvine Company 欧文公司是美国最受尊敬和风格多样的私营房地产公司，注册商标地是加利福尼亚州奥兰治县欧文农场——唐纳德·布伦是欧文公司的董事长。公司拥有和管理 8 500 万平方英尺的高质量投资总额，包括 115 个住宅社区、475 座办公楼、41 家零售中心和 5 座游艇码头。它的资产还包括世界级的旅游胜地——鹈鹕山度假村，由俯瞰太平洋的 204 个房间和套房、128 栋别墅，以及两个高尔夫球场组成。

California Pacific Homes 加州太平洋家园是可靠的、公认的创造优质的生活环境的领导者。它拥有一个多样化的知识团队，其核心优势是与市场保持同步，在单一家庭住宅设计、建设、营销领域具有 50 年的领导历史和客户服务经验。主要产品有公寓社区、高级住宅、校园住房和豪华度假酒店等。

题　记

　　迈克尔·戴尔由于在福布斯杂志评选的10位40岁以下最富有的美国人中名列前茅而备受瞩目。人们称赞他具有远见卓识、勇于创新，是一位稳健、始终如一的领导者。他在大学一年级退学创业的经历激励了一代年轻人，甚至影响到美国教育体制的改革。他从一开始就能用标准化组装程序来直接装配电脑，保持了产品模式整体性制造过程的完美契合。他亲手建立的企业文化——密切关注每一美分的经营成本，并将之转化为至少25美分的经营收入——迅速创造了新经济时代赚钱最快的纪录。戴尔秉持"摒弃存货、倾听顾客需要、直销顾客"的三大黄金法则，在瞬息万变的现代商业环境中深受市场青睐。

The Way to Success in Dell's Personal Life

In 1984, as a first-year college student in Austin, Texas, Michael Dell borrowed $1,000 from his parents to start a computer accessories business. He began by selling kits to help customers upgrade their personal computers, establishing a business model his company, Dell, Inc., still follows today: sell directly to consumers, eliminating the middle step of a retail store or a distributor, and hold on to far more of the profits. In just two decades, Dell's company grew to massive proportions, with more than 47,000 employees and annual revenues of more than $40 billion. Dell himself was squarely① at the top of Forbes magazine's list of the ten wealthiest Americans under the age of forty. He has been praised as a visionary and an innovator, but he has also earned admiration for being a stable, consistent leader. In an industry that changes rapidly, in terms of both technology and personnel, Dell has stood out from his peers by remaining at the helm② of his company from its struggling early days to its current status as a major player in the global field of information

---

① squarely ['skweəli] *adv.* 正好
② helm [helm] *n.* 领导

60

戴尔的人生成功之路

1984 年，迈克尔·戴尔还在得克萨斯州的奥斯汀读大学一年级时，就用向父母借来的 1 000 美元经营电脑配件业务。 他开始销售零部件，帮助客户升级个人电脑，建立一种时至今日他的戴尔公司还在沿用的商业模式：向客户直销，省去零售商店或分销商等中间环节，以便获取更多的利润。 戴尔公司仅用了二十年的时间，就发展成为拥有 47 000 多员工、年收入超过 400 亿美元的庞大公司。 戴尔本人因为在福布斯杂志评选的 10 位四十岁以下最富有的美国人中名列前茅而备受瞩目。 人们称赞他具有远见卓识、勇于创新，是一位稳健、始终如一的领导者。 在技术和人员变化迅速的一种产业中，戴尔领导他的公司从同龄人中脱颖而出，从早期的艰苦创业发展成为全球信息技术（IT）领域的领军人物。

迈克尔·戴尔 1965 出生于得克萨斯州的休斯敦，从小就具备商人的素质。 他在幼年时期表现出超乎一般的智慧和创造力，对上学不感兴趣。 8 岁时，他函购了参加高中同等学力考试的资料，如果他通过这项考试就成为一名高中毕业生，无需忍受剩下来的几年学

technology（IT）.

A businessman from the beginning, Michael Saul Dell was born in 1965 in Houston, Texas. While he displayed intelligence and ingenuity from an early age, he had little interest in school. At the age of eight, he sent away for information on taking a high school equivalency exam, which, if he passed, would make him a high school graduate without having to endure the remaining years of school. His parents insisted he stay in the classroom, and Dell invested his considerable creative energy in after-school ventures. When he was twelve years old, he operated a mail-order trading business for stamps and baseball cards, earning $ 2,000. At the age of fourteen, Dell got his first computer, an Apple II and soon realized that he had a knack for taking computers apart and putting them back together. While in high school, Dell took a job delivering newspapers for the Houston Post. His aggressive selling strategies, which included obtaining mailing lists of newly married people, offering them free trial subscriptions①, and then following up with phone calls, resulted in earnings of $ 18,000. Not one to hold on to his spoils, Dell spent the money on a new BMW.

Dell claims, "What people have never understood is that we're not like other companies." When Dell entered his freshman year at the University of Texas at Austin, his parents hoped he would become a doctor, but Dell's skills lay elsewhere. In examining the personal

---

① subscription [səb'skrip∫n] *n.* 预定

校生活。 父母坚持让他待在教室里，于是戴尔把他巨大的创造能量投入到放学后的风险投资上。 12 岁时，他经营了一项买卖邮票和棒球卡的邮购贸易业务，赚了 2 000 美元。 14 岁时，戴尔得到第一台个人电脑——苹果 II 型机并很快意识到自己在拆装电脑方面的天分。 进入高中后，戴尔找到一份为休斯敦邮报分销报纸的工作。他采取积极的销售策略：首先获取新近结婚人士的邮寄名单，向他们提供免费试用订阅服务，然后电话跟踪反馈，结果赚了 18 000 美元。 没人留意他的战利品：戴尔用这些钱买了一辆崭新的宝马。

戴尔声称，"人们所不理解的是我们与其他公司不同"。 戴尔开始得克萨斯州立大学奥斯汀分校的学业时，父母希望他成为一名医生，但戴尔的才能却在其他方面。 他考察了个人电脑即 PC 行业之后，留意到低价出售个人电脑的时机，正如他所解释的："我发现买一台个人电脑需要约 3 000 美元，而里面的部件仅值 600 美元。IBM 从其他公司购买大部分的元件，将它们组装到一起，然后以 2 000 美元出售给电脑交易商，那个对销售电脑或组装电脑一无所知的中间商，却更加可恶地以 3 000 美元的价格出售。" 戴尔认为他可以组装电脑部件，跳过出售给中间商这个步骤，直接卖给消费者。这样消费者不仅可以低价购买产品，而且戴尔每赚一分就有一分的利润。 于是，戴尔将他的电脑知识与敏锐的商业嗅觉结合起来，开始自己做生意，为个人电脑组装升级包。

戴尔回忆自己在得克萨斯大学宿舍外一个 27 层楼高的宿舍经营

computer, or PC, industry, he noticed an opportunity to sell PCs for less, as he explained, "I saw that you'd buy a PC for about $ 3,000, and inside that PC was about $ 600 worth of parts. IBM would buy most of these parts from other companies, assemble them, and sell the computer to a dealer for $ 2,000. Then the dealer, who knew very little about selling or supporting computers, would sell it for $ 3,000, which was even more outrageous①." Dell realized that he could assemble computer parts, skip the step of selling to a dealer, and go directly to the consumer. That way the consumer could buy the product for less, and Dell held on to every penny of the profits. Dell thus combined his knowledge of computers with his well-developed business sense and began his own business, assembling upgrade kits for personal computers.

Dell recalled operating his new business out of his University of Texas dorm room on the twenty-seventh floor: "People would ride up to the 27th floor with their computers. I'd put in some memory or a disk drive, they'd pay me, and I'd send them on their way." His earnings soon reached about $ 25,000 a month. After one year at the university, Dell had decided that he needed to focus all of his time on his business, and he dropped out of college. His company, then called PCs Unlimited, began building PCs, starting with parts from such established computer companies as IBM and Compaq and adding elements to make the products unique. Dell continued to sell directly to consumers, a strategy that paid

---

① outrageous [aut'reidəʒs] *adj.* 无耻的

他的新业务时的经历说："人们会带着电脑上到 27 楼，我植入某个存储器或一个磁盘驱动，他们付款给我，然后我送他们离开。"他的月收入很快高达 25 000 美元。 在大学待了一年以后，戴尔认为他需要集中所有的时间做生意，于是退了学。 他当时的公司名为"无限电脑公司"，像美国国际商用机器公司和美国康柏公司等已经成熟的公司一样，从部件开始生产电脑，再添加一些让产品独特的元素。戴尔坚持对消费者直销，这一策略获得了巨大的回报：不到一年的时间公司赢利 600 万美元。 戴尔殚精竭虑，年复一年，领导他的公司快速成长壮大。

戴尔是一个让任何公司的 CEO 都羡慕的人。 戴尔 20 岁的时候拥有 30 名员工。 那年夏天，公司开始生产涡轮电脑，首台电脑生产从零开始，而不是套用其他公司的惯用模式。 后来，戴尔将公司"无限电脑公司"改名"戴尔电脑公司"。 那时他开始了一项业内独一无二的项目：戴尔电脑公司为客户提供上门服务，客户不用再带着有故障的电脑到店铺维修。 戴尔指出，这项服务比任何一个对抗竞争者的巧妙策略都更有必要。 他回忆说："这是一项重要的附加服务，因为我们没有任何店铺。"1988 年，戴尔开始对公众提供购买他的公司股票的机会。 戴尔公司成立仅仅 4 年，销售额就达到1.59 亿美元。 戴尔从此在人生路上走向成功。

off in vast sums: within less than a year, his company had earned $6 million. Dell was off and running, leading his company to enormous growth year after year.

Dell is the envy of CEOs everywhere. At the age of twenty, Dell had thirty employees working for him. During the summer of that year, the company began producing the Turbo PC, its first computer made entirely from scratch①, rather than a customized version of another company's machine. In 1987 Dell changed the name of the company from PCs Unlimited to Dell Computer Corporation. At that time he began a program offered by no one else in the industry: rather than having customers bring broken-down computers to a store for repair, Dell Computer would pay house calls to service its customers' PCs. Dell pointed out that this offer came out of necessity rather than an ingenious② plan to outperform competitors: "That was a pretty important plus because we didn't have any stores," he recalled. During 1988 Dell began offering the public the opportunity to buy stock in his company. Just four years after the company had begun, sales reached $159 million. Dell has found the way to success in his personal life.

(893 words)

---

① scratch [skrætʃ] v. (from~)白手起家
② ingenious [in'dʒiːnjəs] adj. 有独创性的

知识链接

Dell Computer Inc. 戴尔公司是一家总部位于美国得克萨斯州朗德罗克的世界五百强企业。它以生产、设计、销售家用以及办公室电脑而闻名，同时也涉足高端电脑市场，生产与销售服务器、数据储存设备、网络设备等。戴尔的其他产品还包括 PDA、软件、打印机等电脑外围产品。

Compaq 美国康柏电脑公司由罗德·肯尼恩（Rod Canion）、吉米·哈里斯（Jim Harris）和比利·默顿（Bill Murto）三位来自得州仪器公司的高级经理于 1982 年 2 月分别投资 1 000 万美元共同创建。2002 年康柏电脑公司被惠普公司收购。康柏奠定其在所在行业内的重要位置是在 1987 年，在这一年，他们推出了第一台采用由英特尔公司设计的新一代 x86 系列中的第一种 32 位处理器——80386PC 机。

题　记

全球投资之父、史上最成功的基金经理邓普顿爵士是邓普顿集团的创始人，他被誉为全球最具智慧以及最受尊崇的投资者之一。在长达 70 载的职业生涯中，邓普顿创立并领导了那个时代最成功的共同基金公司，其运作手法令华尔街眼花缭乱，成为金融界一位是有传奇色彩的人物。作为上个世纪最著名的逆向投资者，邓普顿创造了"在大萧条的低点买入，在互联网的高点抛出，并在这两者间游刃有余"的投资方法。他的投资哲学"行情总在绝望中诞生，在半信半疑中成长，在憧憬中成熟，在希望中毁灭"，已经成为邓普顿基金集团的投资团队以及许多投资人永恒的财富。

Father of the Global Investment
— John Templeton

If, on any day over the past few decades, you had chanced to be strolling in the early morning at Lyford Cay in the Bahamas, you might have seen a wiry, determined figure power-walking in the sea. Keen as a whippet, his thin arms pumping, he headed into the prevailing swell. In his 80s, he would do an hour of this. In his 90s, he still managed 25 minutes.

Sir John Templeton spent his life going against the flow. In September 1939, when the war-spooked① world was selling, he borrowed $10,000 to buy 100 shares in everything that was trading for less than a dollar a share on the New York Stock Exchange. All but four eventually turned profits. In early 2000, conversely, he sold all his dotcom and Nasdaq tech stocks just before the market crashed. His iron principle of investing was "to buy when others are despondently② selling and to sell when others are greedily buying". At the point of "maximum pessimism" he would enter, and clean up. It took fortitude③, he would

---

① spook [spuːk] *vt.* 惊吓
② despondently [disˈpɔndəntli] *adv.* 意气消沉地;沮丧地
③ fortitude [ˈfɔːtitjuːd] *n.* 勇气

全球投资之父——
约翰·邓普顿

几十年前的某一天早晨，漫步巴哈马莱福德群岛的珊瑚礁，你或许会看见一位瘦削、坚毅的身影在海边矫健行走。他奋力挥动细长的双臂，像一只灵巧的猎狗，迎头冲向波涛汹涌的海浪。80 岁时，他可以做一个小时的此类运动。90 岁时，他仍然努力坚持 25 分钟。

约翰·邓普顿爵士一生都在与风浪搏击。1939 年 9 月，经过战争洗劫的世界一派萧条，他用借来的 10 000 美元在纽约股票交易所以每股低于 1 美元的价格购买了 100 股的各家公司股票。这些股票除四只之外，其他最终全部盈利。然而，2000 年初，他逆市卖掉所有网络和纳斯达克科技股不久，股市即崩盘了。他的投资遵循着一条铁定的原则："在大家绝望地卖出时买入，在大家疯狂地买进时卖出。"大家"悲观到极点"的时刻，他却进入市场赚钱。他说，和众人做出完全相反的决策需要坚忍不拔的毅力。刚开始，他只是东海岸华尔街的一个来自南方的青涩男孩，住在一栋没有电梯的公寓里的六楼，家具价值 25 美元，办事近乎鲁莽。但他尝试着从不同于证券市场惯常的角度观察股票，他的逆向思维习惯给他带来了巨

say, to do the opposite of what the crowd was doing. At the very beginning, a southern boy on Wall Street against the east-coast preppies, living in a sixth-floor walk-up filled with $ 25-worth of furniture, it was almost foolhardy. But he learnt to look at shares distinct from the flow and emotion of the market, and his contrarian habits brought him huge success. A sum of $ 10,000 invested in his Class A portfolio, when he set up the Templeton Growth Fund, would have grown to $ 2m, when he sold his stake. That represented an annualised average return of 14.5% . Sir John knew what he liked. Common stocks, like Dow Jones industrials, were unglamorous but usually dependable. Government bonds were steady, if you picked a country with no trade or fiscal deficits and a high savings rate. He disliked speculation, and any instrument over-geared to make money. But he was open-minded, some moments were good for Treasuries, some for equities, some for blue-chip stocks, he favoured market-neutral hedge funds late in life. Diversity was important, in countries as well as instruments. A journey in 1936 round Europe and the Middle East, sleeping on open decks and chewing dry bread to save money, taught him that investment opportunities lay everywhere he looked.

The Templeton Foundation, set up and now endowed with $ 1.5 billion, was another sort of growth fund, monitoring God's performance in various religions and seeking proofs of divine agency in every branch of science, from chemistry to astrophysics. Scholars helped by Sir John's money investigated whether prayer and health were connected, whether water was fine-tuned to promote life, whether purpose guided the universe. Intelligent Design was embraced, then abandoned. The

大的成功。 自他成立邓普顿增长基金、投资 1 万美元进入 A 类有价
证券起，到售出全部股份为止，其投资价值涨至 200 万美元。 这意
味着平均年回报率高达 14.5%。 约翰爵士知道自己喜欢什么。 道
琼斯工业股票之类的普通股诱惑不大但通常可靠。 假如选择一个没
有贸易或财政赤字、高储蓄率的国家，购买政府债券则收益稳定。
他不喜欢做投机买卖和任何超速赚钱的手段。 但他思想开放，有时
偏好政府债券，有时偏好普通股，有时偏好蓝筹股，晚年偏好市场
中立的对冲基金。 他非常注重多国和多种投资手段的多样化投资方
式。 他在 1936 年环游欧洲和中东时，为了省钱，睡开敞的甲板，
嚼干硬的面包。 这次经历使他明白，他眼中的世界各地都存在着投
资机会。

邓普顿基金会自建立至今，捐资金额已达 15 亿美元，它属于另
类发展基金，监测不同宗教中神的行为，探寻从化学到天体物理学
等科学的各个分支中神力的证据。 约翰爵士资助科学家研究祈祷与
健康之间是否存在联系，水是否有助于延年益寿，意识是否支配着
宇宙等问题。 研究问题曾经包括"智能设计"，但后来被放弃。 净
值 100 万美元的邓普顿奖授予在"人生精神层面"取得突出成就的
个人。 约翰爵士坚信邓普顿奖会超越诺贝尔奖，因为后者忽视了精
神贡献。 邓普顿拥有巨额资产，但他仍然在积累财富，尽其所能
"帮助加速神圣的创造性"。

约翰爵士崇尚节俭，惧怕负债。 这是儿时在田纳西州的小镇父
母对他的教诲，这种思想深深扎根于他的心中，即使有能力住在巴

Templeton prize, a neat $1m, was awarded for individual achievement in "life's spiritual dimension". Sir John made sure it surpassed the Nobel prizes, in which spirituality was ignored. His asset might be infinite, but he meant to build it up, doing whatever he could to "help in the acceleration of divine creativity".

Sir John revered thrift and had a horror of debt. His parents had taught him that in small-town Tennessee, instilling it so well that in his white-columned house in the Bahamas, overlooking the golf course, he still cut up computer paper to make notebooks. But he made an exception for love, which needed spending. You could give away too much land and too much money, said Sir John, but never enough love, and the real return was immediate: more love. The Institute for Unlimited Love, founded with his money, was set up to study this dynamic of the spiritual marketplace. His own charity, though, was harder-edged. On earth a free capitalist system was the only way to enrich the poor. No safeguards were needed: an unethical enterprise would fail, "if not at first, then eventually."

But most of all Sir John went long on God. As a lifelong Presbyterian[1] with a devout and curious mind, he reckoned that the market price of the creator of the universe was probably 1% of its actual value. The crowd might have lost interest in this underrated stock, so dully and unerringly[2] recommended by theologians and priests down the centuries, but Sir John

---

① Presbyterian ['prezbi'tiəriən] *n.* 长老派教徒
② unerringly [ˌʌn'əːriŋli] *adv.* 没有偏差地

哈马群岛纯白石柱装饰的别墅，俯瞰高尔夫球场，他仍然用裁剪好的电脑打印纸做笔记本。但是他对爱心的理解却别具一格，他认为，爱心需要付出。约翰爵士曾经说过，一个人可以捐出大量的土地和大量的金钱，但捐赠的爱心却永远不够，而真正的及时回报是更多的爱心。他出资建立了"无限爱心学院"，研究精神市场的动态。他自己的慈善机构采取了更为坚定的立场。他认为自由的资本主义体系是世上造福穷人的唯一方法，他不需要什么捍卫者，因为缺乏职业道德的企业终究会失败，"这种结局只是早晚的事情"。

约翰爵士长期以来坚定地追随上帝。作为一名长老会终身教徒，他有一颗虔诚和好奇之心，他认为宇宙造物主的市场价格可能只是实际价格的1%。神学家和牧师几个世纪以来单调乏味、一成不变的说教让大众对被低估的股票失去了兴趣，而约翰爵士对它未来的主要赚钱期值坚信不疑。他曾经说过，如果以谦卑胸怀去接近神灵，上帝的力量可能会比人们想象中的强3 000倍。批评约翰爵士的人认为他是迷信上帝的右翼分子。人们注意到，为了避免在美国纳税，他曾逃往巴哈马群岛并加入英国国籍，这些都是他自私的表现。然而，他只是把自己的金钱施与个人，没有上缴政府。他公务繁忙，浮躁好奇，反对自我封闭。拜访者发现，他经常连续发问，渴望听到回答，会谈结束时的分析结果非常尖锐。他可以预见房地产市场的破产，也可以宣布股票市场的"崩盘"。

坐在饰有蝴蝶图案的沙发上，邓普顿爵士依旧渴望科学与宗教之间能够调和。"没人知道在我们死后会发生什么，不会比毛毛虫知

bought it up on the firm expectation of stellar① future earnings. Indeed the divine, he once said, if approached in a humble spirit of inquiry, might turn out to be 3,000 times more than people imagined it was. Critics of Sir John considered him a God-obsessed right-winger. It was noted that, for all his selflessness, he once fled to the Bahamas and took British citizenship to avoid American taxes. Yet Sir John gave his money to individuals, not governments. And, with his restless, buoyant curiosity, he resisted pigeonholing②. Interviewers found that they were peppered with questions and keenly listened to, and to the end the analysis was sharp: Sir John could foresee the housing crash, and pronounce the stock market "broken".

From his sofa decorated with butterflies, he continued to yearn for the reconciliation of science and religion. "None of us know what's going to happen after we die, any more than that caterpillar knows." And in the mornings he took to the sea again and again, striding against the flow. Sir John Marks Templeton, the distinguished investment analyst and philanthropist died, aged 95.

(889 words)

---

① stellar ['stelə] *adj.* 主要的
② pigeonholing ['pidʒinˌhəuliŋ] *n.* 分格化

道得更多。"在那些个早晨，他一次又一次奔向大海，大步走向风浪。 著名的投资分析家和慈善家约翰·马克斯·邓普顿爵士在 95 岁时去世。

知识链接

The John Templeton Foundation 约翰·邓普顿基金会是一个慈善组织，旨在发现人类生存的目的与上帝之间的相关性。基金会资助各种复杂类别的研究，包括进化、创造力、宽恕、仁爱和自由意志。基金会鼓励科学家、哲学家、神学家与公众开展文明对话，获取"新的精神信息"，并建立严格的科学研究和相关奖金制度。基金会每年重奖在人文和科学研究上有卓著贡献之士，颁发世界上奖金最丰厚的邓普顿奖。

题　记

　　一位曾经在街头流浪的无家可归者，一位曾经两次过量吸毒而差点送命的瘾君子，一位曾经蹲过监狱的囚犯，如今却成为一位功成名就的软件公司总裁。鲍伯·威廉森的传奇人生揭示了他克服困难和挫折成为成功企业家的秘诀。他是一个勤奋的人，每天第一个到达公司，最后一个离开公司。他极具商业头脑，创建的地平线国际软件公司为学校食堂提供的软件不仅可以让管理层更好地管理食堂的运作，它甚至可以让家长上网浏览自己的孩子今天的午餐都吃了些什么东西。他视市场和营销为商业中的重中之重，几年时间就将地平线国际软件公司的软件安装到国防部下属的包括军事基地、战舰、潜水艇等在内的所有兵种的食堂中。在他眼中，生意场上的挫折和失败与他生活中遭受的磨难相比真是云淡风轻。

From Junkie to Software Success
— Bob Williamson

Accidental entrepreneur Bob Williamson's personal turnaround led to the creation of his 180-employee, $26 million company. Bob Williamson fled a broken home in Mississippi at age 17 to hitchhike around the country. He landed in Atlanta in 1970 at 24, homeless, broke, and addicted to heroin and methamp-hetamine①. When he got a job there cleaning bricks for $15 a week, no one would have guessed that he would start a $26 million software company someday.

Successful businesses often spring from a combination of hard work and dumb luck, and Williamson credits both. Not long after arriving in Atlanta, he was injured in a car wreck and spent months recovering in the hospital. While there, he read the Bible, converted to Christianity, and decided to straighten up his life. It wasn't easy: He had a criminal record, no college degree, and few job prospects. "I was either going to commit suicide, which several of my friends had done, or I was going turn my life around," says Williamson, now chairman and chief executive officer of Horizon Software International, a 180-employee maker of software for food service systems used in schools, hospitals, and

---

① methamphetamine [ˌmeθæˈfetəmin] n. 甲基苯丙胺(一种中枢兴奋药)

从瘾君子到软件成功人士——鲍伯·威廉森

鲍伯·威廉森意外地成为了企业家，他个人的革心洗面造就了一个拥有 180 个雇员、资产达 2 600 万美元的公司。 鲍伯·威廉森 17 岁那年逃离了他在密西西比州的一个破碎的家庭，开始在全国搭便车旅行。 1970 年，24 岁的他踏上了亚特兰大的土地，他无家可归，身无分文，吸食海洛因和冰毒成瘾。 在那里他找到了一份洗刷砖块的工作，每周 15 美元，那时没有人会猜到有一天他会创办一家价值 2 600 万美元的公司。

成功的事业通常源于吃苦耐劳和偶然运气的结合，威廉森对这两者深信不疑。 到达亚特兰大后不久，他在一场汽车交通事故中受伤，在医院休养了数月。 住院期间，他阅读圣经，皈依了基督教，并决定好好整顿一下自己的生活。 但这并非易事，因为他有犯罪记录，又没有大学文凭，几乎没有什么工作前景。 威廉森认为，"我当时要么就像我的一些朋友那样选择自杀，要么选择改变自己的生活"。

威廉森最终得到了一份在地下室往油漆罐上贴标签的工作，效力于亚特兰大的格利登油漆公司。 他不仅在标签部门赚钱，还帮助格利登研发了公司的第一个计算机系统。 他坚持的工作信条是"最

other institutions.

Williamson eventually landed a job putting labels on paint cans in the basement of the Glidden paint company in Atlanta. He cleaned up the labeling department and helped Glidden move to the company's first computer system. His work ethic, he says, was: "First one there, last to leave." Glidden promoted Williamson eight times in two years. He also went on to work at two other paint companies. By then a paint expert, Williamson started working in his basement to develop a better formula for his hobby: airbrush art. "I borrowed $1,000 on my Visa card and bought a bunch of chemicals and made a bunch of paint," he says. At a trade show, artists flocked to his booth to buy the paint he developed, called Polytranspar. He quit his job and started his own paint company, Master Paint Systems, in 1977. He spun that into several other businesses: a magazine for artists, how-to books, an art supply manufacturer, and a mail-order business, teaching himself as he went along. As the business grew, so did his need for organizational tools. It was the early 1980s, and he realized he needed systems for his warehouse, inventory control, and supply-chain management. "Back then you couldn't buy software, so I hired a couple of programmers, and we wrote software for all these different companies," Williamson says.

His recovering from bankruptcy is really a miracle. By 1986, when he was selling 6,000 different art-related items, Williamson prepared to take the company public. But during the audit for his IPO, he discovered an accountant had been embezzling money from the company. "We fought our way through it, and my accountant and my lawyer and everybody told me to just take bankruptcy and forget about it,"

先到达，最晚离开"。 威廉森在格利登的两年工作中被提拔了八次。 接着，他继续在另外两家油漆公司工作。 那时威廉森已成为一位油漆专家，他开始在自己的地下室里开发一种更好的配方来满足自己的兴趣爱好，即油漆喷雾器艺术。 他说："我从维萨信用卡上预支了 1 000 美元，买来一堆化学药品，完成了一堆油漆作品。"在一次交易展中，艺术家们纷纷涌向他的展台，购买他开发的名叫Polytranspar 的油漆作品。 1977 年，他辞职创办了自己的油漆公司：万事达油漆公司。 威廉森还将自己的事业扩展到其他领域，包括为艺术家开办的杂志、指导手册、艺术品供应厂商和邮购业务。随着事业的发展，他对组织工具的需求也不断上升。 20 世纪 80 年代早期，他意识到需要建立自己的仓储、存货控制和供应链管理计算机系统。 威廉森回忆道："那个时候自己是买不起软件的，所以我雇用了几个程序编写员，我们为那些不同的公司编写计算机软件。"

威廉森曾经从破产中恢复元气的经历简直是个奇迹。 当威廉森1986 年还在销售 6 000 件不同的美术相关用品时，他准备把这间公司投向公共市场。 但在首次公开募股的审计过程中，他发现有一名会计师盗用了公司的账款。 威廉森说："我们为此事努力抗争，想找条出路，我的会计师、律师以及每一个人都让我宣告破产并忘记此事。"但威廉森一直坚信自己能够重新站起来。 他极力劝说他的债权人不要提起诉讼，以免导致强制性的清算。 他说："我每周都给他们写信，告诉他们发生的事情，后来我们重新建立起一个超越以往的平台。"

威廉森随后将目光投向学校的自助餐厅。 公司恢复元气之后，

Williamson says. But he was convinced he could recover. Williamson urged his creditors not to file lawsuits that would force a liquidation①. "Every week I would send them a letter and tell them what was happening, and we rebuilt it up beyond its former stage, " he says.

Williamson then focused on school cafeterias. After recovering, he sold off his previous ventures, and in 1992, founded Horizon. The company was built on the back-office software Williamson spent years developing for his own businesses. "We wrote a system for our mail-order business, we wrote software for our manufacturing company, a point-of-sale system for retail, " he says. "We weren't selling that to anybody. We had just written in-house for our own use." The company focused on systems for school cafeterias when Williamson found no one had written back-office software for that market. He was soon selling into other institutions like hospitals, nursing homes, colleges, and military bases. Horizon recently won the contract for the Los Angeles public schools, the nation's second-largest system. Williamson's son, Michael, who is Horizon's chief operating officer, says his father succeeded by jumping on opportunities that chance presented. "You would never have thought that we would be in food service software when we started Horizon, but the path just kind of led that way and we took advantage of it, " he says. "He's always had a great ability to look out into other markets and other products."

Since the founding of Horizon Software International, its employees have been multipling by two to three, and its business is booming day by

---

① liquidation [ˌlikwi'deiʃən] n. 清算

84

威廉森出售了自己原先的风险投资，并于 1992 年创建了地平线国际软件公司。 威廉森花费多年时间为自己的事业研发了后端办公软件，这家公司就建立在此基础之上。 他说："我们为邮购业务编写了一套程序，为我们的制造公司编写了一套零售销售点系统。 我们不对外出售这些软件，只是在内部编写作为己用。" 当威廉森发现尚未有人为市场编写后端办公软件之时，地平线国际软件公司就重点研发了学校自助餐厅系统。 接下来，他很快将这套服务软件卖给医院、疗养院、大学以及军事基地等机构。 地平线近期赢得了与洛杉矶公立学校合作的合同，即将构建全国第二大系统软件。 威廉森的儿子迈克目前担任地平线国际软件公司的首席运营官，他认为父亲靠抓住偶然降临的机遇获得了成功。 他说："我们开始创办地平线国际软件公司的时候，你决不会想到我们会做食品服务软件这一行，但机遇把我们带到了这条路上，我们充分利用了这次机会。 父亲总是很擅长将眼光投放到其他市场和其他的产品上去。"

地平线国际软件公司自创建以来，员工每年以两到三倍的速度递增，而公司的生意也是蒸蒸日上。 威廉森认为，成功机遇的要素就是吃苦耐劳和坚持不懈。 威廉森现在已经成为地平线国际软件公司的主席和首席执行官，管理着 180 位软件设计制造人员，为学校、医院以及其他机构提供食品服务系统的运营。 位于亚特兰大公司总部的面积超过 44 000 平方英尺。 尽管如此，威廉森还是表示，"我是第一个到达公司、最后一个离开的人"。 同时，他将生意上的成功归因于自己皈依了基督教。"我总是尽量使自己的业务朝着上帝指引的方向去发展……我也总是尽力做一个诚实、坦率的人，不说谎，不欺骗，而且不只是找寻简单的出路。" 吃苦耐劳确实是威廉森

day. Williamson considered that the element of chance is hard work and persistence. Williamson now presides over Horizon's 44,000-square-foot headquarters in Atlanta. Still, Williamson says, "I'm the first one there and the last one to leave." And he ascribes his business success to his conversion. "I have always tried to run my business according to the way that God would want me to ... I've always tried to be honest and straightforward, and not lie and not cheat, and not try to take an easy way out." Hard work was certainly part of Williamson's improbable personal turnaround: He recalls years of working 20-hour days and says he still only sleeps four or five hours a night. But chance guided his entrepreneurial success as well: a car accident that jolted him out of a destructive life, a paint recipe that became a hit, and early exposure to the burgeoning① software industry. And in some ways, Williamson's arrival in Atlanta at the nadir of his life set the foundation for his rise.

"I'd been through so much in my life, I don't get discouraged, " he says. "The trials I've had in business are mild compared to what my life was like."

(943 words)

---

① burgeoning [ˈbəːdʒəniŋ] *adj.* 迅速发展的

罕见的个人转变的必要条件：他回忆起那些每天工作 20 个小时的岁月时，说自己仍然每晚只睡 4 或 5 个小时。 但是，机遇同样也对他企业的成功有引导作用：一场使他从消极而否定的生活中清醒过来的交通事故，一种畅销一时的油漆配方，以及他对迅速发展的软件业的早期探索。 某种意义上来说，威廉森在生活的低谷期来到亚特兰大，这也为他的崛起奠定了基础。 他声称："我一生经历了风风雨雨，但我并没有气馁。 我在生意场上遇到的磨难与我的生活比起来真是微不足道。"

知识链接 ⌕

Horizon Software International 地平线国际软件公司于 1992 年创办，总部位于乔治亚州的德卢斯市，在得克萨斯州、佛罗里达州、科罗拉多州、加利福尼亚州以及乔治亚州的亚特兰大市均设有分部。公司为食堂的管理运作提供软件解决方案、服务性工作和技术，包括库存管理、采购、菜单计划编制、营养分析、产品和仓库分布状态。公司服务于医院、高级会所、公共餐厅、私立学校和高等教育市场，并提供综合温度管理解决方案。

IPO IPO 的全称是 Initial Public Offering，即首次公开募股，指某公司(股份有限公司或有限责任公司)首次向社会公众公开招股的发行方式。有限责任公司首次公开募股后成为股份有限公司。为了保证该企业的规范性以及资金的安全性，国家相关监管部门必须在进行严格的 IPO 审核之后才允许企业进行募股。其中，要求企业的申报会计师完成审计业务、准备会计师报告、资产评估报告(资产评估师)、复核盈利及营运资金预测。

题　记

在华盛顿这座充满了太多必然和绝对的城市里，人们习惯像观看棒球赛胜负一样来断定经济与政治的得失——多少次击打，多少次失误，哪些人成为赛场上的英雄，哪些人成为替罪羔羊，而格林斯潘却从未按此理行事。他那著名的含糊其词的做法并非是为了掩饰自己的真实想法，而是因为他没有得出确切答案的表达方式。梅尔文·金在谈到格林斯潘的为官之道时指出：对经济理解的关键在于如何思考而不是该去思考什么。当人们都自以为手握真理的时候，格林斯潘始终能清醒地认识到自己并非知道每个问题的答案。格林斯潘从美国的经济舞台上谢幕之后，华盛顿政府将很难再找到具有如此谨慎思维的理性伟人。

Alan Greenspan's Humility

Fed Chairman Alan Greenspan has been an unusual figure in Washington because of his willingness to admit that he doesn't have all the answers. In that state of uncertainty，Greenspan developed an economic approach that he described in a farewell speech as "risk management" let more of our cocksure① politicians and analysts share his humility.

Washington is a city that lives on certainties. People want to score political and economic debates like a baseball game— how many hits，how many errors，who are the heroes and who are the goats. Greenspan wouldn't play by those rules. His famous mumble② wasn't always an attempt to mask his real conclusions. It was often a way of expressing the reality that he wasn't sure yet what the answers were. A telling example of Greenspan's agnosticism③ appeared in a profile by Edmund L. Andrews in the New York Times. He cited a comment Greenspan made at the height of the tech boom，to a closed meeting of the Fed："We really do not know how this system works. It's clearly new. The old models just are not

---

① cocksure [ˌkɔkˈʃuə] *adj.* 过分独断的

② mumble [ˈmʌmbl] *adj.* 含糊地说

③ agnosticism [ægˈnɔstisizəm] *n.* 不可知论

艾伦·格林斯潘的谦卑

美联储主席艾伦·格林斯潘因坦言自己并非万事皆通而成为华盛顿令人瞩目的人物。 格林斯潘面对荆棘丛生的局面，制定了一套经济学的方法，在一场告别演讲中将其描述为"风险管理"，让更多独断专行的政治家和分析人士见证了他谦逊的一面。

华盛顿是一座循规蹈矩的城市。 人们习惯像观看棒球比赛一样来断定政治与经济方面的得失——击中多少次，失误多少次，谁成为赛场上的英雄，谁又是替罪羊。 格林斯潘却不按这些常规行事。他以含糊其词著称，但这并不总是为了掩饰其真实的想法。 这通常是表达现实的一种方式，即他尚未找到确切的答案。《纽约时报》特约撰稿人埃德蒙多·L. 安德鲁斯从侧面剖析的格林斯潘不可知论，即是一个有说服力的例证。 他引用了格林斯潘在技术景气鼎盛期召开的一次美联储会议结束时发表的评论："我们真的不知道这个体系是如何运行的。 它是一个全新的机制。 旧的模型已经不适用了。"格林斯潘这样告诉他的同事们。

知道自己并不了解真实的经济发展形势，格林斯潘凭直觉选择了一种务实的经济形式。 他与商界执行者交谈，研究零碎的统计数

working." Greenspan told his colleagues.

Knowing that he couldn't be sure of what was going on in the real economy, Greenspan opted for a pragmatic, seat-of-the-pants kind of economics. He talked to business executives. He studied odd bits of statistical data. He reread his old economics texts. He made decisions about the economy the way most of the people try to make decisions about personal matters, often by asking: What's the penalty if I'm wrong? How do I reduce the likelihood of a really bad event? Sometimes that pragmatism made Greenspan cautious— keeping interest rates higher than critics wanted because he still worried about inflationary expectations. Other times, it made him very bold, as when he pumped massive liquidity into the system after the stock market crash of October 1987; after the collapse of Long-Term Capital Management in September 1998; and after the Sept.11,2001, terrorist attacks.

Through the ups and downs of his 18 years as Fed chair-man, Greenspan tried to remain supple and adaptive— and to avoid becoming locked in his own dogma. His genius seems to be that by leaning one way, then the other, he managed to achieve a series of "soft landings" for economic problems that many analysts thought would produce a crash. Greenspan was candid for him in explaining his approach at the conference on monetary policy in Jackson Hole, Wyo. He noted how the economic certainties of earlier decades had dissolve: People no longer believed in the "Phillips Curve" that described a long-term trade-off between inflation and unemployment; they lost faith in controlling the money supply — the famous "M1" and "M2." Greenspan described the state of economic uncertainty this way in his farewell speech: "Our knowledge about many critical linkages is far from complete and, in all

据，反复研读他的经济学旧作。 他根据大多数人处理个人事务的方式做出决定。 他经常拷问自己：如果我做错了会受到怎样的惩罚？我怎样真正做到减少坏事发生的可能性？ 有时务实会让格林斯潘谨小慎微，例如他因为害怕通货膨胀期望值，将利率维持在高于评论家希望的水平。 而务实有时又会让他敢作敢为，例如 1987 年 10 月股票市场崩溃之后、1998 年 9 月长期资本管理瓦解之后以及 2001 年 9 月 11 号恐怖袭击之后，他曾三次为金融体制注入大量的资产流。

在担任美联储主席 18 年跌宕起伏的生涯中，格林斯潘努力维持着自身的灵活性和适应性，并尽量避免自身思维定式的束缚。 他的天赋就是依托这样或那样的方式，在许多分析家认为即将产生崩溃的经济问题时，他却设法完成一系列的"软着陆"。 在怀俄明州杰克逊·荷尔镇举行的关于货币政策的会议上，格林斯潘坦诚地解释了他的方式。 他指出近几十年来经济的必然性是如何消失的：人们不再信任描述通货膨胀与失业率之间长期权衡的"菲利普斯曲线"，他们对货币的供给控制（即著名的"狭义货币供应量"和"广义货币供应量"）失去信心。 格林斯潘在他的告别演讲中提到经济的不确定性时指出，"在很多关键环节上，我们的知识远非完整，而这种情况完全可能继续存在下去"。 他在继续谈论无确定性答案这一问题时认为，对政策制定者来说，最可贵的优点是维持经济弹性。"经济体系越灵活，对相应不可避免的、通常不可预见的动乱进行自我修复的能力也会更强。"

likelihood, will remain so." Lacking certain answers, he continued, the most valuable asset for policymakers is an economy's flexibility. "The more flexible an economy, the greater its ability to self-correct in response to inevitable, often unanticipated disturbances."

Mervyn King, the governor of the Bank of England, explained what he had learned from Greenspan about how to be a central banker. "The key is to recognize that economics tells you how to think, not what to think. It is not a set of settled conclusions about issues." Right now, Greenspan's critics are taking a poke at him for what they claim has been an overly expansionary monetary policy, which has created a real estate bubble that's about to burst. New York Times columnist Paul Krugman denounced Greenspan for his flip-flopping — warning of budget deficits now when he didn't four years ago, cautioning about a housing bubble that he said would be manageable. He accused Greenspan of playing games with his changing views, But to the most people, that flexibility is precisely what has made Greenspan so successful. He may not always get it right the first time, but he analyzes, considers, adjusts.

Greenspan has been thought as Washington's last great rationalist. At a time when people are screaming certainties and dogmas at each other, he's smart enough to admit he doesn't know all the answers. When he makes mistakes, he goes back and rethinks. He's willing to risk small problems to avoid big ones. He never puts a huge stack of chips on a bet when he's unsure of the odds. It's a prudent turn of mind that Washington government will badly miss when Greenspan retires from the Ameican economic stage.

(779 words)

英格兰银行的总裁梅尔文·金指出，格林斯潘担任央行行长的为官之道令他学会了很多。"关键是要意识到经济学告诉我们如何思考，而不是思考什么。它可不是解决问题的一系列固有结论。"现在，格林斯潘的批评者们正在对其指指点点，他们认为，过度的经济扩张政策引发了即将破裂的房地产泡沫。《纽约时报》专栏作家保罗·克鲁格曼指责格林斯潘翻手为云覆手雨，警告他4年前没有出现的财政赤字现在已经凸显，提醒他对曾经认为可设法控制的房地产泡沫持谨慎态度。但对大多数人而言，正是灵活性成就了格林斯潘。也许他不能总是在第一时间找到正确的解决方式，但他会分析、思考，然后做出调整。

格林斯潘一直被人们认为是华盛顿最后的一位伟大的理性主义者。当人们彼此大声疾呼确定性和独断见解之时，格林斯潘足够聪明，他承认自己并不知晓所有的答案。一旦犯错，他会回到原地，并重新思考。他愿意为小事麻烦，从而避免大问题的产生。他在成败的可能性不确定之前，绝不会轻易拿大把的货币下赌注。格林斯潘从美国经济的舞台上退休之后，华盛顿政府将很难再找到具有如此谨慎思维的人。

知识链接 🔍

M1M2 货币供应量是指某一时点一个国家流通中的货币量。它是分布在居民个人中、信贷系统、企事业单位金库中的货币总计。M1指狭义货币供应量，是流通中现金M0+企业活期存款+农村存款+机关团体部队存款+个人持有的信用卡类存款。M2 指广义货币供应量，是 M1 加上机关、团体、部队、企业和事业单位在银行的定期存款、城乡居民储蓄存款、外币存款和信托类存款。

Soft landings　"软着陆"是一种回落方式。指国民经济的运行经过一段过度扩张之后，平稳地回落到适度增长区间。国民经济的运行是一个动态的过程，各年度间经济增长率的运动轨迹不是一条直线，而是围绕潜在增长能力上下波动，形成扩张与回落相交替的一条曲线。国民经济的扩张，在部门之间、地区之间、企业之间具有连锁扩散效应，在投资与生产之间具有累积放大效应。当国民经济的运行经过一段过度扩张之后，超出了其潜在增长能力，打破了正常的均衡，于是经济增长率将回落。

Phillips Curve　菲利普斯曲线通货膨胀说 (phillips curve) (或称需求面)：需求带动理论主要集中于货币供给，通货膨胀与流通中的货币数量与经济供应力 (其潜在输出) 相关。

题 记

　　蛮横的垄断者、骄傲的王者、一手缔造世界信息产业的霸主——微软公司的比尔·盖茨，没有菲利浦·卡恩那样的热情，没有史提夫·贾伯斯那样的高雅，更没有拉里·埃利森那样的舞台阵势，但是他却带来了计算机工业的革命。随着微软在世界信息产业链上攻城掠地、唯我独尊，"垄断"这个词汇成为与比尔·盖茨联系最密切的词语。尽管比尔·盖茨为推动计算机工业的发展所做出的贡献比其他任何人都多，但微软企业四处伸展的触手也让比尔·盖茨备受"产业独夫"称号的指责。所以说，微软既应该为刺激了计算机产业的革新而被歌功颂德，又应该为扼杀计算机产业的繁荣而受到口诛笔伐。

Monopolist Bill Gates

He's a merciless competitor, a shameless "fan" of other people's ideas and an unapologetic monopolist. And because of all that, Bill Gates has done more to create the thriving computer industry than anybody else. As Gates prepares to retire from full-time work at Microsoft, after 33 years of doing everything from writing code to defending his company's business practices in court, many people are saying 'good riddance' to the man most techies loved to hate. What the critics won't acknowledge is that it was Gates' most obnoxious① qualities that made it possible for the tech industry to grow as large as it has.

"In his prime, Gates combined the monomania of the compulsive software programmer with the competitiveness of Attila the Hun," said Nicholas Carr, author of Does IT Matter and The Big Switch. And that was a good thing. "A lot of people see Microsoft as the enemy of openness and innovation, but it's worth remembering that it was the open architecture of the Microsoft-based PC that spurred② massive creativity in both

---

① obnoxious [əb'nɔkʃəs] *adj.* 极讨厌的
② spurred [spəːd] *vt.* 激励

98

垄断者比尔·盖茨

他集残酷无情的竞争者、掠夺他人思想的不知廉耻"爱好者"和毫无歉意的垄断者于一身。正因为如此，比尔·盖茨为创造繁荣的计算机产业比他人做出了更多的努力。在微软33年的职业生涯中，从写代码到出庭为公司辩护，比尔·盖茨事必躬亲。当盖茨准备全身隐退之时，很多人都说"谢天谢地"，大多数搞计算机的人都对盖茨爱到了要恨的地步。批评家们不愿承认的是，正是盖茨最令人讨厌的品质才使得技术产业的发展壮大成为可能。

《IT重要吗》和《巨大的转变》的作者尼古拉斯·卡尔认为："青壮年时期的盖茨有着患强迫症的软件程序员一样的偏执和匈奴大帝阿提拉一般的竞争力。"这本是件好事。卡尔说，"许多人视微软为开放性和创新性的仇敌，但千万不要忘了，正是基于微软个人计算机开放式的体系结构刺激了硬件和软件的大规模创新，并加速了家用电脑和办公电脑的安装"。事实上，微软曾经在电脑操作系统上占据垄断地位，这对计算机行业的发展至关重要，它强化了一个实际标准，催生了数以千计生产软件和硬件的企业繁荣兴旺。

hardware and software and sped the adoption of computers both at home and at work, " Carr said. In fact, the monopoly that Microsoft once had on computer operating systems was essential to the development of the computer industry, enforcing a de facto standard that permitted thousands of software and hardware companies to blossom.

The Microsoft monopoly was one part luck, one part business acumen①. The lucky part: When IBM asked Microsoft to provide an operating system for its new personal computer in 1980, Gates got the contract, even though he didn't have an OS to sell. No problem. Gates immediately bought the rights to another operating system, QDOS, which he then recast as MS-DOS and sold to IBM. The savvy part: Gates' fledgling company was able to retain rights to the new operating system, securing Microsoft's place at the hub of the PC industry. Later, Gates leveraged that monopoly into such complete dominance of the PC industry that Microsoft was able to collect payments from PC manufacturers for every PC they sold — even if those PCs didn't carry a Microsoft operating system. That monopoly was bad for competitors who had arguably superior operating systems — including, later, IBM's OS/2. And it was built in large part on appropriating the best ideas of other companies, from Gary Kildall's CP/M to Apple's Macintosh.

But the upside was enormous because the monopoly created a stable environment where entrepreneurs could develop new companies and new

---

① acumen [əˈkjuːmen] n. 敏锐

　　微软之所以能够垄断市场，一部分靠运气，一部分靠敏锐的商业头脑。 幸运的是：当美国国际商用机器公司在 1980 年要求微软为他们新开发的个人电脑提供操作系统，甚至在还没有产品可卖的情况下，盖茨就签下了合同。 不费吹灰之力，盖茨随即买下了另一项操作系统 QDOS 的专利，改写一番之后，以微软磁盘操作系统卖给美国国际商用机器公司。 此举的精明之处在于：当年盖茨这家羽翼未丰的公司能够保住对新操作系统的专利权，确保微软作为计算机行业的枢纽地位。 之后，盖茨将垄断的优势扩大，完全主导了个人计算机行业，计算机厂商必须为他们售出的每一台电脑——甚至包括那些没有安装微软操作系统的电脑——向微软付费。 这种垄断对那些生产性能更优越的操作系统包括美国国际商用机器公司后来的 OS/2 的竞争者来说可不是什么好事。 其垄断地位在很大程度建立在盗用其他公司最优秀的理念上，从加里·基尔德尔的 CP/M 到苹果的麦金托什机，这些先进理念都曾被微软盗用过。

　　但反过来看，垄断的好处是巨大的，因为它创造了一个稳定的环境，企业家们可以在一个公共的平台上发展新公司和开发新产品。 如果没有这样一个标准，那么 20 世纪 90 年代的计算机工业就会类似于今天的互联网：虽然丰富的创新活动形式多样，充满活力并层出不穷，但也会因为不同产品之间最基本的连接互不兼容，导致崩溃现象时有发生。 弗雷斯特研究公司的创始人乔治·克勒尼在

products around a common platform. Without that standard, the computer industry in the 1990s would have resembled the web today: diverse, vibrant and flowering with abundant innovation, but also frequently broken because of the inability of disparate products to make the most basic connections with one another. "Unlike oil, pharmaceutical① or steel, monopolies are a necessary ingredient in the technology business," Forrester Research founder George Colony wrote in a blog post. "It's only when de facto standards like Windows or de jure standards like HTML become dominant that usefulness soars."

Contrast that to the state of the internet today. While the web abounds in standards, a frequent problem is that companies don't hew to them and since 1996, Microsoft has been guilty of this behavior too. Having trouble syncing your Google calendar with your Yahoo calendar? Wondering why your camcorder won't upload to your new Macbook, your iPod can't share files with your friends. MP3 players and your mobile phone can't display webpages properly? All of these problems are traceable to a lack of widely supported standards. Just imagine if the same chaos had reigned throughout the 1980s and early 1990s. Hardware manufacturers like Dell, Hewlett Packard, Compaq and IBM would still be battling it out with incompatible systems. And software like Lotus 1-2-3, WordPerfect and, yes, even Microsoft Office never would have achieved widespread success. "Bill Gates made an unbelievable

---

① pharmaceutical [ˌfɑːməˈsjuːtikəl] *adj.* 制药的

网络日志中写道："不像石油、制药或钢铁行业，垄断在科技行业中是必不可少的因素。只有像微软公司生产的'视窗'操作系统那样的实际标准、或者像超文本链接标示语言那样的法律标准占据主导地位的时候，有效性才能凸显出来。"

互联网的现状与之形成了鲜明对比。尽管互联网的标准很多，但经常发生的问题是那些公司没法坚持这些标准，自 1996 年以来，微软也一直存在类似的不良行为。你是否发现让谷歌日历与雅虎日历同步有一定的困难？你是否纳闷为什么自己的可携式摄像机无法安装到新款的麦金塔笔记型电脑上？为什么 iPod 拒绝和朋友的 MP3 分享文件？为什么自己的手机不能完全显示网页？所有这些问题源于互联网没有一个广泛的支撑标准。设想一下，如果同样混乱的局面发生在上世纪整个 80 年代和 90 年代早期会怎样。戴尔、惠普、康柏和美国国际商用机器公司之类的硬件制造商仍在为不兼容的系统角逐胜负。而 Lotus1-2-3、WordPerfect，甚至微软 Office 等类似的软件永远不会取得广泛的成功。身为网景公司、Opsware 软件公司和 Ning 软件公司三家企业创始人的马克·安德森说道："比尔·盖茨做出的贡献，让人感到难以置信。很难想象如果没有当年微软给操作系统定下的规矩，计算机行业今天会是怎样的一个惨状……我认为如果没有微软的垄断，这个行业会小得多。"这种论调与约翰·巴特利当年在旧金山 Web2.0 博览会上的主题发言如出一辙。

contribution," said Netscape, Opsware and Ning founder Marc Andreessen, while speaking at a keynote with John Battelle at the Web 2.0 Expo in San Francisco that year. "It's hard to conceive what this industry would look like today if Microsoft hadn't standardized the OS ... I think the industry would be much smaller if that hadn't happened."

Of course, success breeds resentment, and Gates' aggressive business practices — and less-than-polished personal style — made him many enemies. "The problem is when you're the biggest sequoia in the woods, everyone wants to cut you down," said Paul Santinelli, a general partner with North Bridge Venture Partners, a venture capital firm. Gates didn't help matters by overreaching once his company's monopoly was firmly established. "Gates became kind of a Godfather figure in the industry, demanding tributes from his partners and whacking those who threatened his power," Carr said. "So Microsoft deserves both praise for stimulating innovation and criticism for stifling it."

And then there was the problem that many of Microsoft's products simply didn't work that well. Indeed, as the chorus of complaints about Windows Vista grows louder day by day, it could be said that Gates is leaving Microsoft at exactly the right time, before the company's long decline sullies his reputation. "If all that stuff worked right out of the box, we'd all be out of a job," said David Strom, an independent technology consultant and speaker in St. Louis. Strom has a speech praising Gates for, among other things, effectively guaranteeing full employment

　　当然啦，成功也滋生出了怨恨，盖茨具有侵略性的商业活动以及缺乏圆滑的个人风格使他树敌颇多。风险投资公司北桥风险的一般合伙人保罗·桑提奈利如是说："问题是你成为了丛林中最大的一棵美洲杉，每个人都想把你砍倒。"一旦微软的垄断地位牢固地建立起来，盖茨无法遏制延伸得过头的局面。卡尔认为，"盖茨差不多就成了计算机行业的教父，一边从合作伙伴那里收钱，一边无情地打击那些威胁到他权力的人。所以说，微软应该受到赞扬，因为它促进了创新；但同时又该受到批评，因为它也扼杀了创新"。

　　接下来的问题是，微软的许多产品性能似乎不怎么好。确实，人们对 Windows Vista 操作系统的抱怨之声日渐壮大，应该说，盖茨此时离开微软正是时候，免得公司一天天衰败玷污了他的名声。圣路易斯的一位独立技术顾问兼发言人大卫·斯特勒姆认为："如果电脑不用装软件都能运转的话，我们大概都会失业。"斯特勒姆曾发表演讲赞扬盖茨，其中之一就是他有效地保证了 IT 人员充分就业，使微软的产品能够正常运行。尽管有些技术人员可能会诅咒盖茨的侵略性做法和微软软件存在的漏洞，可既然盖茨要离开计算机行业了，他们还是该为他离开计算机行业举杯祝福。桑提奈利指出："他没有菲利浦·卡恩那样的热情，也没有史提夫·贾伯斯那样的高雅，更没有拉里·埃利森那样的舞台阵势。但是这家伙带来了个人计算机行业的革命，这是人们需要铭记的。"

for IT people called in to make Microsoft products work properly. But while technologists may curse Gates' aggressiveness and the buggyness of Microsoft software, they should also raise a glass to toast him as he departs the computer business. "He didn't have the zest of a Philippe Kahn, or the elegance of a Steve Jobs, or the stage presence of a Larry Ellison. But the guy revolutionized the PC industry, and that's what people need to remember," said Santinelli.

(984 words)

知识链接 🔍

Netscape 网景是一个自 1994 年开始的品牌。它亦是网景通讯公司（Netscape Communications Corporation，1994 年 4 月 4 日—2003 年 7 月 5 日）的常用简称。网景通讯公司曾经是一家美国的电脑服务公司，以其生产的同名网页浏览器而闻名。就市场占有率来说，网景的网页浏览器曾占首位，但在"第一次浏览器大战"中被微软的 Internet Explorer 所击败。1998 年 11 月，网景被美国在线（AOL）收购，而美国在线之后又成为时代华纳的一部分。美国在线现时依然使用网景品牌。

Forrester Research 弗雷斯特研究公司于 1983 年 7 月创建，是一家独立的技术和市场调研公司，针对技术给业务和客户所带来的影响提供务实和具有前瞻性的建议。在过去的 30 年当中，弗雷斯特研究公司已经被公认为思想的领导者和可信赖的咨询商，它通过所从事的研究、咨询、市场活动和高层对等交流计划，帮助那些全球性的企业用户建立起市场领导地位。

题 记

　　阿玛尼代表柔和的结构裁剪，普拉达代表尼龙，香奈儿让人联想到开襟羊毛衫，而王薇薇则是婚纱礼装的标志。一件王薇薇婚纱的价格足够买下一辆名车，但照样让人趋之若鹜。在王薇薇时代到来之前，许多新娘只能想象戴安娜王妃婚礼服上那些令人眼花缭乱的蛋白色亮片，更多地期待小女孩典藏在化妆盒中的婚礼梦幻。当王薇薇推出时代性和精巧时尚轮廓相融合的理念之后，她在婚纱礼服市场引发的效应不亚于一场革命。王薇薇在成功地为好莱坞顶级大牌女星们设计一件又一件精妙的婚纱礼服的同时，也成功地收获了自己婚纱时尚女王的称号以及随之而来的巨大财富。她的成功离不开她那过人的天赋和对时尚的狂热与执著，更离不开她对这份事业不懈的努力和探索。

Wedding Belles
Vera Wang

Even if you were only dimly aware of Wang's reign on the red carpet — at Oscars, Michelle Williams's canary yellow gown and Keira Knightley's bordcaux silk taffeta dress were both hers — you'd have been hard pressed to meet a bride over the past decade who hasn't nurtured a fantasy about wearing a Vera Wang dress on her big day. As she points out herself, Wang's name is to bridalwear what Armani is to softly-constructed tailoring, what Prada is to nylon, what Chanel is to the cardigan jacket. In the years before Vera, many brides— those who couldn't afford an haute couture dress from Paris, or a lovely hand-me-down from their mother— couldn't see beyond a Princess Di meringue, blizzards of sequins and a fantasy that had more in common with a little girl's dressing-up box than anything seen on a contemporary designer catwalk. When Wang introduced the idea of modernity and subtly fashionable silhouettes, she effected nothing less than a revolution on the bridalwear market.

Wang not only introduced a fashionable sensibility to wedding dress design but also benefited from dozens of high-profile celebrity nuptials, at a time when there was no obvious bridal "brand" on the fashion landscape. Sharon Stone, Uma Thurman, Jennifer Lopez and Mariah

婚纱女王王薇薇

即使人们只能模糊地感受到王薇薇在红地毯上的影响——在奥斯卡颁奖礼上，米歇尔·威廉的淡黄色礼服着装和凯拉·奈特莉的枣红色丝制塔夫绸裙装均出自她之手，但在过去的十年间，人们一直惊讶于每个新娘都梦想着在自己大喜的日子穿上王薇薇设计的婚纱。 正如她自己所说的，阿玛尼代表柔和的结构裁剪，普拉达代表尼龙，香奈儿让人联想到开襟羊毛衫，而王薇薇则是婚纱礼装的标志。 在薇薇时代到来之前，许多新娘只能想象戴安娜王妃婚礼服上那些令人眼花缭乱的蛋白色亮片，更多地拥有小女孩藏在化妆盒中的婚礼幻想，而不是亲眼见证当代时尚设计师的猫步，他们无法支付巴黎昂贵的高级女装，或是只能穿着母亲传下来的礼服。 当王薇薇推出时代性和精巧时尚轮廓相融合的理念之后，她在婚纱礼服市场引发的效应不亚于一场革命。

王薇薇不仅为婚纱设计引入了时尚的敏感性，也从许多名人大腕的婚礼中取得了丰厚的回报，而当时的时尚设计界还没有一个响当当的婚纱"品牌"。 莎朗·斯通、乌玛·瑟曼、詹妮弗·洛佩兹和玛丽亚·凯利等明星都是王薇薇的座上宾客。 维多利亚·贝克汉姆婚礼上穿的那款象牙白缎面、下摆呈玛丽·安托瓦内特式的宽大

Carey, among others, have all walked up the aisle in Vera Wang; the designer's UK profile was raised considerably when Victoria Beckham chose an ivory satin gown with a broad skirt worthy of Marie Antoinette.

"That was a 'transatlantic' dress," recalls Wang. "The underpinning was flown back and forth. I had thought, God, she's going to want something asymmetric and very sexy because she's — you know — body-conscious. But she wanted it to be all about a bustier, very cinched in, with an enormous skirt. It was a lot of work to create that silhouette." Although uncluttered, dramatic silhouettes are probably most typical of Wang's vision, over the years, she says, "there's almost nothing I've not done. We brought everything that was happening in fashion and translated it into a wedding vocabulary. Deconstructed. Constructed. Micro-minis. I've done dresses with 20-foot trains. I've been able to explore the world of dressmaking through bridal."

"She started off the corset-with-a-big-skirt look," says Bryony Toogood, fashion editor at Brides magazine. "But she's not a one-trick pony. She's very current and keeps on top of trends, but also keeps all the elements of a sophisticated wedding dress." Toogood believes that Wang's perceived kudos[1] as a former fashion insider has benefited the business as a whole. "I think other designers used to think bridal was naff. But it's more acceptable now — and she's bridged that gap. A lot of bridal designers do things that are really safe."

Wang's entry into the fashion world reads like scene from The Devil Wears Prada, the forthcoming film starring Meryl Streep: having

---

① kudos ['kjuːdɔs] n. 荣誉

裙摆礼服，使王薇薇在英伦的名声大噪。 王薇薇回忆到："那是条'美式'裙子，下摆的衬裙支架会前后晃动。 我当时想，天哪，她喜欢不对称而又性感的，你知道，她的曲线意识很强。 她只想要一件紧身胸衣，很贴身的那种，下面搭配一条宽大无比的裙子。 设计这样一件婚纱装着实花费了我不少心血。"尽管剪裁整洁，戏剧化影像无疑是王薇薇设计的最佳诠释。 她在多年后承认："我几乎尝试了所有的设计手法。 我们引进了一切可能发生的时尚元素，并将其转化为婚纱语言。 分解、构造、微型迷你，我用 20 英尺长的下摆来做裙子。 我已经能够通过婚礼来探索女装裁剪的世界。"

《新娘杂志》的时尚编辑布莱妮·涂古德认为："她以女性胸衣结合大摆下裙的造型开启了自己的设计生涯。 但她并不只是个仅有一技之长的小巧女子。 她非常时尚，紧跟前沿潮流，还能将所有的元素融入精细的婚纱裙装。"涂古德相信，王薇薇天生的时尚感知力对她的整体事业起到了推波助澜的作用。"我想其他设计师过去常常认为，新娘用品毫无时尚价值可言。 然而更多的人现在接受了这一观点——王薇薇填补了这一空白。 许多婚纱设计师做事确实是保守了。"

王薇薇进入时尚界的经历与电影《穿普拉达的女魔头》中梅丽尔·斯特里普所扮演的角色经历颇为相似：放弃孩童时代成为一名花样溜冰运动员的抱负，这位 23 岁的前哥伦比亚大学和巴黎大学艺术史学生成为一名美国《时尚杂志》助理，她在工作的第一天就接到卡尔万·克莱因亲自打来的电话。 但是与电影中那个有些莽撞的女主角不同，薇薇已经对圣·洛朗有了自己的品位，她的母亲在巴黎购物，为她的衣橱添置衣物，她没有任何后顾之忧。 实际上，成

abandoned a girlhood ambition of becoming a figure-skater, a 22-year-old former art history student of Colombia and the Sorbonne is taken on as an assistant at American Vogue and finds herself taking calls from Calvin Klein himself on her first day. Unlike that film's gauche① young heroine, however, Vera, who had already developed a taste for Saint Laurent and whose mother shopped in Paris for her wardrobe, wasn't fazed at all. In fact, so precociously chic was she, the legendary fashion editor Polly Mellen sent her home on her first day in the photographic studio for being over-dressed. "I didn't know what to wear. In Funny Face the editors had all dressed up as if they were going to a ball. So I came in wearing a white YSL shirt waister and red nails. She said, 'Put on some jeans — we are going to work.' And I never dressed up at Vogue again."

Wang remained at Vogue for 16 years, working as a fashion editor and revelling in the discovery of previously unknown labels. "I loved trawling Chelsea for young designers. I remember when Isaac Mizrahi started, when Marc Jacobs started. It was astonishing that the magazine let me do it. They let me bring in Norma Kamali. It was a dream job." She idolises Vivienne Westwood, she says, and "I collect Comme, Yohji and wear a lot of Prada and Marni. I respect other talent." You get the feeling much of her ambivalence about her success as a bridalwear designer is borne out of a niggling fear that designing fantasy dresses— however chic— for white weddings isn't quite as avant-garde a calling as she would prefer.

Nonetheless, she started out with a boutique on Madison Avenue that

---

① gauche [gəuʃ] *adj.* 笨拙的

熟漂亮的她在摄影工作室上班的第一天就被传说中的时尚编辑波莉·梅兰遣送回家，原因竟是她穿着不得体。"我真的不知道该穿什么。 在《滑稽面孔》工作时，编辑们都浓妆艳抹，仿佛准备去参加一场化装舞会。 所以去摄影工作室时我系了一条伊夫·圣洛朗的白色腰带并涂了红指甲。 编辑当时便对我说，'牛仔裤就行了——我们是来工作的。' 从那以后，去《时尚杂志》上班我再也没有打扮过。"

王薇薇在《时尚杂志》一待就是 16 年，做过时尚编辑，也痴迷地挖掘过先前不知名的品牌。 她将维维恩·韦斯特伍特奉为偶像："我喜欢帮年轻设计师搜罗切尔西品牌。 我仍清楚地记得艾萨克·麦兹拉西和马克·雅可布何时起的家。 我很惊讶杂志让我做这一切。 他们让我引进了诺玛·卡玛丽品牌。 这真是份梦幻般的工作。 我收集恤之王者和优基服装，穿了许多普拉达和阿玛尼品牌。我尊重那些有才华的人。"人们会察觉她作为一名成功的婚纱礼服设计师具有太多的矛盾情绪，这种心理出于一种过于琐碎的担忧，即由她设计的梦幻礼服不管对白色婚礼来说有多么别致漂亮，总是没有她所希望的那么前卫、紧贴时尚。

虽然如此，她还是在麦迪逊大道开了一间专营手工婚纱礼服的时尚小店。 她谓之为"一个商业决策"。 她逐渐引入自己的设计并在店中销售。 如今，她掌管的横跨各洲、覆盖各生产领域的公司即使没有达到保罗·拉夫·劳伦的规模，也可称之为帝国。 可以预见，该品牌满足了时尚新娘们的多元化需求：家具、瓷器、香水，甚至还有王薇薇设计的"一晚五千五百美金"的蜜月套房，该套房最近已在夏威夷哈利库拉尼风景胜地揭幕营业。 王薇薇的特许经营

sold a hand-picked selection of wedding dresses. "It was a business decision," she says. Gradually, she introduced her own designs— and they sold. Today, she helms an empire that, if not on a Polo Ralph Lauren scale, sprawls across continents and product categories. Predictably, the brand attends to the multifaceted requirements of the modern bride: stationary, china, fragrance and even a $ 5,500-a-night Vera Wang-designed honeymoon suite, which recently opened at the Halekulani resort in Hawaii. A dedicated Vera Wang concession opened at Selfridges on Oxford Street, the only bridalwear available at the store. Her dresses have a reputation for being expensive, but, actually, the brand has three "levels", with the most affordable starting just below £2,000 and the most costly running into several tens of thousands of pounds. Personal fittings with Wang herself at her New York atelier① inflate prices to around £75,000. "You know, I do try to bring a high level of thought to my bridal collections," she reflects. "I always think I've done everything there is to do in bridal, but then I always come up with another idea that looks new — to me. Of course, from far away all big white dresses tend to look the same. But not when you're close up."

(964 words)

---

① atelier ['ætəljei] *n.* 制作室

店在牛津大街的塞尔福里奇百货大厦落成开业，店中只出售新娘婚纱礼服。 她的礼服以昂贵出名，但实际上品牌共分为三个"档次"，最便宜的低于两千英镑，而最贵的则高达几十万英镑。 在位于纽约的私人定制工作室里，一件由王薇薇亲自为新娘量身定制的礼服价格飙升到七万五千英镑左右。 她慎重地表达了自己的想法："你知道，我绞尽脑汁地将自己的所思所想注入婚纱设计之中。 我常常认为自己在婚纱设计上已是江郎才尽，但脑子里又常常不经意地再次迸发出新的思想。 当然，长期来看，所有的大型白色婚纱都趋于一种模式。 然而这绝非我收手之时。"

知识链接

Ralph Lauren 拉夫·劳伦(Ralph Lauren)是有着浓厚美国气息的高品位时装品牌，款式高度风格化是拉夫·劳伦旗下的两个著名品牌"Ralph Ralph Lauren"(拉夫·劳伦女装)和"Polo Ralph Lauren"(拉夫·劳伦马球男装)的共同特点。拉夫·劳伦品牌还包括香水、童装、家居等产品。拉夫·劳伦勾勒出的是一个美国梦：漫漫草坪、晶莹古董、名马宝驹，它的时装设计融合幻想、浪漫、创新和古典的灵感呈现，所有的细节架构建立在一种不被时间淘汰的价值观上，无论是服装还是家具，无论是香水还是器皿，都迎合了顾客对上层社会完美生活的向往，而舒适、好穿、价格适中的拉夫·劳伦POLO衫无论在欧美还是亚洲，几乎已成为人人衣柜中必备的衣着款式！

题　记

　　大卫·卡尔霍恩担任尼尔森的首席执行官期间，为公司设置了一个简单的目标：大量的赚钱和重塑市场营销与传媒业的未来。他让尼尔森在世界的每一个角落大展身手，通过最丰富、最全面的媒体和市场资讯，业内最具专业性的服务和分析工具，获取市场知识、专业技巧和洞察市场最可靠的源泉。客户、竞争对手和同事都认为卡尔霍恩的管理为尼尔森注入了活力和竞争激情，通过把市场数据转换为具有可操作性的市场和经营策略促进了客户业务的增值。卡尔霍恩在重塑阿瑟·尼尔森创建的商业信誉，即公正、全面、准确的"尼尔森代码"过程中，展现了自身的人生价值和魅力。

Reshaping Nielsen Code

CEO David Calhoun has a simple plan for Nielsen: Make gobs① of money and reshape the future of marketing and media.

The son of a cement salesman, Calhoun grew up in Allentown, Pa., and joined GE's management training program right after finishing his accounting degree at Virginia Tech. Known at GE for a willingness to tackle big jobs, Calhoun takes pride that despite wearing an insulin pump to treat diabetes, he has an athletic life. Calhoun says there was no friction with GE CEO Jeff Immelt. What made him jump when he did, he says, was the realization that he would be on the road 90% of the time in one year, much of that abroad. He decided he wanted to spend more time with his wife, Barbara, and the two of their four kids who hadn't yet left for college. At Nielsen he works mostly out of a bland satellite office in Wilton, Conn., a short drive from his house. "I miss the breadth of GE today," says Calhoun. "I can't tell you I don't miss that. So whatever I had to do had to be really different."

His biggest concern about taking the Nielsen gig② was whether six

---

① gob [gɔb] *n.* 大量
② gig [gig] *n.* 职业

重塑尼尔森代码

首席执行官大卫·卡尔霍恩为尼尔森制订了一个简单的计划：大量的赚钱和重塑市场营销与传媒业的未来。

卡尔霍恩是一个水泥销售商的儿子，他在宾夕法尼亚州的阿伦敦长大，取得弗吉尼亚理工大学会计学位之后，进入通用电器的管理培训项目部。卡尔霍恩在通用电器以心甘情愿处理重要的工作而出名，尽管需要靠注射胰岛素来治疗糖尿病，他仍然在生活中坚持运动，并以此为骄傲。卡尔霍恩认为他与通用电器的首席执行官杰夫·伊梅尔特之间没有摩擦。他一年里有 90% 的时间在路上度过，而且大多数是在国外，基于这样一个事实，他才跳了槽。他决定花更多的时间陪伴妻子芭芭拉和四个孩子中两个尚未上大学的孩子。在尼尔森，他大多数情况下会在康涅狄格州威尔顿一间普通的附属办公室工作，这儿离他家的车程很近。卡尔霍恩说："我现在仍然怀念通用电器的氛围。我一直在告诉人们，那些日子我铭记于心。所以我不管做什么都必须真正做到与众不同。"

六个独立的私人股东是否可以共存是他履行尼尔森职责以来最大的担忧。但他认为到目前为止还算一帆风顺。尼尔森要保证第一年的营业收入至少增长 20%，并使目标不会受到影响。卡尔霍恩

private-equity egos could coexist. But so far, he says, it's been smooth sailing. It can't hurt that Nielsen looks to be on track to achieve ownership's first-year goal of raising operating income by at least 20%. Calhoun has cut costs and acquired new, higher-growth businesses. On a pro forma basis, revenues for the nine months ended Sept.30 were $ 3.4 billion, up 11% from last year, while operating income increased 19% to $ 196 million. If Calhoun can keep it up, he'll double the profits of the company within five years of its changing hands. And thanks to the magic of leverage, the $ 4 billion in equity that the company's owners invested could double or triple in value.

During his first two months on the job Calhoun met with the CEOs of clients and got personally involved in big contracts — including P&G, Coca-Cola, NBC, and KFT— that were up for renewal. Since then he has opened up his thick GE management playbook — doing everything from importing Six Sigma productivity gurus to hiring several former colleagues to key corporate posts. He renamed the company after its core brand. And he's given longtime Nielsen executives, such as research chief Susan Whiting, expanded duties while bringing in a couple of media industry mavericks, like former Grey Advertising exec Jon Mandel, to help shake up the business. Nielsen has announced a raft of deals and alliances, including one with potential rival Google. And it has been working on entirely new ways to measure things that it hopes will ensure its hegemony in decades to come, including one new service to monitor the impact of in-store advertising (e.g., video-screens) and another that takes the coding Nielsen embeds in all TV shows as part of its ratings — gathering apparatus and uses it as a watermark to protect the shows from

已经削减了成本，并获得了新的高增长业务。 据估计，到9月底，公司9个月的盈利达34亿美元，相比去年同期增长11%，而营业收入增长了19%，达1.96亿美元。 如果卡尔霍恩能够保持这种增长，公司利润将在他获得公司管理权之后5年内增加一倍。 由于神奇的杠杆作用，拥有40亿股票的公司股东们的投资将会增值一倍或者两倍。

卡尔霍恩在就职的头两个月里就会见了几家客户公司的首席执行官，并亲自参与了这些大合同的续约工作，其中包括宝洁、可口可乐、美国国家广播公司和卡夫食品公司。 自那以后，他充分发挥了在通用电气公司学到的丰富的管理经验，尽一切可能引进六西格玛管理法的生产权威，并雇用以前的几个同事担任公司要职。 他以公司的核心品牌重新为其命名。 他扩大了长期担任尼尔森主管（如研究部首席苏珊·怀廷）的职责，同时引进了几个传媒业的巨头，如前灰色广告主管乔恩·曼德尔，帮助公司重新组合业务。 尼尔森宣布了一系列协议和联盟，其中有一项是与其潜在的竞争对手谷歌签订的。 他一直致力于用全新的方式作为衡量标准，希望确保今后几十年的霸权地位，其中包括两项新的服务项目，一个用来监测店内的广告影响（例如，视频屏幕），另一个是尼尔森对所有电视节目嵌入的编码，作为收视率收集仪器的一部分，并把它当做水印使用，以防止未经授权的在线节目的播出。

迄今为止，客户、竞争对手和同事都认为卡尔霍恩的管理为尼尔森注入了活力和竞争激情。 信息资源部的主席、尼尔森最大的单一竞争对手罗梅什·瓦德万尼认为："与以前的业主竞争让我感到更愉快。"尼尔森的长期雇员乔·维尔克这样总结了卡尔霍恩对公司的

unauthorized play online.

So far clients, competitors, and colleagues alike say that Calhoun's management has injected energy and competitive fire into Nielsen. "I was much happier competing with the previous owners," says Romesh Wadhwani, the chairman of Information Resources, Nielsen's largest single competitor. Joe Willke, a longtime Nielsen employee, summed up Calhoun's impact on the company this way: "It's like you're playing in AA baseball, and suddenly Roger Clemens has come to pitch for you." It's still early innings①, of course. And Roger Clemens hasn't had an easy time lately either. There are plenty of challenges to keep Calhoun on his toes. In television Nielsen might be facing its first real threat, well, ever. Everyone from TiVo to DirecTV to Comcast (CMCSA) is now working on a way to use set — top boxes to provide real-time TV viewing data that rival Nielsen's — at a fraction of the cost.

One of Nielsen's biggest pushes is what it calls "anytime, anywhere media measurement." Calhoun believes Nielsen NetRatings can be the currency of Internet advertising, just as Nielsen ratings are for TV. For now, though, figuring out who really visits what on the web is a chaotic② exercise, with several competitors often producing wildly different numbers. Whether the criticism is valid or not, some wonder if some of Nielsen's current quality issues are linked to its new ownership and financial situation. Although Nielsen is within its covenants③, it has

---

① inning ['iniŋ] *n.* 局,回合
② chaotic [kei'ɔtik] *adj.* 无秩序的
③ covenants ['kʌvənənt] *n.* 盟约

影响:"这就像正在进行世界棒球赛时,罗杰·克莱门斯突然出现在球场,助你一臂之力。"当然局势才刚打开。 罗杰·克莱门斯最近也在艰难度日。 卡尔霍恩面临很多挑战,需要谨慎行事。 对尼尔森来说,第一次真正的威胁可能来自电视信息市场,或许任何时候都是如此。 从蒂沃公司到美国直播电视公司,每家公司都在以一种低成本的方式使用置顶盒,提供现时电视查访数据对抗尼尔森。

尼尔森的核心竞争力之一被称为"随时、随地的媒体测量"。卡尔霍恩认为,尼尔森的网络评级体系可以成为互联网广告的主流,其影响将不亚于尼尔森电视节目收视率评级。 不过,目前很难推测谁真正在网站上访问了什么,网站仍然呈无序状态,几个竞争对手对此给出的结论往往很不一致。 不管批评合理与否,一些人怀疑尼尔森目前的质量问题是否与其新的所有权和财务状况有关。 尽管还在订立的公约范围之内,但尼尔森需要支付其所有的债务。 不过,私人股本合作伙伴已经同意卡尔霍恩使用营运储蓄业务,他采取了新的举措,并倡议增加基金收购。 但这也意味着公司每年需要支付将近 7 亿美元的利息,而这影响到卡尔霍恩可以继续投资多少资金。 有传闻说公司要出售商业信息部门和内部预映部,重心转向研究,对此他给予否认。 哥伦比亚广播公司的首席研究官戴伟·波特里克指出,在任何情况下,他都会警惕卡尔霍恩做出的调整。 波特里克说:"我们理解业务的现状。 但在这个时刻,我们关注的是确保他们不会削减到公司的核心部门。"

让人放心的是,根据卡尔霍恩发布的信息,之前他在塑料、机车和喷气发动机等行业也遇到过类似的挑战。 如果他把重点放在执行上——当然是衡量标准——其他的一切将迎刃而解。 但他需要保

yet to pay down any of its debt. Instead, the private equity partners have allowed Calhoun to use operational savings he's made to fund acquisitions and new initiatives — but that also means that the company is paying close to $ 700 million in interest each year, which raises questions about how much Calhoun can continue to invest. One rumored option, which he denies, is to sell the business information and trade show division and focus on research. In any case, David Poltrack, chief research officer at CBS, says he is wary of some of the restructuring Calhoun has done.

"We understand the business reality of that, " says Poltrack. "But at this point in time we are concerned to make sure that they are not cutting to the bone."

The reassuring, take-charge message from Calhoun is that he has faced challenges like this before, in everything from plastics to locomotives to jet engines. If he focuses on executing— and of course on measuring— everything else will work out. But he needs to keep his troops on track too. As the Florida retreat wound to a close, Calhoun praised and thanked his people but added a note of caution. He reminded them that Arthur Nielsen and his son built their business on integrity — a "Nielsen code" of impartiality, thoroughness, and accuracy. And in their role as caretakers of that legacy, nothing less than the future of honest commerce is at stake. "We're temporary, all of us, " he said. "This is bigger than us, and bigger than me. Nielsen is a powerful name. It matters in the world." In other words, he might have added, Nielsen counts.

(1,010 words)

证自己的管理团队走上正轨。 佛罗里达州务虚会即将结束之时，卡尔霍恩略带谨慎地赞扬并感谢了他的团队，他提醒大家，阿瑟·尼尔森和他的儿子建立了商业信誉，即公正、全面、准确的"尼尔森代码"。 他们的任务是看护好这一遗产，诚信商业的未来岌岌可危。 他认为，"我们，包括我们所有人，都只是过渡性人物。 这比我们、比我本身更重要。 尼尔森是一个强有力的名字。 它在世界上举足轻重。" 换句话说，他很可能会补充：尼尔森价值无量。

知识链接 🔍

AC Nielsen AC 尼尔森是全球领先的市场研究、资讯和分析服务的提供者，服务对象包括消费产品和服务行业，以及政府和社会机构。在全球 100 多个国家里有超过 9 000 的客户依靠 AC 尼尔森认真负责的专业人士来测量竞争激烈的市场的动态，来理解消费者的态度和行为，以及形成能促进销售和增加利润的高级分析性洞识。AC 尼尔森总部位于美国纽约，并在伊利诺伊州的商堡(Schaumburg)、比利时的瓦韦尔(Wavre)、中国香港、澳大利亚的悉尼、阿根廷的布宜诺斯艾利斯以及塞浦路斯的尼科西亚建立了区域业务中心。

Roger Clemens 罗杰·克莱门斯。罗杰·克莱门斯是一位活跃于 20 世纪 80 年代至 21 世纪初的美国职棒大联盟的投手，外号"火箭人"。

题 记

　　美国钢铁大王安德鲁·卡耐基杰出的经商能力、孜孜不倦的奋斗精神和他的真知灼见使他聚集了惊人的财富，但他更因两面人性的光辉留存世间一段不朽的传奇。他是有两个长着一个躯体和一个脑袋的卡耐基：一个是腰缠万贯的巨商；一个是奉献了百万家产的慈善家。作为商人，卡耐基与竞争对手进行谈判协商的概念是对方必须完全妥协；而作为雇主，他则挖空心思地从工人身上赚取每一分能够落到自己腰包里的钱。作为儿子，他在母亲有生之年保持单身；作为爱人，他恪守对妻子的那份责任和真诚。卡耐基将自己的成功归因于自己周围所有人的共同努力。无论是在他生前还是在他死后，人们对他的评价都是褒贬不一。

Double-faced Humanity of Andrew Carnegie

Generous and naive while often grasping and ruthless, Andrew Carnegie personally embodied the contradictions that divided America in the Gilded Age. At a time when America struggled — often violently — to sort out the competing claims of democracy and individual gain, Carnegie championed both. He saw himself as a hero of working people, yet he crushed their unions. The richest man in the world, he railed against privilege. A generous philanthropist, he slashed the wages of the workers who made him rich.

The roots of Carnegie's internal conflicts were planted in Dunfermline, Scotland, where he was born, the son of a weaver and political radical who instilled in young Andrew the values of political and economic equality. His family's poverty, however, taught Carnegie a different lesson. When the Carnegies emigrated to America in 1848, Carnegie determined to bring prosperity to his family. Pittsburgh then was already a bustling① industrial city. But the city had begun to pay an environmental price for its success. The downtown had been gutted by fire in 1845; already the newly constructed buildings were so blackened by

---

① bustling ['bʌsliŋ] *adj.* 熙熙攘攘的,忙乱的

安德鲁·卡耐基的
双面人性

安德鲁·卡耐基个性化地体现了划分淘金时代美国的矛盾集合体：慷慨天真而又贪婪残忍。在那个美国奋斗的年代，人们常常采用暴力方式提出民主诉求，争取个人利益，卡耐基赢得了两者。他把自己看作工人阶级的英雄，却又压制他们的联盟。作为世界上最富有的男人，他又拒绝特权。作为一位慷慨的慈善家，他却大幅度削减给他带来财富的工人们的工资。

卡耐基这种内在冲突的根源深植于他的出生地——苏格兰的丹佛姆林。作为一名纺织工和政治激进派的儿子，安德鲁从小就被灌输了政治和经济平等的价值观。然而，家庭的贫困给他上了不同的一课。当卡耐基一家 1848 年移居美国时，他决定为自己的家族带来繁荣。此时的匹兹堡已经是一个繁忙的工业城市。但这座城市已经开始为它的成功付出环境代价。商业区被 1845 年的一场火灾损毁，新建筑由于被烟灰熏得发黑，已经看不出和旧建筑有什么区别。工业废料相继污染了卡耐基家的邻近地区——被称为赤脚广场和石板镇的地方。他们在丽贝卡街的家是一处极易受损、外观发黑的木屋——与他们在苏格兰舒适的石头房舍简直无法相比。经济条件刚一好转，卡耐基就把全家搬到了市郊，以便远离匹兹堡被污染的空气。卡耐基摒弃他一贯乐观的腔调，描写了当时的境况："任何一篇准确描述那个时期的匹兹堡的言论都极尽夸张。弥漫的烟雾

soot that they were indistinguishable from older ones. Industrial waste fouled the the Carnegies lived in a neighborhood alternately called Barefoot Square and Slab town. Their home on Rebecca Street was a flimsy①, dark frame house— a far cry from their cozy stone cottage in Scotland. As soon as he could afford it, Carnegie would move his family to the suburbs, away from Pittsburgh's tainted air. "Any accurate description of Pittsburgh at that time would be set down as a piece of the grossest exaggeration," Carnegie wrote, setting aside his usually optimistic tone. "The smoke permeated and penetrated everything .... If you washed your face and hands they were as dirty as ever in an hour. The soot gathered in the hair and irritated the skin, and for a time life was more or less miserable."

Carnegie's climb from the slums of Pittsburgh to the mansions of New York paralleled America's transformation from a sleepy agricultural nation into the world's foremost industrial power. By 1868 Carnegie, then 33, was worth nearly $5 million today. But his wealth troubled him, as did the ghosts of his radical past. He wrote himself a telling letter, promising that he would stop working in two years and pursue a life of good works: "To continue much longer overwhelmed by business cares ... must degrade me beyond hope of permanent recovery." Yet Carnegie's business cares held him in sway. For three decades, he dominated the steel industry, and although he allowed himself time for vacations in Scotland and for his troubled courtship of Louise Whitfield, his thoughts rarely strayed from his mills.

Carnegie did not forget his radical roots. In a period of turbulent

---

① flimsy ['flimzi] *adj.* 易坏的,脆弱的

渗透了每个角落……如果你洗干净脸和手，不到一个钟头又依然肮脏如故。 头发里堆积着烟灰，皮肤过敏，生活一度或多或少地令人痛苦不堪。"

卡耐基从匹兹堡的贫民窟攀升至纽约的高楼大厦，相当于美国由落后的农业国向世界最先进的工业国的转变。 到 1868 年卡耐基 33 岁时，他身价已接近现在的 500 万美元。 可财富困扰着他，像他激进的过去那样阴魂不散。 他给自己写了一封劝告信，承诺两年后停止工作，追求一种推举慈善行为的生活："继续更长时间地工作就会被生意上的事务压垮……那么我想要永久恢复健康的希望肯定会越来越渺茫。"而卡耐基对生意的关注使他进退两难。 30 年来，他控制着钢铁行业。 尽管他许诺要给自己时间去苏格兰度假，解决向露易丝·惠特菲尔德求婚时碰到的麻烦，可他脑子里想的尽是些工厂的事情。

卡耐基不会忘记他激进的根源。 在劳工动乱的混乱期间，卡耐基曾公开表示支持工会。 然而在自己的工厂里，他的立场并不鲜明。 他通常避免使用罢工破坏者，而且拼命地讨价还价，总能得到自己想要的结果，最显著的例子发生在 1892 年荷姆斯泰德工厂血腥地抵制工人的要求而停工事件。 卡耐基和搭档亨利·克莱·弗里克一起，解散了钢铁联盟。 卡耐基的钢铁帝国就此崛起。 到 1900 年，卡耐基钢铁厂生产的钢铁较之整个英国的钢铁工业还要多。1901 年他把公司卖给 J.P 摩根时，个人身价相当于现在的 45 亿美元。 随后，卡耐基把他旺盛的精力转移到慈善事业和追求世界和平上来。 他把财产捐献给慈善事业，希望藉此或许可以拂去财富累积过程中的尘垢。 从公众的记忆来看，他也许做对了。 今天，人们因为他慷慨的捐赠：音乐礼堂、教育拨款以及将近 3 000 个公共图书馆而牢牢地记住了他。

labor unrest, Carnegie publicly supported the unions. In his own mills, though, his position was less clear. He usually avoided using strike breakers, but drove a hard bargain and typically got his way, most notably during the bloody lockout at his Homestead works in 1892. With his partner Henry Clay Frick, Carnegie broke the steel unions. His empire grew. By 1900, Carnegie Steel produced more steel than the entire British steel industry. When he sold the company to J. P. Morgan in 1901, Carnegie personally earned approximately $4.5 billion today. Carnegie then turned his enormous energies to philanthropy[①] and the pursuit of world peace, hoping perhaps that donating his wealth to charitable causes would mitigate the grimy details of its accumulation. In the public memory, he may have been correct. Today he is most remembered for his generous gifts of music halls, educational grants, and nearly 3,000 public libraries.

Andrew Carnegie also played his double-faced humanity in his marriage. In 1880, Carnegie, at age 45, began courting Louise Whitfield, age 23. Carnegie's mother was the primary obstacle to the relationship. Nearly 70 years old, Margaret Carnegie had long been accustomed to her son's complete attention. He adored her. They shared a suite at New York's Windsor Hotel, and she often accompanied him— even to business meetings. Some have hinted that she exacted a promise from Carnegie that he remain a bachelor during her lifetime. Louise was the daughter of a well-to-do New York merchant and a semi-invalid mother. Like Carnegie, Louise was devoted to her mother, who required constant medical attention. Unlike Margaret Carnegie, however, Mrs.

---

① philanthropy [fiˈlænθrəpi] *n.* 慈善事业

安德鲁·卡耐基在婚姻中也展示了他的双面人性。 1880 年，45 岁的卡耐基开始和 23 岁的露易丝·惠特菲尔德谈恋爱。 卡耐基的母亲是这场恋情的最大阻碍。 快 70 岁的玛格丽特·卡耐基已经习惯了儿子将全部的注意力都放在她身上。 他敬爱她。 他和母亲住在纽约温莎公爵旅馆的一间套房，她经常陪伴着他——甚至出席商务会议也陪着他。 有人透露说，她强烈要求卡耐基保证在她有生之年保持单身。 露易丝的父亲是位富有的纽约商人，母亲半身瘫痪。 像卡耐基一样，露易丝专心照顾母亲。 她母亲经常需要药物治疗。 然而与玛格丽特·卡耐基不同的是，惠特菲尔德夫人鼓励女儿花时间与她的追求者交往。 而卡耐基的母亲其时却最大可能地破坏他们的关系。

但这对无畏的情侣还是在 1883 年 9 月订婚。 可进展并不顺利。 关于订婚，卡耐基的传记作家这样写道："感情越来越深厚，谈话越来越真诚，可情绪从欢乐变为悲哀。"露易丝开始怀疑，虽然她依然继续去看望卡耐基，却开始接受别的追求者的邀请。 1884 年 4 月 23 日，他们悔婚了，但并没有持续多久。 那年秋天，卡耐基和露易丝又开始约会。 几周后，婚礼再次提上日程。 即使卡耐基和露易丝感到非常幸福，为了母亲玛格丽特的缘故，他们依然为婚约保密。 1886 年，玛格丽特的健康状况再次恶化。 7 月，卡耐基在宾夕法尼亚州克雷森的家中避暑时写信给露易丝："我没有给你写信是因为看起来我和你有责任保持分离。 所有的事都让我母亲感到困扰，包括我和你——我们的责任是一样的，那就是坚持到最后。 我每天都感觉到这一点。"

1886 年 11 月 10 日，玛格丽特·卡耐基去世。 即便如此，出于对母亲的尊敬，卡耐基不情愿地对外公布了他和露易丝订婚的信息。 卡耐基写给露易丝说："看起来这么快就宣布这一消息似乎并

Whitfield encouraged her daughter to spend time with her suitor. Carnegie's mother meanwhile did her best to undermine the relationship.

Undaunted, the couple were engaged in September 1883. It did not go well. With the engagement, Carnegie's biographer wrote, "the emotions became deeper, the talks more earnest, and the moods shifted from joy to dolefulness①." Louise began to have doubts and started accepting invitations from other suitors, though she continued to see Carnegie. On April 23,1884, they broke off the engagement, but it didn't last. By the fall, Carnegie and Louise began to see each other again. Within weeks the wedding was back on. For all their happiness, however, Carnegie and Louise kept the engagement a secret — for the sake of mother Margaret. In 1886, Margaret's health was again failing. In July, Carnegie wrote to Louise from his summer home in Cresson, PA.

"I have not written to you because it seems you and I have duties which must keep us apart, " he wrote. "Everything does hang upon our mothers, with both of us— our duty is the same, to stick to them to the last. I feel this every day."

On November 10,1886, Margaret Carnegie died. Even then, Carnegie was reluctant to make the engagement public, out of respect for his mother.

"It would not seem in good taste to announce it so soon, " Carnegie wrote Louise. They were finally married on April 22,1887, at the Whitfield home. The wedding was very small, very quiet, very private. There was no maid of honor, no best man, no ushers, and only 30 guests.

(988 words)

---

① dolefulness ['dəufulnis] *n.* 悲哀,寂寞

不得体。" 1887 年 4 月 22 日，他们最终在惠特菲尔德家里举行了婚
礼。 婚礼排场很小，很安静，很隐秘。 没有伴娘，没有伴郎，没
有引座员，只有 30 位宾客。

知识链接

United States Steel Corporation 美国钢铁公司的前身卡耐基钢铁公司通过
白手起家建立成一个生产钢铁的大型钢铁联合企业而获得优势，且数十年保
持世界最大钢铁厂的地位，几乎垄断了美国钢铁市场。卡耐基与洛克菲勒、
摩根并立，是当时美国经济界的三大巨头之一。安德鲁·卡耐基从不名一文
的移民到堪称世界首富的"钢铁大王"，而在功成名就后，他又将几乎全部的
财富捐献给社会。他生前捐赠款额之巨大，足以与死后设立诺贝尔奖金的瑞
典科学家、实业家诺贝尔相媲美，由此成为美国人心目中的英雄和个人奋斗
的楷模。

Homestead Strike 荷姆斯泰德罢工。美国内战结束后不久，社会大震荡已
经是山雨欲来。只不过，这一次金融贵族代替了上次遭到弹压的奴隶主贵
族，金融贵族成了美国人与生俱来的民主思想与平均主义思想的重要威胁。
社会剧变通常都伴随着你死我活的暴力事件。1892 年的荷姆斯泰德罢工，
反对的是安德鲁·卡耐基钢铁厂对工人的压迫和剥削，平克顿 (Pinkerton) 破
坏了工人的团结，导致罢工最终失败，当时鲜血染红了孟农加希拉河
(Monongahela River)。

题　记

　　安东尼·艾柯卡是一名风头盖过杰克·韦尔奇的商界奇
才，曾先担任过福特汽车公司的总裁，被炒鱿鱼后又担任克
莱斯勒汽车公司的总裁，奇迹般地东山再起，把这家濒临倒
闭的公司从危境中拯救过来。他那在逆境中锲而不舍、转败
为胜的奋斗精神使人们为之倾倒。他善于与人沟通交流，尊
重和维护人才的创造性和积极性；他明智地占据汽车市场的
竞争优势，在不断的推陈出新之中引导汽车消费的时尚潮
流；他履行精明的管理制度并果断地冒险，从不享受缓慢迟
疑地做出决定这种奢侈。艾柯卡跌宕起伏的人生经历和事业
给我们留下了太多的思考空间。

Summoning up Strength from Adversity — Lido A. Iacocca

Lido A. Iacocca is an American businessman most commonly known for his revival of the Chrysler Corporation in the 1980s, once serving as President and CEO and additionally as chairman, until his retirement. Among the most widely recognized businessmen in the world, he was a passionate advocate of U.S. business exports.

Iacocca was born in Allentown, Pennsylvania, Italian immigrants who had settled in Pennsylvania's steel making belt. Iacocca graduated from currently named William Allen High School, in Allentown, and Lehigh University, Pennsylvania, with a degree in industrial engineering. After graduating from Lehigh, he won the Wallace Memorial Fellowship and went to Princeton University, where he took his electives in politics and plastics. He then began a career at Ford Motor Company as an engineer. Eventually becoming dissatisfied with that job, he switched career paths at Ford, entering the company's sales force. He was quite successful in sales, and he moved up through the ranks of Ford, moving ultimately to product development.

Iacocca struted his stuff[①] in sales and marketing where his career

---

① strut one's stuff 大显身手

在逆境中崛起——
安东尼·艾柯卡

里度·安东尼·艾柯卡是一位美国商人，他由于在 20 世纪 80 年代复苏克莱斯勒公司而成为大众最熟悉的人物，他曾担任克莱斯勒公司的总裁和首席执行官，随后又担任过公司主席直到退休。 他属于世界上最出名的商界精英一族，也是美国商业出口的热情倡导者。

艾柯卡出生在宾夕法尼亚州阿伦敦，家人是定居宾夕法尼亚州炼钢地带的意大利移民。 艾柯卡在阿伦敦现在名为威廉姆艾伦中学高中毕业后，进入宾夕法尼亚州的理海大学攻读工业管理学。 他毕业后获得了华莱士纪念奖学金，前往普林斯顿大学，在那里他选修了政治学和塑料学。 接着，他开始在福特汽车公司担任工程师。 但他最终对这份工作并不满意，跳槽到福特公司的销售部门。 他做销售相当成功，不断得到晋升的机会，最后进入产品开发部。

艾柯卡在市场营销部大显身手，事业由此进入鼎盛时期。 艾柯卡在做区域销售时，凭借他开展的 "56 换 56" 活动赢得了全国范围的认可，该活动每月提供 56 美元的分期付款用以购买 1956 年度的新型汽车。 他的活动在全国进行了推广，艾柯卡被调到迪尔本，并很快得到晋升，40 岁生日时便担任福特分部的总经理。 艾柯卡参与

flourished. While working in a local district for sales, Iacocca gained national recognition with his "56 for 56" campaign, offering $56 monthly payment loans for 1956 model year cars. His campaign went national and Iacocca was called to Dearborn where he quickly moved through the ranks to become President of the Ford Division on his 40th birthday. Iacocca was involved with the design of several successful Ford automobiles, most notably the Ford Mustang. He was also the "moving force," as one court put it, behind the notorious Ford Pinto. He promoted other ideas which did not reach the marketplace as Ford products. These included cars ultimately introduced by Chrysler — the K car and the minivan. Eventually, he became the president of the Ford Motor Company, but he clashed with Henry Ford II and ultimately, was fired by Ford, despite the company posting a $2 billion profit for the year.

After being fired at Ford, Iacocca was aggressively courted① by the Chrysler Corporation, which was on the verge of going out of business at the time, the company was losing millions, largely due to recalls of the company's Dodge Aspen and Plymouth Volare, cars that Iacocca would later claim should never have been built. Iacocca joined Chrysler and began rebuilding the entire company from the ground up, laying off many workers, selling Chrysler's loss-making European division to Peugeot, and bringing in many former associates from his former company. Also from Ford, Iacocca brought to Chrysler the "Mini-Max" project which, bore fruit in the wildly successful Dodge Caravan and Plymouth Voyager. Interestingly, Henry Ford II had wanted nothing to do

---

① court [kɔːt] vt. 献殷勤

设计了几款成功的福特汽车，其中最出名的要数福特野马了。 正如一位支持者所言，他也是声名狼藉的福特斑马的幕后"推手"。 他提出的其他想法并没有像福特产品一样进入市场。 这些想法包括由克莱斯勒推出的 K 型车和微型货车。 后来，他成为福特汽车公司的总裁，但是因为和亨利·福特二世的冲突而被福特解雇，尽管当年公司宣布盈利 20 亿美元。

艾柯卡被福特炒鱿鱼之后，收到克莱斯勒公司的盛情邀请，该公司当时正处在濒临破产的边缘，主要是因为道奇白羊和普利茅斯飞驰招回事件使公司损失数百万美元，艾柯卡后来宣称从来就不应该生产这些车。 艾柯卡加盟了克莱斯勒公司，开始从基础上重建整个公司，他解雇了许多工人，将克莱斯勒老是亏损的欧洲分区卖给标致，还从前公司拉拢了许多以前的同事。 艾柯卡还将福特的"最小-最大"计划引进克莱斯勒，使大获成功的道奇捷龙和普利茅斯捷龙受益匪浅。 有趣的是，亨利·福特二世对这个本该命中注定属于福特的"最小-最大"项目没有任何想法。 福特"最小-最大"计划的幕后推手赫尔·斯帕里奇在艾柯卡被炒前的几个月就已被解雇，正在克莱斯勒等待艾柯卡的到来，他们俩共同创造了汽车界的历史。

艾柯卡来后不久便引进了微型道奇欧米尼和普利茅斯地平线。这些前轮驱动的欧米尼和地平线很快成为畅销产品，初登卖场的当年便各自卖出 30 多万辆，显示出克莱斯勒的未来风范。 具有讽刺意味的是，欧米尼和地平线倚靠克莱斯勒地平线设计的很多产品来自公司被艾柯卡砍掉的欧洲分部。 艾柯卡认识到，如果无法注入大笔资金维持公司的运转，公司将面临停产危机。 于是他取道美国国

with the Mini-Max, which doomed the project at Ford. Hal Sperlich, the driving force behind the Mini-Max at Ford had been fired a few months before Iacocca and was waiting for him at Chrysler, where the two would make automotive history.

Iacocca arrived shortly after the introduction of the subcompact① Dodge Omni and Plymouth Horizon. The front-wheel drive Omni and Horizon became instant hits, selling over 300,000 units each in their debut② year, showing what was to come for Chrysler. Ironically, the Omni and Horizon had been designed alongside the Chrysler Horizon with much input from the European division of the company, which Iacocca axed. Realizing that the company would go out of business if it did not receive a significant amount of money to turn the company around. So Iacocca approached the United States Congress and asked for a loan guarantee. While it is sometimes said that Congress lent Chrysler the money, it, in fact, only guaranteed the loans. Most thought this was an unprecedented move, but Iacocca pointed to the government bail-outs of the airline and railroad industries, arguing that more jobs were at stake in Chrysler's possible demise③. In the end, though the decision was controversial, Iacocca received the loan guarantee from the government.

After receiving this reprieve, Chrysler released the first of the K-Car line, the Dodge Aries and Plymouth Reliant. Like the minivan which would come later, these compact automobiles were based on design proposals that Ford had rejected during Iacocca's tenure there. Coming

---

① subcompact ['sʌbkɔmpækt] *n.* 超小型汽车
② debut ['deibjuː] *n.* 初次登场
③ demise [di'maiz] *n.* 死亡

会，申请贷款担保。 大多数人认为这是一个史无前例的举动，但艾柯卡据理力争，指出政府曾经对航空业和铁路业采取应急措施，而克莱斯勒的存亡关乎着更多的就业机会。 最后，虽然决议仍有分歧，但艾柯卡还是得到了政府的贷款保证。

经历缓冲期之后，克莱斯勒开启了 K 型车道奇阿力士和顺风礼兰的第一批生产线。 就像后来的微型货车，简约型汽车基于艾柯卡在福特任期里遭弃的设计提议。 这些体型小、效率高、价格便宜的前轮驱动车正好在 20 世纪 70 年代石油危机爆发后上市，销路很好。 克莱斯勒在 1983 年秋季推出微型货车，它基本上都是斯帕里奇的"孩子"。 25 年后，克莱斯勒继续在微型货车销售方面引领汽车行业。 因为 K 型车和微型货车的出现，以及艾柯卡实施的改革，公司很快有了好转，比预期早 7 年的时间还清了由政府担保的贷款。 艾柯卡还负责对美国汽车公司的求购，从而将利润可观的吉普部门置于克莱斯勒的法人保护伞下。 这一举动也创造了由美国汽车公司遗留下来的部分组成的短期鹰牌公司。 此时，美国汽车公司已经与吉普大切诺基合作完成了大部分业务，而这正是艾柯卡十分期待的结果。

艾柯卡认为，成功管理的关键是集中精力和明智地使用时间的能力，必须能够确定优先权和成为问题的解决者。 管理者需要成为决策的行动人和制定者，而激发人们行为的最佳方式是跟他们沟通交流。 一名好的管理者既要善于交谈，更要善于倾听。 在做生意的时候，要记住的最重要的事情之一就是，如果想在今天的全球市场上占据竞争优势，那么每个问题都不能被结构化、简化为一个案例。 在企业生活中，总有人觉得自己需要做额外的研究，但当相关

right after the oil crisis of the 1970s, these small, efficient and inexpensive, front-wheel drive cars sold rapidly. Chrysler introduced the minivan, which was by and large Sperlich's "baby," in the fall of 1983. Twenty-five years later, Chrysler continues to lead the automobile industry in minivan sales. Because of the K-cars and minivans, along with the reforms Iacocca implemented, the company turned around quickly and was able to repay the government-backed loans seven years earlier than expected. Iacocca was also responsible for Chrysler's acquisition of AMC, which brought the profitable Jeep division under Chrysler's corporate umbrella. It also created the short-lived Eagle division, formed from the remnants of AMC. By this time, AMC had already finished most of the work with the Jeep Grand Cherokee, which Iacocca desperately wanted.

Iacocca feels the keys to successful management are the ability to concentrate and use time wisely. Establishing priorities and being a problem solver are a must. Managers need to be decision makers as well as motivators. The best way to motivate people is to communicate with them. A good manager needs to listen at least as much as he talks. One of the most important things to remember in business is that every problem can not be structured and reduced to a case study if you want to stay ahead of the competition in today's global market place. In corporate life there are always people who feel they need additional research, but after a certain point when most of the relevant facts are in, a decision must be made. A certain amount of risk taking is necessary. Businesses don't have the luxury of slow decision making today.

(969 words)

的事实大部分集中在某个点时，你必须做出决定。 一定的冒险是必需的，今天的商场承受不起缓慢做出决定这种奢侈。

知识链接 🔍

Ford 福特汽车公司是世界上第四大工业企业和第二大小汽车和卡车生产商。1903 年由亨利·福特先生创办于美国底特律市。现在的福特汽车公司是世界超级跨国公司，总部设在美国密执安州迪尔伯恩市，它有三个战略经营单位——汽车集团、多样化产品集团和金融服务，在全世界大约有 36 万名职工服务于汽车、农业、金融和通信领域。福特公司的多样化经营范围分别包括电子、玻璃、塑料、汽车零部件、空间技术、卫星通信、国防工程、地基开发、设备租赁和汽车出租。

Chrysler Corporation 克莱斯勒(Chrysler) 公司创建于 1912 年，是以创始人沃尔特·克莱斯勒姓氏命名的美国三大汽车公司之一，公司总部设在密歇根州海兰德帕克。它的图形商标像一枚五角星勋章，体现了克莱斯勒家族和公司员工们的远大理想和抱负，以及永无止境地追求和在竞争中获胜的奋斗精神；五角星的五个部分，分别表示五大洲(亚、非、欧、美、澳) 都在使用克莱斯勒汽车公司的汽车，克莱斯勒汽车公司的汽车遍及全世界。

题　记

　　李·斯科特在沃尔玛打拼 20 多年，一步步攀上公司权力的最高峰——沃尔玛百货公司总裁兼首席执行官。他接受了父亲的商业教育启蒙，工作勤奋而努力；他做事不喜张扬，继承了山姆·沃尔顿一贯的勤俭作风；他不善言辞，总是神情轻松出现在他主持的沃尔玛周六晨间例会或是和他的管理团队共同参与的营销会议上，尽管他和他的同事们有时候在这些会议上做出关系几十亿美元的决定；他恪守沃尔玛的低价经营模式，却毫无疑问地制约着整个行业的货品价格与设计；他设计了一种辐射型配送网，保证货架可以及时更新和低价销售；他通过减少沃尔玛每一种类的商品数目、快速流通销售滞缓商品、确保供应商供给数量少的商品等措施，削减了多余量库存。李·斯科特在销售规划上的成功证明了他是一位精干的多面手，给谦和的创始人沃尔顿精神感染的公司注入了一种全新的职业理念。

A Capable Generalist
— Lee Scott

Lee Scott grew up in Baxter Springs, Kan., a tiny town in the southeast corner of the state where his father owned a local gas station. Baxter Springs was once a rowdy cow town, and later a prosperous mining community, but it had fallen unfortunately on hard times. Situated on Route 66, the gas station was threatened by a new interstate that took away its regular supply of customers. Mr. Scott's father sold the business, an event the CEO sometimes talks about in speeches. "I know that change isn't necessarily fun, but understand also that change isn't necessarily someone's fault," he once said, referring to the interstate, during Wal-Mart's press tour.

To support himself while studying at Kansas' Pittsburg State University, Scott worked nights at a factory making steel molds for tires. In his junior year, he married fellow student Linda Aldridge. By his senior year, the couple were parents of a baby boy and lived in a 10-by-50-foot trailer in the Lone Star Trailer Court not far from campus. After graduating with a degree in business, he went to work for Yellow Freight System, a trucking company, as a dispatcher① in Joliet. "I had one job offer, so it

---

① dispatcher [dis'pætʃə] n. 调度员

精干的多面手——李·斯科特

李·斯科特在美国堪萨斯州东南角落的一个小镇巴克斯特斯普林斯长大，他的父亲在小镇开了一家本地加油站。 巴克斯特斯普林斯曾是个喧闹的牛镇，后来发展成为繁荣的矿区，但在岁月艰难时期不幸衰落。 加油站坐落在66号公路，遭到州际新厂的威胁，并抢走了常来的客源，斯科特的父亲只好卖掉了加油站。 斯科特总裁有时在演讲中谈到这件事，他曾在沃尔玛举办的一次记者参观活动中提及洲际兼并大潮："我知道改变未必是一件令人开心的事，但也明白改变未必就是某个人的错。"

在堪萨斯州匹兹堡州立大学就读期间，斯科特为了维持自己的生活，每天晚上都会到当地的一家工厂上班，制造生产轮胎的钢模。 大三时，他和自己的同学琳达·奥尔德里奇结婚。 到大四时，夫妇俩有了自己的儿子，住在校园附近独立星活动房屋停放场一辆宽10英尺长50英尺的拖车里。 获得商业管理学位毕业后，斯科特进入载重汽车运输公司耶路货运工作，在乔利埃特负责调度。他说："我拿到了一个工作录用函，那时我理所当然地认为从事货运就是我的未来。"

1977年，斯科特第一次接触沃尔玛，但他并不喜欢自己所看到

made sense to me to think that trucking was in my future, " he says.

In 1977, Scott had his first encounter with Wal-Mart and didn't like what he saw. Still working for Yellow Freight, one of Wal-Mart's shippers, Mr. Scott went to Bentonville to collect a disputed $ 7,000 bill. David Glass, who was then head of distribution and finance, refused to pay. As Scott started to exit in a huff, Glass offered him a job. "I liked the way he handled himself, " recalls Glass, who eventually became Wal-Mart chief executive and Mr. Scott's predecessor①. "He was articulate and made his point very well." The feeling, however, wasn't mutual. "Why in the world would I leave a good job for a company that couldn't even pay a $ 7,000 bill, " both men recall Scott saying at the time. Glass pursued him for the next two years, eventually convincing him to work for Wal-Mart as an assistant director of transportation where he was charged with building an in-house trucking fleet. Scott says he changed his mind based on Glass's description of a company that was good to its employees and rewarded talent.

At the time, Wal-Mart had 276 stores in 11 Southern and Midwestern states and had just hit $ 1 billion in annual sales. But the young executive hated speaking to large groups of people. As he drove to weekly Saturday meetings at Wal-Mart's headquarters, Scott tried recalling which side of the room had been questioned the previous week. That's where he would sit, hoping that Sam Walton, the company's founder, would start elsewhere. If his turn came before the time ran out, "I would shake and my voice would crack, " he recalls. In small

---

① predecessor ['priːdisesə] *n.* 前任

的情况。 当时他还在耶路货运工作，这家公司是沃尔玛货运代理商之一，有次他去本顿维尔讨还一笔 7 000 美元颇有争议的债务。 当时主管配售和财政的大卫·格拉斯拒绝付账。 斯科特正要气呼呼地离开时，格拉斯向他提供了一份工作。 后来成为沃尔玛总裁、斯科特的前任格拉斯回忆说："我喜欢他表达自己的方式。 他口齿伶俐，非常善于说服别人赞成自己的论点。"然而，这种感觉并不是相互的。 两人都还能记起斯科特当时的话："我究竟为什么要辞掉一份好工作，跳槽到一家连 7 000 美元都还不起的公司就职呢？"接下来的两年里，格拉斯一直在劝说斯科特，最终说服他到沃尔玛担任运输主管助理，斯科特在这里承担了建立公司内部卡车车队的任务。 斯科特认为他之所以改变主意，是因为格拉斯说公司善待员工，奖励人才。

沃尔玛当时在南部和中西部的 11 个州有 276 家商店，年销售额达 10 亿美元。 但是年轻的主管讨厌对着大批的人群演讲。 开车去参加沃尔玛总部每周六召开的例会时，斯科特总会试图回忆上周被提问过的成员坐在房间的哪个位置，然后他就会选择那个位置坐下来，希望公司的创始人山姆·沃尔顿从别处开始找人发言。 他回忆说，如果会议结束前轮到他发言，"我就会浑身发抖，嗓音沙哑"。相反，人少时斯科特则显得生硬粗暴。 在一次会上，他试着说服货仓经理加快卸货速度。 时任沃尔玛副总裁的唐纳德·萨德奎斯特会后就此事强硬地提醒了斯科特。 斯科特说："他告诉我，如果我的目的是激怒和惹恼屋子里的每一个人，那么我成功了。"

斯科特作为团队老板经常发表权威性的意见，如要求货车司机慢速驾驶，减少事故率。 如果司机工作时喝酒或者被抓到和女朋友

groups, by contrast, Scott could be abrasive①. During one meeting, he tried to convince warehouse managers to unload trucks faster. Don Soderquist, then a Wal-Mart vice chairman, cornered him after the meeting. "He told me that if my intention was to irritate and annoy everyone in the room, I had succeeded," Scott says.

As boss of the crew, Scott frequently delivered dictums②, for example, demanding truckers drive slower to reduce accident rates. If a driver drank on the job or was caught visiting a girlfriend, Scott would write scolding letters to all Wal-Mart drivers, who were infuriated by these broadsides. Some complained directly to Mr. Walton and asked the boss to fire Scott. Instead, Mr. Walton made Scott listen to the drivers. complaints and thank each one individually for using the company's "open-door policy." Scott said it was a humbling experience but one that gave him a good introduction to the company's culture.

By 1993, Scott was heading Wal-Mart's vast logistics division. Wal-Mart was the first discount retailer to have its own distribution centers, a move that cut costs by removing a layer of middlemen. It was a key to the company's success. Mr. Scott designed a hub-and-spoke distribution network with warehouses serving a series of stores not more than a day's drive away. That allowed shelves to be replenished quickly and inexpensively by keeping less inventory on hand.

Though he had spent his entire career in logistics, Mr. Scott was tapped in 1995 to run Wal-Mart's merchandising division, the unit

---

① abrasive [ə'breisiv] *adj.* 粗鲁的
② dictum ['diktəm] *n.* 权威的断言

约会，斯科特就会写信给沃尔玛的全体司机，严厉叱责，司机们被这些广泛的抨击给激怒了。有些人直接向沃尔顿先生投诉，要求老板解雇斯科特。不过，沃尔顿先生还是让斯科特倾听司机们的抱怨，感谢每一位使用公司"开放政策"的人。斯科特认为那段经历令人感到羞辱，但却让他很好地融入了公司的文化。

斯科特在 1993 年时主管了沃尔玛庞大的后勤部门。沃尔玛是首个拥有自己的配送中心的打折零售商，这一举动省去了中间商这一环节，降低了成本。这是公司成功的一个关键。斯科特设计了一种辐射型配送网，仓库对一系列商店提供货物的发货时间都不超过一天。这种配送网络能够通过保持较少的手头库存，保证货架可以及时更新和低价销售。

虽然斯科特全身心地投入到后勤部门，1995 年，斯科特还是被调到沃尔玛的商品营销部，负责挑选和采购货物。沃尔玛曾经遭受重创，那时它一直在为收购几家商店努力，为开辟新的超级购物中心、销售从钻石到自行车一应俱全的大型商店而分散了精力。公司当年的报告显示，第一季度的利润 25 年来首次下滑。斯科特通过减少沃尔玛每一种类的商品数目、快速流通销售滞缓商品、确保供应商供给数量少的商品等措施，削减了 20 亿美元的多余量库存。然而，斯科特一直在幕后操作。每当他要在公司会议上发表演讲时，他通常和当时主管沃尔玛各个商店的库格林先生步调一致。库格林先生更加健谈一些。

斯科特在销售规划上的成功证明他是一位精干的多面手，这对他晋升公司高层起了作用。斯科特根据既定的继任方案，担任首席运营官后接管了公司执行总裁的职务。他带给公司一种职业理念，

responsible for selecting and buying goods. Wal-Mart had hit a rough patch. It was struggling with several acquisitions and distracted by rolling out new supercenters, gargantuan stores selling goods from diamond rings to bicycles. That year, the company reported its first quarterly profit decline in a quarter of a century. Scott cut $ 2 billion of excess inventory by reducing the number of products Wal-Mart sold in each category, zapping slow-moving merchandise and convincing suppliers to ship smaller amounts. Yet he remained in the background. Whenever Scott addressed company meetings, it was often in tandem with the more-garrulous① Mr. Coughlin, who was then running Wal-Mart's stores.

His success in merchandising showed Mr. Scott to be a capable generalist. It helped secure his ascension to the top spot. After a planned succession, in which he served as chief operating officer, Mr. Scott took over as CEO. He brought with him a corporate professionalism that had been missing from a company still imbued with the spirit of its folksy founder Walton. From the outset, Scott was a little more willing than his predecessor to address the growing chorus of disapproval. From gender discrimination to low pay and benefits, Wal-Mart agreed to improve its monitoring of labor conditions in overseas factories and insist on standards for its suppliers.

(956 words)

---

① garrulous [ˈgærələs] *adj.* 饶舌的

在谦和的创始人沃尔顿精神感染的公司里，缺失的正是这种专业水准。 从一开始，斯科特就表现出较之前任更乐意解决日益增长的不和谐之声。 沃尔玛同意改善海外工厂劳工条件的监管，坚持供应商标准，解决性别歧视、低工资和福利待遇等问题。

知识链接 🔍

Wal-Mart 沃尔玛百货有限公司由美国零售业的传奇人物山姆·沃尔顿先生于 1962 年在阿肯色州成立。经过四十余年的发展，沃尔玛百货有限公司已经成为美国最大的私人雇主和世界上最大的连锁零售商。目前沃尔玛在全球 10 个国家开设了超过 5 000 家商场，员工总数 160 多万，分布在美国、墨西哥、波多黎各、加拿大、阿根廷、巴西、中国、韩国、德国和英国。每周光临沃尔玛的顾客近一亿四千万人次。

题 记

　　迈克·米尔肯，这个曾经创造了金融新天地的垃圾债券大王、自 J．P 摩根以来美国金融界最有影响力的风云人物之一，在改变美国证券发展史的同时，个人命运也发生了几乎毁灭性的转变。他不仅因为恶意收购的罪名成立被送上法庭，而且在被诊断出患有晚期前列腺癌时被告知只剩 12 到 18 个月的时间。他没有放弃，选择了抵抗，争分夺秒地恢复他的健康和声誉。他成为一名重要的癌症慈善家，为自己的想法而充满激情地工作，对传统的颠覆常常带来曲径通幽的豁然开朗。米尔肯不带一丝幽默或讽刺，声称他这辈子人生哲学的基础就是："繁荣等于金融技术的总和乘以人力资本、社会资本和房地产三者的总和。"

The Reincarnation① of Mike Milken

He is not wasting a minute trying to restore his health and reputation.

It's on a brilliant Sunday morning and Mike Milken, looking tanned and fit, is wide-eyed and eager to show off his library and new kitchen. Both are paneled in a blonde shade of pine that, Milken says, helps him to relax. "Listen," he says quietly, pointing to a small fountain running just outside. Milken had that installed, too. Out by the pool, a garden is bursting with flowers. "Honeysuckle② and jasmine③" the former financier says wistfully, his head tilting back as he savors the faint scents in the air. Having just finished up his yoga routine, Milken continues his meditation technique: He sits cross-legged, his elbows resting on his knees, hands extended, eyes closed.

The miracle about Michael R. Milken is that he is breathing at all. Diagnosed with terminal prostate④ cancer in 1993, Milken was told by his doctors that he had 12 to 18 months to live. Rather than give up,

---

① reincarnation [ˌriːinkɑːˈneiʃən] n. 再生
② honeysuckle [ˈhʌnisʌk(ə)l] n. 金银花
③ jasmine [ˈdʒæsmin] n. 茉莉
④ prostate [ˈprɔsteit] n. 前列腺

迈克·米尔肯的涅槃

他正在争分夺秒地努力恢复健康和声誉。

在一个阳光灿烂的星期天早晨，皮肤晒成棕褐色的迈克·米尔肯看上去身体健康，他睁大了眼睛，迫不及待地要炫耀他的图书馆和新厨房。两者都镶嵌在松树的金色树荫中，米尔肯说，这样会帮他放松心情。他指着外面一个流动的小型喷泉，平静地说，"听"。池塘外的花园里，花儿竞相开放。这位前金融学家若有所思地说道："金银花和茉莉花。"他在品味空气中淡淡的清香时，头向后倾斜。米尔肯习惯性地做完瑜伽后，接着练习他的沉思技巧：他盘腿而坐，胳膊肘放在膝盖上，手掌摊开，双目关闭。即使是在放松，竞争欲望强烈的米尔肯看上去也在制定目标。

迈克·米尔肯的奇迹在于——他还在呼吸。1993 年，米尔肯被诊断出患有晚期前列腺癌时，医生告诉他说，他只能活 12 至 18 个月的时间。米尔肯没有放弃，与癌症展开了抗争。他学习一切跟他的疾病有关的知识，练习瑜伽和冥想来减轻压力，成为严格的素食者，不再食用肉饼和煎炸食品，取而代之的是清蒸西兰花和大豆昔。到目前为止，米尔肯已经证实医生的结论是错误的：他的癌症完全缓解。

Milken counterattacked. He learned everything about his disease, took up yoga and meditation to reduce stress, and became a strict vegetarian, abandoning his diet of burgers and fries for steamed broccoli and soy shakes. So far, Milken has proven his doctors wrong: His cancer is in full remission.

Had Milken not beaten the odds, cancer would have taken one of the most storied, vilified business figures of our time. In the public's mind, Milken was the iconic white-collar criminal, a symbol of everything wrong with Wall Street. It has been eight years since Milken went to jail, but the debate over who Mike Milken is and how bad his crimes were goes on. Junk-bond villain or brilliant financial innovator? There are plenty who think Milken got sandbagged with trumped up, politicized charges, and plenty more who think he simply got what he deserved. And long after many of the less reputable characters he financed have been forgotten, Milken remains controversial.

That debate will never be fully resolved. All that is certain is that Mike Milken has moved on. As far as Milken is concerned, he has paid his penalties— a total of $ 1.1 billion— and done his time. But that doesn't mean he has faded from the scene. Far from it. For the past six years, Milken has used every waking moment to rebuild his life and his reputation. First, he became a major cancer philanthropist, raising some $ 75 million for research and appearing regularly on such TV programs as Larry King Live and The Charlie Rose Show to push efforts to cure prostate cancer. And since 1996, he's moved back into business in a big way, founding Knowledge Universe (KU), a new venture that he hopes to build into a huge presence in the $ 800 billion educational-services

如果米尔肯没有胜算的可能，癌症将会把我们这个时代最具有传奇色彩、受中伤最多的商界人物之一给带走。 在公众眼里，米尔肯是白领罪犯的形象，是华尔街诸事道德败坏的标志。 米尔肯入狱至今已有八年之久，但是关于米尔肯究竟是谁、他的罪行有多么恶劣的争论还在继续。 垃圾债券的恶根还是才华横溢的金融创新者？很多人认为米尔肯遭到了无中生有的政治陷害，而更多的人则认为他是罪有应得。 许多受过他资助的人名誉比他更差，却早已被人们遗忘，但米尔肯仍然备受争议。

这场争论永远不会有圆满的结果，唯一确定的是，米尔肯已经在采取行动。 就米尔肯来说，他已经交付了惩罚——总数 11 亿美元，并结束了自己的时代，但这并不意味着他从此退出了舞台。 远非如此。 在过去的六年中，米尔肯利用每个清醒的时刻来重建他的生活和声誉。 首先，他成为一名重要的癌症慈善家，募集了约7 500万美元用以研究，还频频现身于拉里·金现场直播、查理·罗斯秀等电视节目中，以推动对前列腺癌症的治疗。 自 1996 年以来，他又轰轰烈烈地返回商界，创建了知识寰宇公司（KU），希望将这项新投资构建成8 000亿美元的庞大的教育服务产业。 这两项追求共同给予了米尔肯一个新的平台，用他自己的话来说，他再次成为平台上的玩家。 爬得越高摔得越惨，之后拾起碎片继续前进。但这从来就不是件容易做到的事情。 人们忍不住会问，米尔肯这个人过去十年的生活究竟是什么样子？ 那段经历是怎样改变了他？今天的迈克·米尔肯又是个什么样子？ 当我们最终跟这位 20 世纪80 年代的传奇面对面时，他最让我们想起的不是别人，而是理查德·尼克松，还有他对恢复正常生活不屈不挠的追求。

industry. Together, his twin pursuits have given Milken a new platform from which, on his own terms, he is once again a player. To have risen so high, to have crashed so hard, and then, to just pick up the pieces and move on. That could not have been easy. People can't help but wonder what the past 10 years of this man's life have really been like. How has that experience changed him? What's it like to be Mike Milken today? As we finally come face-to-face with this legend of the 1980s, he reminds us of no one so much as Richard Nixon and his own relentless quest for rehabilitation[1].

Is Milken, too, driven mainly by the desire to win back his good name? That is certainly a part of it. But it doesn't take long to realize that, despite all he has been through; Mike Milken seems much the same intense and compulsive guy he always has been, passionately worked up by his ideas. He's perpetually in motion, and every minute of his day is scheduled. He strikes us as the opposite of an introspective man. At work and at play, he continues to surround himself with the same loyal family members and business associates who've stood by him since the 1980s. There is about Milken an air of unreality, a need to rewrite history on much of what he has done. Cancer doesn't seem to have slowed him. The man works — really works —15 hours a day, seven days a week. He seems almost too focused, lacking the little flaws and weaknesses that make the rest of us fallible[2], susceptible to distraction, and in a word, human. He doesn't touch coffee, alcohol, or even soda.

---

[1] rehabilitation [ˈriːhəˌbiliˈteiʃən] n. 复原
[2] fallible [ˈfæləbl] adj. 易错的

是重新赢得好名声的欲望，在推动着米尔肯吗？ 这肯定只是一部分原因。 尽管他历经磨难，但要恢复名誉不会用去很长的时间。迈克·米尔肯看上去仍然是之前那个为自己的想法而充满激情地工作、热情又放荡不羁的小伙子。 他永远充满活力，白天的每一分钟都安排得满满的。 他留给人们的印象与好反省之人截然不同。 无论是工作还是娱乐，他周围总是围绕着同样忠诚的家人和生意伙伴，他们自 20 世纪 80 年代以来就一直支持他。 米尔肯似乎有几分不真实的色彩，需要重写他已经创下的大部分历史。 癌症似乎没有放慢他的脚步，他每周工作 7 天，每天工作 15 个小时，这就是他真实的工作状态。 他几乎是全神贯注，做事几乎没有我们常人容易犯错的缺陷和弱点，甚至痴迷到一种发狂的程度，总之，使我们更像凡人。 他不碰咖啡不喝酒，甚至连苏打水都不沾。 他从不诅咒，他讲的笑话内容健康但平淡无奇。 即便是孩子的时候，他也从不叛逆。 他 22 岁时和劳拉结婚，两人从九年级开始就一直在约会。

他的一些朋友和那些在他周围工作的人都认为，米尔肯对完美的追求既令人振奋，又令人气恼。 约瑟夫·科斯特洛说："在很多方面，你会希望你的孩子们都像他那样。 他勤劳、忠诚、善于倾听、做事有理有据、持之以恒、乐观、认错态度达观大方。 但也缺少一些东西。 他看上去从来都不会完全放松，总有一个目标，一种目的。 如果他可以失去这个目标，让它随风而逝，他会更容易被理解。"这也是为什么米尔肯如今比以前更加集中精力的原因。 他要用自己剩下的时光，竭尽全力消除过去十年所遭受的痛苦。 这从来就不是简单的事情。 对于米尔肯来说，唯一的答案是保持一颗进取之心。 霍尔顿认为："如果我是他的话，我就会在法国的里维埃拉

He never swears. His jokes are always hopelessly wholesome and corny. Even as a kid, he never rebelled. When he married Lori, at the age of 22, the pair had been dating since the ninth grade.

Some of his friends and those who've worked closely with Milken say his drive for perfection are both inspiring and maddening. "In so many ways, he is who you hope your kids become. He is diligent, loyal, a great listener, grounded, persistent, optimistic, generous to a fault, " says Joseph Costello, " But something is missing. He never seems completely relaxed. There is always a point, a purpose. If he could just lose it, let go, he would be easier to relate to." That's why Milken is more focused than ever these days. With the time that's left to him, he is striving to erase the painful episodes of the last decade. It hasn't been easy. For Milken, the only answer is to keep pushing. "If I were in his position, I would be in the French Riviera, " says Holden. "He loves to work hard. As long as he is doing something where he works tirelessly, he is happy. As Mike and I part company, I feel relieved." He's an exhausting guy to be around and, at the core, a tragic character. But his way of dealing with his situation is to work twice as hard to win everyone over. That ought to keep Mike Milken very busy indeed. Milken claims, without a trace of humor or irony, that his philosophical underpinning for his entire life has been "Prosperity is the sum of financial technology times the sum of human capital plus social capital plus real assets."

(1,037 words)

潇洒。他热爱工作。只要他不知疲倦地工作，他就开心。迈克和我各司其职，我感到非常欣慰。"总体上看，米尔肯是一个让人精疲力竭的家伙，从本质上讲他是一个悲剧性的人物。为了赢过所有人，他加倍拼命地工作，这就是他应对自己处境的方式。而这确实会让迈克·米尔肯非常忙碌。米尔肯不带一丝幽默或讽刺，声称他这辈子的人生哲学基础就是："繁荣等于金融技术的总和乘以人力资本、社会资本和房地产三者的总和。"

知识链接 🔍

Knowledge Universe 知识寰宇公司是一家全球领先的教育机构，拥有3 700多家网站，雇佣40 000多名教育专业人士，经营大型网上学校、学院、国际学校和学校管理系统，日常注册学生人数400多万。知识寰宇公司采用行之有效的教学方法、严谨的课程和复杂的教育技术，聘用充满热情的教育工作者为婴儿和幼儿、小学生和中学生以及成年人服务。知识寰宇公司还提供知名品牌、世界级的教育资源和基础设施。

题 记

瑞安航空公司总裁迈克尔·奥利里为人自信、果断、不拘常理。他以激进的性格、乐观的言论以及多样化的资本手段被称为航空界的坏小子。他坚持超低价的运营方式，使欧洲人趋之若鹜，公司业务大幅上升，客流量成倍增长。他可以在公司利润下降的情况下实施更为猛烈的价格战，令各大航空公司不寒而栗。瑞安航空在他的领导下拥有强大的征服能力，以务实的方式减少冗余支出，以各种方式维护世界环保。旅行者们欣喜地看到，廉价航班是有远见者创造的一个更为平等的社会。

The Advocate of Budget Airlines — Michael O'Leary

David Cameron prefers pedalling around the lanes of Cornwall to jetting off overseas. Gordon Brown drove to his Suffolk beach hut. As oil prices take off, more people are staying at home. Ryanair announced an 85 percent fall in profits, while British Airways admitted that it, too, was tipping into the red. But not everyone thinks that the death knell is tolling for the airline industry. "Rubbish," says Michael O'Leary, the Ryanair chief executive, who is famed for his pugnacious① manner, bullish optimism and showman's approach to marketing. He could just take three of his flights in ten hours, from Dublin to Bologna and on to Frankfurt then home again.

House prices are falling, food costs are rising but Mr. O'Leary is convinced that everyone needs a holiday, particularly in a recession. "It will never go horrendously② wrong when you're offering the cheapest fares in Europe. We just have to keep flying more aircraft, opening up more routes and offering people more cheap flights." He expects that Ryanair passenger numbers will grow from 51 million to 58 million annualy, which is why its profits will fall as "we have guaranteed no

---

① pugnacious [pʌɡ'neiʃəs] *adj.* 好斗的
② horrendously [hɔ'rendəsli] *adj.* 可怕的，令人惊骇的

廉价航班的创导者——
迈克尔·奥利里

英国保守党领袖戴维·卡梅伦宁可骑脚踏车在康沃尔郡的乡间小路环游也不愿坐飞机出游海外；英国首相戈登·布朗则驱车前往他位于萨克福马海滩的小屋；当油价节节攀升的时候，更多的人选择待在家里。瑞安航空宣布公司盈利下降 85%，而英国航空公司也同样宣告亏损。但并非所有人都认为航空业已经走到了尽头。瑞安航空的总裁迈克尔·奥利里认为这是"胡说八道"。奥利里在航空界以激进的风格、乐观任性的个性以及张扬炫耀的营销方式而著称。他可以在 10 小时内乘坐三趟航班，从都柏林到博洛尼亚，再直飞法兰克福，然后返家。

房价下跌，食品价格上涨，但奥利里先生仍然坚信每个人都需要度假，尤其是在经济不景气的时候。"在欧洲，如果你提供最为低廉的机票决不会令人惊骇。我们必须坚持飞行更多的航班，开通更多的航线，给人们提供更便宜的航班。"他预计瑞安航空的乘客数量将会从每年 5 100 万增至 5 800 万，这就是利润下降的原因，因为"我们保证不管油价上升幅度多大，都不收取燃油附加费"。奥利里没有退却，继续展开了攻击性的价格战。他试图将票价再降低 5%，开辟飞往意大利和德国的新航线，瑞安航空甚至打算提供 100

171

fuel surcharges whatever oil increases there are". Far from retreating, he is going on the offensive with a price war. He intends to cut fares by a further 5 percent and is opening new routes to Italy and Germany, even Ryanair will offer a million flights for £1 each. Many are just waiting for Mr O'Leary — the self-described "bad boy" of the airline industry — to fail.

No-frills airlines have been blamed for everything from the rise in skin cancer to the melting ice-caps at the North Pole. President Sarkozy of France sued Ryanair for using a picture of him and his wife, Carla Bruni, without permission. "We paid €60,000 to their charity but we got more than €5 million worth of free publicity so we're happy," O'Leary says. "I'm available to kiss and make up with Mrs Sarkozy any time she wants." British Airways, he says, are the real villains. "Willie Walsh, the chief executive of BA, is the one with the high fares and the fuel surcharges. BA's neither on time nor efficient. They used to claim to be the world's favourite airline now they're not even Britain's favourite airline, Ryanair is. We have twice as many passengers." He thinks that the critics of the budget airlines are hypocrites. "People may pretend they don't fly Ryanair but everyone does it. Tony Blair, half the Royal Family. If I showed you our passenger list, we'd have half the House of Lords, lots of MPs. Green protesters are our best passengers. They're always flying off to their demonstrations. The chatterati① hate mass tourism but they travel with us to their Italian villas. They all love a bargain. If they use it, why should they exclude others? It's just snobbery."

The budget airlines are visionaries who are creating a more equal society. "Low fares have transformed Europe politically. There's much more

---

① chatterati [ˌtʃætəˈrɑːti] *n.* 名嘴精英

万张仅售 1 英镑的机票。 许多人都在等待这位自称为航空界"坏小子"奥利里的倒下。

只提供起码必需品的航空服务已经受到来自各方的指责，从皮肤癌几率的上升到北极正在融化的冰帽。 法国总统萨科奇状告瑞安航空，说公司未经他和妻子卡拉·布鲁尼允许就擅自使用了他们的一张照片。"我们仅为他们的慈善行为支付了 6 万欧元，但在公开场合使用这些照片却让我们获利 500 多万欧元，因此我们感到很高兴。"迈克尔·奥利里说道。"如果萨科奇夫人愿意，我随时希望与她达成和解。"他认为英国航空公司才是真正的恶棍。"英国航空行政总裁威利·沃尔什是个收取高票价和燃油附加费的家伙。 英航既不准时效率又低。 过去他们常常宣称是世界上最受欢迎的航空公司，可现在他们根本不值一提，瑞安航空才是最受欢迎的航空公司。 我们拥有他们两倍的客流量。"奥利里认为那些批评廉价航空者都是伪君子。"他们假装不会乘坐瑞安航空，但每个人都是乘客，包括托尼·布莱尔和半数的皇室成员。 如果我给你看乘客名单，就会发现半数的上议院成员和很多下院议员。 环保主义者是我们最好的乘客，他们经常乘坐我们的航班就是最好的证明。 名嘴精英阶层厌恶如此大众化的旅行，但依旧和我们一起飞往他们位于意大利的别墅。 他们都爱占小便宜。 如果他们乘坐廉价航班，又凭什么排除他人？ 只不过是摆架子罢了。"

廉价航班是有远见者创造的一个更为平等的社会。 迈克尔·奥利里对政治家们在英国度假修建沙堡不以为然："低价收费使欧洲变得更加政治化。 年轻人有更多的机会跨大陆旅行。 在欧洲一体化进程中，我们比那些在布鲁塞尔大放厥词的政治家们做得多多了。

movement of young people across the Continent. We've done more for European integration than any old fart① politician in Brussels." Mr O'Leary is not impressed by politicians spending their holidays building sandcastles in Britain. "Typical political posturing. England's a wonderful country but it isn't right for every family or every holiday. Sometimes you need to get away."

He is not concerned that by increasing air travel he is shortening the life-cycle of polar bears and shrinking the ice-cap. "The green lobby are like those old guys in the medieval market-place, shouting about the end of the world. Climate change is not the biggest threat to mankind. If it is, why is the summer so crappy?" O'Leary seems determined to reverse the "green madness". "I drive a car and a tractor, I have a herd of 600 cows on my farm in Ireland who probably make a more damaging impact on the environment than my airplanes do." He uses low-energy bulbs but only because "it's cheaper". The one thing he recycles is cow pats, which he uses as fertiliser. "This global warming nonsense is no different to some of the more lunatic movements you've had throughout history. They were excommunicating Galileo 500 years ago for suggesting the Earth might go round the Sun. Now the ecologists say we're boiling the planet to extinction. This is just the crazy idea."

The economic downturn will end the eco-fad. "All this climate change stuff is an inevitable byproduct of a period of economic growth and low unemployment." And politicians are manipulating people's fears to make them pay more tax. "They call them eco-taxes but that's just spin— it's just taking more money off us." Airport taxes are "highway robbery" even though "air transport accounts for less than 2 percent of

---

① fart [fɑːt] n. 放屁

这是典型的政治作秀，英国虽然是一个非常美好的国家，但不适合每一个家庭或者是每一个假期都在这里度过。有些时候你需要到处走走。"

增加飞行次数就意味着减少北极熊的寿命，缩减极地冰帽，这样的说法让他不屑一顾："环保说客就像中世纪市场上的那些老家伙，叫嚣着世界末日的来临。气候变化其实并不是人类最大的威胁。如果真是这样，夏天为什么还如此糟糕?"奥利里似乎下定决心要颠倒"环保疯狂"："在爱尔兰农场我拥有一辆汽车、一辆拖拉机和 600 头牛，这些东西对于环境的破坏力肯定要比飞机大。"他使用节能灯只是因为"更便宜"。他回收牛粪这件事只是用作肥料。"这种关于全球变暖的无稽之谈和历史上曾有过的一些愚蠢举动没有什么两样。500 多年前，伽利略因认为地球可能是绕着太阳旋转而被逐出教会，现在生态学者又说我们正将地球推向灭亡，这真是个疯狂的想法。"

经济衰退会结束对生态的狂热。"整个气候变化是经济增长和低失业率不可避免的一种副产品。"政治家利用人们对环境的担忧让他们承担更多的税赋。"他们将这些税收称之为生态税，但这仅仅是找了一种说法，为的是从我们身上榨取更多的钱。"他认为，航空税就是"拦路打劫"，尽管"航空交通只占不到 2% 的二氧化碳排放量。海上运输的二氧化碳排放量占 5%，是航空业的两倍，但从没听说对海运业实施税收"。奥利里坚持认为瑞安航空非常环保："我们的飞机可以搭载更多的乘客，我们拥有一批更节能的新式飞机，我们携带更轻的重量。巴西热带雨林的损耗来自英国航空公司，他们携带过多的行李，飞机老旧，商务舱浪费了大量空间。"他也不认为碳抵消就能解决问

CO_2 emissions", he says. "Marine transport accounts for 5 percent, double the aviation industry, but you don't hear saying let's tax the the ferries." Ryanair is, he insists, quite green. "We can put more passengers in our planes, we have a fleet of new aircraft that are more fuel efficient, we take less weight. Entire Brazilian rainforests of waste come off BA's aircraft with all that extra packaging, the ancient planes, the waste of space in business class." Nor does he think that carbon offsetting is the answer. "Where do all these offsets go? Corrupt African dictatorships and staff in New York. The money doesn't actually go to planting trees."

O'Leary would rather "be in a lunatic asylum[①]" than be a politician but that doesn't stop him giving the party leaders advice. "David Cameron can hug trees because he won't have to do much to get into power but it is not a way to run a country." He has even less time for Mr. Brown. "It's just Government by poll and spin-doctor Thatcher and Blair didn't dither[②] they just made their decisions." He wants the next leader "whether it is Dave or David" to run the country in the same no-frills way as he does his business.

Michael O'Leary may have made his fortune flying the masses to the Med but he prefers to spend his own summer on his farm. "I don't like to go abroad on holiday. I'm an Irish peasant farmer— I don't like sunshine. When I can stay at home in Ireland what the hell would I want to go away for?"

(1,068 words)

---

① lunatic asylum n. 疯人院, 精神病院
② dither ['diðə] vi. 慌张

题："这些补偿款项何去何从？ 都落到了腐败的非洲独裁统治和纽约幕僚的口袋。 那些钱并没有真正地用于植树造林。"

奥尼尔宁愿"待在疯人院"里，也不愿成为一名政客，但这并不妨碍他给政党领袖们提建议："大卫·卡梅隆可以拥抱树木，因为他不用多大努力就可以得到执政的权力，但以那样的方式治理国家却不是一个好的选择。"奥利里与首相布朗接触的时间更少："由投票和高级幕僚撒切尔和布莱尔组织起来的政府不会令人兴奋，他们从来都是自己做决定。"迈克尔·奥利里希望下一任首相不管是"戴夫还是大卫"，都能够跟他运营航空公司一样，能以务实的做法来治理国家。

迈克尔·奥利里可能靠送大量的人飞往地中海发了财，但他更喜欢在自己的农场中度过夏天。"我不喜欢到国外度假。 我是一名爱尔兰农夫，我不喜欢阳光。 可以待在爱尔兰的家中时，为什么我还想走远呢？"

知识链接

Ryanair 瑞安航空公司（Ryanair）是欧洲廉价航空的领头羊，它由克里斯蒂·瑞安（Christy Ryan）创立于 1985 年，总部设在爱尔兰都柏林，枢纽包括伦敦斯坦斯特机场、都柏林国际机场、洽米皮诺机场、法兰克福·哈恩机场等。多年来，瑞安航空公司已经逐步发展成世界上最赚钱的航空公司。

British Airways 英国航空公司是全球最大的国际航空公司之一，全球航班网络覆盖 75 个国家的 150 多个目的地，每年乘载约 3 600 万名乘客。英航总部设在英国伦敦希思罗机场（Heathrow Airport），并以此为枢纽基地。

题 记

　　路易·威登品牌箱包自问世以来，渐渐从巴黎传遍欧洲，成为旅行用品最精致的象征。不论是时髦的仕女或成熟的男性，甚至是活泼的年轻人，都可以在 LV 找到符合自己的皮件用品，尝试"LV 旅行哲学"。在时尚界呼风唤雨的美国设计师马克·雅各布斯加入 LV 之后，他为这个象征巴黎传统的精品品牌注入了一股新的活力。雅各布斯的设计理念因典雅、奢华和性感赢得无数美人的芳心，受欢迎的程度已俨然打破国界。他将波西米亚的浪荡不羁、英伦新浪漫主义的风流、美国著名游戏软件公司的反叛时尚态度等运用到自己的服装系列中，更成功地将纽约的喧嚣与巴黎的奢华高贵相融合，让马克·雅各布斯服装保有一贯的贵族休闲风格。

Marc Jacobs' Design Philosophy

It was just a store opening, but the festivities taking place behind New York City's Lincoln Center could have rivaled the christening of the new Queen Mary. A giant tent glowed with the image of a logo-laden Louis Vuitton trunk, a beacon for the handbag obsessed. On the ceiling inside, tiny stars shaped like Vuitton's LV logo twinkled above the crowd. Kirsten Dunst, Maggie Gyllenhaal and Rudy Giuliani swept in to congratulate LVMH Moet Hennessy Louis Vuitton chairman and CEO Bernard Arnault on his spectacular four-story Fifth Avenue emporium.

The 150-year-old Vuitton brand may have been the star of the night, but on the ground, the talk was all about Marc Jacobs, the designer who has been widely credited with boosting Vuitton's profile and bottom line ever since he was named creative director. Rumors were flying around the tents at the New York fashion shows that Jacobs was unhappy with the way LVMH was handling his signature label and that he had been approached by rival Gucci Group N.V. to design the Yves Saint Laurent line. Arnault dismissed the chatter, saying that the relationship was very good and that Jacobs had the potential to become as big as Ralph Lauren or Donna Karan.

The designer, 40, is perhaps already more influential among fashion's Young Turks than those brands are. The disheveled-1950s-

马克·雅各布斯的
设计哲学

这仅仅是一个商场的开张,但是在纽约的林肯中心举办的庆祝活动却可以与新女王玛丽的洗礼仪式相媲美。 一个点缀着 LV 包箱标志的熠熠生辉的巨型帐篷,就像手提包堆砌的灯塔。 帐篷里的天花板上,小星星形状的 LV 标志在人群的上空闪闪发光。 柯尔斯滕·邓斯特、玛吉·盖伦霍尔和鲁迪·朱利亚尼鱼贯而入,前来祝贺路易·威登董事长和首席执行官伯纳德·阿诺特壮观气派的四层第五大道百货商场的开张。

150 岁的路易·威登品牌也许一直都是夜晚的恒星,但在地面上的发言人就是设计师马克·雅各布斯。 他自从被任命为创意主管之后,在提升路易·威登的形象和设计方面获得了广泛的称誉。 帐篷周围弥漫着纽约时尚界的传言,称雅各布斯不满路易·威登发放他的签名标签,被竞争对手逼近而去设计伊夫·圣罗兰系列。 阿诺特驳回了传言,认为马克·雅各布斯和路易·威登关系良好,而且雅各布斯具备成为拉尔夫·劳伦或唐娜·卡兰等大人物的潜能。

这位 40 岁的设计者,在时尚的土耳其年轻人心中也许比其他品牌更有影响力。 例如,他的设计首次出现于雅各布斯 2003 年时装展,就改变了 20 世纪 50 年代以来家庭主妇的形象,使她们一拨一

housewife look that stalked runway after runway, for example, first appeared in Jacobs. spring 2003 show. And renditions of his brightly colored accessories have recently turned up in mass venues like the Gap for which a onetime Jacobs accessory designer now works. "He certainly has made it really cool to look back to the past, and now other designers are following him in the way they put together a collection," says Julie Gilhart, vice president and fashion director at Barneys New York, marveling at Jacobs'. growing influence. In fashion schools around the world, students reference Jacobs almost exclusively. "They revere① him," says Timothy Gunn, chairman of the department of fashion design at the Parsons School of Design in New York City. "It's his design innovation and flea-market sensibility but also the fact that there's a little bit of mystery about him."

If Calvin Klein is the icon of minimalism, Ralph Lauren the elegant esquire and Donna Karan the workingwoman's tailor, Jacobs is the eclectic sampler who has ushered in an era of sophisticated charm in fashion. His uncanny ability to give street-wise looks a luxurious twist— a thermal② undershirt made of cashmere, or cropped cargo pants turned into tuxedo pants — has made him one of the most carefully watched — and desired — designers in the business. The $ 1,000-plus Murakami bag, a collaboration with Japanese artist Takashi Murakami, generated more than $ 300 million in sales for Vuitton. "He has a vision of what people will want tomorrow," says Yves Carcelle, chairman and CEO of Louis Vuitton. "With the Murakami bag, he came to me and said,

---

① reverer [ri'viə] *vt.* 崇敬
② thermal ['θə:məl] *adj.* 热的

拨地开始追求潮流。 他那色泽鲜艳的配件处理方式已于近期出现在加普等地的公众场合，雅各布斯曾经的配件设计商正在操作该项目。 副总裁兼纽约巴尼斯的时装总监朱莉·吉哈特对雅各布斯日益增长的影响力惊讶不已："确实，他的作品怀旧味道真的很酷，现在其他设计师也开始学着他把许多小玩意放在一起。"世界各地时装学校的学生几乎一丝不漏地参照雅各布斯的风格设计。 纽约市帕森设计学校时装设计系主席悌穆斯·戈恩说："学生们崇拜雅各布斯，崇拜他的设计创新和对廉价商品市场的敏感性，还有他身上存在的一点点神秘感。"

如果卡尔文·克莱恩是极简抽象主义的偶像，拉尔夫·劳伦代表优雅的绅士，唐娜·卡兰为职业女性剪裁师，那么雅各布斯就是兼收并蓄的样板，他引领着时装界富有精致魅力的时代。 他那不可思议的创造都市时装的能力似乎是一种奢侈的扭曲，他用开司米编织的保暖内衣，或将剪裁不规范的工装裤变成晚礼服的裤子，这些使他成为业界最受关注、最受期待的设计者。 他与日本艺术家塔卡斯·木拉米合作，推出价值 1 000 多美元的村上包，为路易·威登创造了 3 亿多美元的收益。 路易·威登公司董事长兼首席执行官伊夫·卡斯利说："他具有比普通人更广阔的视野。 随着村上包的诞生，他来对我说，'看，我们度过了 9·11 以后的困难时期，我们需要乐观，用一种新鲜、甚至天真的视野看世界'"。 当那些明亮、鲜艳的手包出现在 T 台时，是如此的释放，那么新鲜，这正是人们所想要的。

但是，尽管他的产品姿态鲜明，雅各布斯本人并非如此。 他与许多和媒体关系更友好的同事不一样——这里要提到汤姆·福特和

'Look, we've been through such a gray period after Sept.11, and we need optimism, a fresh, even naive, vision of the world. ' And when those bright, colorful bags came out on the runway, it was such a relief, so new, so what people wanted."

But while his products are high profile, Jacobs himself is not. Unlike many of his more media-friendly colleagues — Tom Ford and Donatella Versace come to mind— the low-key Jacobs would rather cultivate his grunge-kid image than kowtow to Hollywood stars or join the society party circuit. Born in New York City, Jacobs was raised by his grandmother, whom he still cites as a fashion muse, having introduced him to places like Bergdorf Goodman and encouraged him to sketch. He now lives in Paris, works almost 365 days a year and pals around with longtime friends like artist Elizabeth Peyton and director Sofia Coppola. His grunge-meets-glamour aesthetic, often inspired by his friends, has quietly permeated the fashion world, influencing both luxury and mass-market designers. If Ford's louche Gucci Amazons symbolized the excesses and decadence of the past, then Jacobs. offhand, sexy thrift-store style is shaping up to be the fashion leitmotif① of today. Jacobs is particularly deft② at attracting different kinds of customers. At Vuitton he appeals to the consumer's lust for "trading up" — buying something slightly out of her price range because of the status that attends it. And with his less expensive Marc line, he has created high fashion for a younger customer.

It was only seven years ago that Jacobs and his business partner of 20 years, Robert Duffy, were struggling to keep their business afloat,

---

① leitmotif ['laitməuti:f] *n.* 主乐调
② deft [deft] *adj.* 灵巧的

多纳泰拉·范思哲——低调的雅各布斯宁愿培养乏味的孩子般的想象力也不愿对好莱坞的明星叩头或加入社会党派的圈子。 雅各布斯出生于纽约市，由祖母带大，而祖母一直是他心中的时尚缪斯，她曾经推荐雅各布斯到贝格多福·古德曼等地，并鼓励他学习素描。他目前居住在巴黎，几乎一年 365 天都在工作，经常与艺术家伊丽莎白·佩顿和导演索菲亚·科波拉等朋友交流切磋。 他的油渍荟萃魅力审美感就是来自朋友们的灵感启迪，这种审美感已经深深渗透时尚界，影响了奢侈品和大众市场的设计师。 如果说福特声名狼藉的古奇亚马逊象征着过往的放肆和颓废，那么雅各布斯随意、性感的节俭商店风格正在成为当今的时尚主色调。 雅各布斯特别擅长吸引不同类型的客户，在路易·威登，他激起消费者"购买更高价值物品"的欲望，即购买价格略高的商品，因为那里面包含了身份和地位。 对于不太昂贵的马克系列，他则为更年轻的顾客创造出高级时尚。

就在 7 年前，雅各布斯和他已经相处 20 年的商业伙伴罗伯特·杜菲还在尽力维持生意的顺畅，为其他设计工作室做顾问，重新募集资金投入自己的工作室。 雅各布斯说："关于我自己，更准确的说法是我比万圣节的杰米·李·可悌斯更容易复原。 我和罗伯特在很长的一段时间里都坚持不放弃。"他们两人在帕森斯晚宴上相识，当时雅各布斯正在展示他的一些收藏品，而杜菲当时受雇于第七大道的制造商罗本·托马斯，正在寻找新的人才。 后来雅各布斯被任命为佩里·爱丽丝的女装设计师，设计出他今天称之为用下层社会的态度来看上流社会的服装品牌。 但是在出名的印花条纹 T 恤衫作为特色的蹩脚货收购活动之后，雅各布斯被解雇了，于是，他和杜

consulting for other design houses and refinancing their personal homes for cash. "The most accurate thing that was ever said about me is that I've had more comebacks than Jamie Lee Curtis in Halloween, " says Jacobs. "Robert and I have a long history of not giving up." The two met at a Parsons dinner, at which Jacobs was presenting a collection and Duffy, then employed by the Seventh Avenue manufacturer Ruben Thomas, was looking for new talent. Then Jacobs was named womenswear designer at Perry Ellis and made his mark designing what he now calls uptown clothes with downtown attitude. But after his famous grunge collection, which featured floral-print dresses over striped T shirts, Jacobs was fired, so he and Duffy teamed up to create a Marc Jacobs line, which they produced on a shoestring until Arnault came calling three years later. Jacobs quickly reprised the LV logo in varnished① leather and then, with the first collection of handbags designed under his own name, raised the bar for American accessories, an area usually stronger in Europe.

For all his commercial success, Jacobs doesn't put much stock in the marketplace as a design engine. He develops collections through discussions with his design staff and endless sketching. He thinks the secret is in the spontaneity of his clothes. "We got somewhere by making something we thought was right, " says Jacobs, "not by sitting and thinking what we could contrive that millions of women will want." Although he seems to be pretty good at that too.

(1,011 words)

---

① varnished ['vɑːniʃt] *adj.* 涂漆的

菲合作创建了马可·雅各布斯系列，他们以小本经营，直到阿诺特三年后使用他们的设计。 雅各布斯迅速在漆皮上重启路易·威登商标，随后，以他的名字设计的第一批手提包提高了美国配件市场的占有率，欧洲通常在该领域占有更多的份额。

尽管他在商业上取得了成功，雅克布斯没有像设计发动机一样对市场投放大量的货物。 他通过与设计伙伴的讨论，不断地绘图收集素材。 他认为秘密在于服装的行为冲动。 雅克布斯说："我们通过制造我们认为正确的东西取得一些成就，而不是坐下来思考我们可以设计什么，从而满足数百万女性的愿望。"尽管他似乎很擅长这样做。

知识链接

LV 路易·威登(Louis Vuitton)创立于1854年，现隶属于法国专产高级奢华用品的路易·威登集团。创始人路易·威登革命性地创制了平顶皮衣箱，并在巴黎开了第一间店铺，从此路易·威登成为时尚的潮流。路易·威登品牌延伸出来的皮件、丝巾、笔、手表，甚至服装，都是其150年来崇尚精致、品质、舒适的"LV旅行哲学"的真正象征。

题 记

　　今天，当我们回忆伟大的美国金融家的名字时，我们往往会想起 J. P 摩根和华伦·巴菲特，甚至迈克尔·米尔肯这样的人物。但是，他们当中没有任何一个人像查尔斯·爱德华·美林那样影响了美国人的生活。他是第一个意识到连锁店有一天将主导零售市场的投资银行家，第一个预言1929年大萧条的华尔街大玩家，也是第一个公开倡导股市不应该仅仅是华尔街业内人士的玩物，也应该成为美国广大民众致富渠道的金融思想家。美林所传递的投资理念和市场信仰使"好时代查理"孤独的声音成为美国人的共同智慧——股市不再只属于业内人士，它属于我们所有的人。我们现在都参与其收益，正如我们分享其损失。

Sapiential① Investment Banker—Charles Merrill

With a fervent belief in the small investor as the foundation of the stock market, "Good Time Charlie" made America the shareholder nation. In 1940, the year Charles Edward Merrill founded the firm we now know as Merrill Lynch & Co., he was 54 years old and had already lived an extraordinarily productive and visible life. A poor boy from the backwaters of Florida, Merrill was forced to leave college by lack of funds. But he schemed his way to Wall Street and made himself wealthy by the time he was 31.

He was the first investment banker to realize that chain stores would one day dominate retailing, and he got rich by underwriting and often controlling such future powerhouses as K Mart and Safeway Stores. He set up one of America's first wire houses — brokerage firms with branch offices in different cities connected to the main office by Teletype.

He was also the first big-name Wall Streeter to predict the Great Crash of 1929. Indeed, in the months leading up to the Crash, Merrill pleaded to no avail with President Calvin Coolidge to speak out against speculation. By February 1929, Merrill was so sure the end was near that

---

① sapiential [ˌsepiˈenʃəl] *adj.* 智慧的，表现智慧的

智慧的投资银行家——
查尔斯·美林

凭借小型投资者是股市根基这一强烈的信念，"好时代查理"使美国成为股东之国。1940 年，查尔斯·爱德华·美林创立了现在我们称之为美林的公司，当时他已 54 岁，过着十分富足和显赫的生活。美林这个穷小伙子来自落后的佛罗里达州，他曾因交不起学费而被勒令退学。但他想方设法来到华尔街发展，并在 31 岁那年成为有钱人。

他是第一个意识到连锁店有一天将主导零售市场的投资银行家，通过对凯马特和赛福威等未来大型连锁企业的承保和经常性控制而发财。他是美国首批建立电讯化经纪公司中的一员，即通过电传打字电报机将位于不同城市的区域办公室与总部相连的经纪公司。

他也是第一个预言 1929 年大萧条的华尔街知名人士。实际上，在大萧条将至的前几个月，美林请求当时的美国总统卡尔文·柯立芝出面反对投机行为，但无功而返。1929 年 2 月，美林十分肯定他判断的结局即将降临，他清算了公司的股票投资组合，这一举动使其在当年 10 月大萧条最终到来之时声名远扬。

美林是个身材矮小、自我专注、目中无人、派头十足的人，朋

he liquidated① his firm's stock portfolio, an act that made him famous in October, when the Crash finally came.

A short, self-absorbed, prideful, flamboyant fellow— "Good Time Charlie Merrill," his friends called him— he had the unconscious expectation that Great Men always have: that he should be at the center of any orbit he entered. And so he was. As his son once wrote, "Whatever he decided to serve, the victim was meant to choke it down② and be grateful."

Merrill can't be dismissed as a moneybags who made a lucky guess on the Crash. He truly deserves to be remembered for what he did during that second career of his, the one that began when he was deep into middle age. In founding Merrill Lynch— his partner and sidekick, Edmund C. Lynch, was a soda-fountain-equipment salesman— Merrill created an important and enduring institution. But more than that, he started the country down an important and enduring path. Merrill was the first person to openly advocate that the stock market should not just be a plaything for Wall Street insiders but should also be an avenue to become rich for the broad mass of Americans. Decades before founding Merrill Lynch, he coined the phrase "Bringing Wall Street to Main Street." For the last 17 years of his life, that's what he tried to achieve with his new firm, which became a laboratory for his grand experiment. Today when we conjure up the names of the great American financiers, we tend to think of people like J.P. Morgan and Warren Buffett and even Michael

---

① liquidate ['likwideit] v. 清算
② choke down 用力咽下;强抑制住

友称呼他"好时代查理·美林"。 他的潜意识中蕴含着伟人常有的期望: 他应该位于他进入的任何领域的中心。 情况确实如此。 正如他儿子曾写到的那样，"不管他决定提供什么样的服务，受害者都有意要承受这样的服务，并心存感激"。

不能简单地视美林为有幸预测到大萧条的富翁。 他的确值得为他始于中年后期的第二次职业生涯中的所作所为而被世人铭记。 他与合伙人和合作伙伴、冷饮柜设备销售商爱德蒙·C.林奇创建了美林，使之成为一个重要而持久的机构。 更重要的是，他推动这个国家开始沿着一条重要而持久的道路前进。 美林第一个公开倡导股市不应该仅仅是华尔街业内人士的玩物，也应该成为美国广大民众的致富渠道。 他在美林建立的前几十年就杜撰了"使华尔街成为主街"的短语。 他在生命中的最后 17 年，一直设法完成这一目标，新公司成为他实施宏伟实验的实验室。 今天，当我们回忆伟大的美国金融家的名字时，我们往往会想起 J.P摩根和华伦·巴菲特，甚至迈克尔·米尔肯这样的人物。 但是，他们当中没有任何一个人像查尔斯·美林那样影响了美国人的生活。 事实上，甚至无人能接近美林的影响。

毫无疑问，市场民主化是过去半个世纪以来唯一最深刻的财政趋势。 统计数据当然证实了这一点: 目前有一半的美国家庭参与投资，单单共同基金就比银行持有更多的美国金融资产。 甚至可以得出一个有力的结论: 数量远多于专业交易员的小型投资者一直是建立现代牛市的真正基础。 看看我们已经变得多么关注每日跌宕起伏的道琼斯指数吧: 当市场上升时我们的心跳得多么快，而当市场下降时我们变得多么沮丧。 或者，看看我们已经如何将共同基金经理

Milken. But none of them had the effect on American life that Charlie Merrill had. In fact, they're not even close.

No doubt that the democratization of the markets is the single most profound financial trend of the past half-century. The statistics certainly bear this out: by some measures, half of America's households now invest, and mutual funds alone hold more of America's financial assets than banks do. Indeed, a strong argument can be made that the small investor, far more than the professional trader, is the true foundation upon which the modern bull market has been built. Look at how fixated we've become with the daily ups and downs of the Dow — how our hearts race when the market is up and how we sag① when the market does. Or look at how we've turned mutual-fund managers like Peter Lynch into celebrities. Most of all, look at the extraordinary extent to which we now rely on stocks to fund our retirement, send our kids to college and allow us to lead the kind of comfortable lives we view as middle class. We believe in the market today with something approaching religious faith, which, it turns out, is a pretty fair description of how Merrill always viewed the market. Its ability to create wealth broadly was to him an undeniable proposition. And while this is now a more or less universal truth, it was not always so. After all, the Street was largely a rigged game. Insiders manipulated the market from behind the curtains, behavior that, while unseemly, was legal then. Small investors were scorned — or fleeced. Yet Merrill was untouched by the cynicism that pervaded Wall Street. Like so many American visionaries, he was marked by naive and exaggerated

---

① sag [sæg] v. 物价下跌

彼得·林奇之流变成名人。 最重要的是，看看我们现在对股票的依赖程度有多么惊人：我们依赖股票基金退休养老、送孩子上大学、过那种我们认为是中产阶级的舒适生活。 现在，我们对市场的信任程度接近于对宗教的信仰，结果正好公平地描述了美林始终是如何看待市场的。 对美林来说，市场广泛创造财富的能力是一个不可否认的命题。 尽管这一命题目前或多或少是一个普遍真理，但并非总是如此。 毕竟在很大程度上，华尔街上演的是一场受人非法操作的游戏。 业内人士在幕后操纵市场，尽管行为不适宜，在当时也是合法的。 小投资者受到鄙视或欺诈。 然而，美林对弥漫华尔街的犬儒主义无动于衷。 他像美国的许多梦想家那样，其特征是天真夸张的乐观，这种乐观不可动摇，即使是面对周围更加黑暗的现实也是如此。

回想起来，美林公司是查尔斯·美林真正的"白宫"，通过这个平台，他可以宣扬股票市场的美德和对美国展示小投资者可以在华尔街公平交易。 詹姆斯·美林后来在他的回忆录中写道："启蒙已经成为我父亲取得巨大成功的关键。 不再有专门研究小组中哈佛人的繁文缛节，即使是小投资者也可以理解股市今后的运作。"为此，公司发表了数不清的标题为"如何投资"之类的报告、杂志和小册子。 在美林的带领下，公司在全国各地举办研讨会，并提供儿童保育，使丈夫和妻子都可以参加。 它在县一级的集市上设立促销帐篷。 它马不停蹄地开办经纪业务。 有一次，它甚至为了支持惠特斯赞助的一项竞赛而放弃股票。

1956 年美林去世时，公司拥有大约 40 万客户，已经成为全国最大的股票和债券代理公司，这一殊荣一直保持到今天。 但是，美林

optimism that was unshakable, even in the face of the darker reality he saw all around him.

In retrospect, Merrill Lynch was really Charlie Merrill's bully pulpit①, the platform from which he could preach the virtues of the stock market and show the country that the small investor could get a fair shake on Wall Street. "Demystification had been the key to my father's great success," James Merrill later wrote in his memoir. "No more mumbo-jumbo② from Harvard men in paneled rooms; let the stock market's workings henceforth be intelligible even to the small investor." To that end, the firm published an endless stream of reports, magazines, pamphlets with titles like How to Invest. Under Merrill the firm gave seminars across the country, with child care provided so that both husband and wife could attend. It set up promoting tents in county fairs. It ran a brokerage on wheels. Once, it even gave away stock in a contest sponsored by Wheaties.

By Merrill's death, in 1956, the firm had some 400,000 clients and had become the largest brokerage in the country, a distinction it holds to this day. But Merrill died a sorely disappointed man. Wall Street had not rushed to follow his example, as he had hoped, and the majority of the country, still scarred by the memory of the Depression, was not ready to plunge back into stocks. He was simply too far ahead of his time.

(992 words)

---

① bully pulpit *n.* 天字第一号讲坛(白宫)
② mumbo-jumbo [ˈmʌmbəuˈdʒʌmbəu] *n.* 繁文缛节

去世时失望得有点心酸：华尔街没有像他所希望的那样贸然追逐他的足迹，美国大部分人仍然饱受大萧条的记忆留下的创伤，他们来不及重投股市。美林只是太过于超前了自己的时代。

知识链接 🔍

Merrill Lynch　创办于 1914 年的美林证券（Merrill Lynch & Co.）曾是世界领先的财务管理和顾问公司之一，总部位于美国纽约。作为世界上最大的金融管理咨询公司之一，它在财务世界响当当的名字里占有一席之地，在底特律、芝加哥、丹佛、洛杉矶和都柏林都有办公室。2008 年金融风暴期间，已有 94 年历史的美林公司同意以大约 440 亿美元的价格出售给美国银行（Bank of America Corp.）。

K Mart　凯马特公司（Kmart）是现代超市型零售企业的鼻祖，也是美国国内最大的打折零售商和全球最大的批发商之一。凯马特公司经营包括传统的凯马特和凯马特大卖场以及凯马特超市，在美国、波多黎各、关岛和维尔京群岛等地区的 50 个州提供方便的购物。2004 年，凯玛特公司与西尔斯公司合并，成立"西尔斯控股（Sears Holdings）"，成为美国第三大零售商。

Safeway Stores　赛福威于 1915 年创建、1926 年命名，总部设在加州的奥克兰。它是北美最大的食品和药品零售商之一，在美国西部、西南部、落基山脉周边地区、中西部、亚特兰大中部地区以及加拿大西部地区、墨西哥中部地区共开设了将近两千家分店。

题　记

　　当科学家劳伦·欧瑞特放弃稳定的工作，雄心勃勃地走进商界，创办了属于自己的环境保护企业之时，就已经注定要用敏锐的科学方法挑战企业的管理和发展。借助于其在电化学液体监测和微电子过程中的专门技术，Neosens 公司已经研究出了一系列创新性的传感器件。这些器件不仅能够实现传感器的小型化和低成本，而且还提高了其检测的精确性和对恶劣环境的良好适应性。这些高水平水质监测技术已经因其连续性、工作现场化和实时性得到了广泛的应用，例如冷却系统、纸制造行业、食品和饮料行业等。对欧瑞特来说，创办一家公司就像发明了一种病毒，没有什么东西可以阻止你继续去创办其他的公司。最终，欧瑞特将会看到他的科学视野在商业成功中获取的回报。

A Business Scientist —
Laurent Auret

Laurent Auret likes to say he has four children: two boys, a girl and a company. Yet it is the last, just seven years old, that is likely to sever its paternal ties first, he believes.

Most entrepreneurs clasp their first-born company close to their chest. Mr Auret sees things differently. Having just brought in a deputy managing director, he plans one day to relinquish① control of Neosens to a trade buyer. In time, he expects to move on from the business, which creates and sells devices for detecting contaminants in the water systems of paper-makers, utilities and hospitals. For a company that employs just 17 people, had its first sales, and generated revenues of only € 300,000, the idea of a multinational buyer sweeping in sounds like big talk. But Neosens is no ordinary business. It is a technology pioneer in a conservative industry where change is slow. Driving it from start-up to the brink of commercial success has taken seven years of toil for its scientist founder. Sales of the company's monitoring solutions, which tell users about the levels of oxygen, biofilm or chlorine in industrial water systems, are expected to reach $ 1.4m and triple again next year. Finally, Auret is seeing his scientific vision rewarded with commercial success.

---

① relinquish [riˈliŋkwiʃ] vt. 让出(权利等)

商界科学家——
劳伦·欧瑞特

劳伦·欧瑞特喜欢说自己有四个孩子：两个儿子，一个女儿和一家公司。尽管这家公司是最小的，只有 7 岁大，但他认为公司有可能最先挣脱父亲的管制。

许多企业家都将其第一家公司视若珍宝。欧瑞特先生却有所不同。他刚刚引进了一名副总经理，计划有一天将 Neosens 公司的控制权转让给一位商业买家。他期望能够及时地继续在这里生产和销售检测造纸器械、城市管理服务行业以及医院水流系统中污染物的设备。对于一个只雇佣 17 个人、初次上市、只获得 30 万欧元利润的公司来说，跨国买家大规模买进的想法听起来像是说大话。但是 Neosens 不是普通的商业公司。在变革缓慢的传统行业中，它是技术的先驱者。从公司启动到商业取得初步成功，这位科学家出身的创建者付出了 7 年的艰辛。公司的监控系统可以告诉用户工业污水系统中氧气、生物膜或氯的含量水平，这个系统的销售量预计可达到 140 万美元，明年将会翻三倍。最终，欧瑞特将会看到他的科学视野在商业成功中获取的回报。

棱角分明、骨瘦如柴、皮肤黝黑的欧瑞特给企业的挑战带来一种敏锐的科学方法。欧瑞特没有受过正式的管理训练，只是根据自己的设想追求商业机会，利用对单晶片硅的复数分析过程（一个微

An angular①, scrawny② figure with a deep tan, Auret brings an acutely scientific approach to the entrepreneurial challenge. He has no formal management training, gleaning③ techniques from advisers along the way, as he has pursued a personal vision of the commercial opportunities for using multiple analytical processes on a single wafer of silicon — a microsystem — to transform sensor technology. Fouling in industrial processes is a multibillion-dollar problem, yet traditional tests were often little more sophisticated than the litmus paper used in school laboratories to check for acidity. Monitoring systems were expensive, required a lot of maintenance and disrupted the industrial process. Auret realised that electrical sensors connected to computer programmes on a single microchip could provide far more sensitive tests to detect contamination before it becomes a corrosion or health problem. Today, sensors developed by Neosens have vast potential for utilities, as well as in alerting staff to the risk of Legionella in the water systems of cooling towers, hospitals and other buildings.

It has been a tough slog, though. Raised in Périgueux, Auret took his first degree in Toulouse in the physics of solids but completed his PhD in micro-electrical -mechanical-systems at Johns Hopkins University, Baltimore, a world leader in medical and scientific research. On returning to France, he joined Elta, a subsidiary of Areva, the French state nuclear engineering group. The 50-person company designs electronic systems for hostile environments, including devices designed to detect corrosion risks in nuclear power plant cooling systems. "I started out in research and

---

① angular [ˈæŋgjulə] *adj.* (人)瘦骨嶙峋的
② scrawny [ˈskrɔːni] *adj.* 细而瘦的
③ gleaning [ˈgliːniŋ] *n.* 拾遗

观体系）转变传感器技术，在这个过程中，他一直从顾问那里学习各种管理方法。 工业化进程中的污染涉及上亿美元的问题，而传统检测比学校实验室使用的检验酸碱度的石蕊试纸复杂不了多少。 昂贵的监控系统需要大量的维护工作，还会使工业程序陷入混乱。 欧瑞特认识到，单个集成电路板连接电脑程序的电力传感器对检测污染物具有更高的敏感度，并且在污染物产生腐蚀或者成为健康问题之前完成检测。 Neosens 公司目前开发的传感器具有巨大的潜在效用，它也可以提醒工作人员关注冷冻塔、医院和其他建筑物污水系统中军团杆菌含量的风险。

然而，这是一项艰巨的苦差。 在佩里格长大的欧瑞特在图卢兹大学拿到的第一个学位是固体物理，但是他在位于巴尔的摩的约翰·霍普金斯大学获得了微电子技术系统的博士学位，该校在医学和科学研究领域中处于世界领先地位。 欧瑞特返回法国后进入法国国家核能工程集团阿海珐的附属企业爱尔达。 公司有 50 名职员，针对有害环境设计电子系统，包括用来检测核能工厂冷却系统中腐蚀风险的设备。 欧瑞特先生回忆道："我开始了我的研究和开发生涯。 我就像个自由电子。 我完全拥有自主，独立预算，并直接与总经理对话。"

爱尔达到 2000 年已拥有 200 名员工，然而当他试着说服老板更广泛地运行微型系统时，老板却对此不理不睬。 他向一位挚友、国家电子研究科学中心（CNRS）主任丹尼尔·埃斯特韦提到了这件令人失望的事情。"他对我说，'唯一的解决方式就是创办自己的公司'。"他从来没有过这种想法。 欧瑞特说："我直接找到老板，对他说'我要在污水检测部门创办自己的公司，如果你能成为我的第一个顾客我会很高兴'。"

development engineering," recalls Mr Auret. "I was a bit of a free electron. I had complete autonomy. I had my own budget. I answered directly to the chief executive."

By 2000 Elta had 200 employees, but when Mr Auret tried to convince his boss his microsystems work could be used much more widely, he got the cold shoulder. He raised his frustrations with a close contact, Daniel Esteve, director of the electronic research systems wing of the state-run Centre National de la Recherche Scientifique (CNRS). "He said to me: 'the only solution is that you start your own company'." It was an idea that had never occurred to him. Auret says: "I went straight to my boss and said to him 'I am setting up my company in the water-monitoring sector, and if you want to be my first customer I shall be delighted'."

Mr Auret's parents were deeply shocked that he would give up a safe job. But his wife Muriel, a laboratory analyst, was strongly supportive, as were 20 or so family and friends who backed him with their savings. In 2001, he moved into the regional scientific "incubator" unit in Toulouse— one man and a computer. His first recruit was a graduate from Toulouse business school to work on marketing. "I knew the commercial preparation was going to have to start at once, alongside the research and development," says Auret. For the next couple of years, the company financed itself largely through winning awards, including a € 200,000 national innovation prize. It moved home three times, arriving at its present quarters in a sun-blasted business park at Labè ge, on the outskirts of Toulouse at last.

Development work was financed by a € 1m funding round, drawing money from venture funds and private equity. That was followed by a € 2.5m round that brought Sofinnova Partners, Capricorn Cleantech Fund

　　欧瑞特先生放弃了一份稳定的工作，对此他的父母感到非常震惊。 但身为实验室分析员的妻子穆里尔却十分支持他，大约 20 位家人和朋友用自己的储蓄给予他财力上的支持。 2001 年，他独自一人带着一台电脑搬进了图卢兹当地的科研"孵化器"。 他的第一个员工是来自图卢兹商学院的毕业生，做市场营销的工作。 欧瑞特声称："我知道，商业准备工作随着研发的进程马上就将启动。"在接下来的几年中，公司很大程度上通过赢取各项奖金维持运营，包括 20 万欧元的国家创新奖。 公司三次搬家，最后迁移至现在的总部，位于图卢兹郊区拉伯格一个阳光普照的工商区。

　　研发工作获得风险投资和私募资金约 100 万欧元的资助。 来自比利时和加里亚管理的摩羯洁净科技基金的合作伙伴索菲诺瓦的入股，给公司又注入了约 250 万欧元的资金。 欧瑞特说："我的抱负一直十分远大，所以我愿意吸收外来投资者。"他开始工作后就计划直接出售给用户一套便携式测试用品，以炫耀他的先进技术。 然而许多公司都希望继续监控，且比起技术优势来说，对可行性更感兴趣。

　　欧瑞特采取相应措施重新设计了商业模式。 与大型化工或者水资源治理公司的合作使 Neosens 公司进入了广阔的市场。 威立雅环境或苏伊士环境等公用事业公司和阿法·拉伐等制度制定者有潜力打开通向世界范围内的客户大门。 德国小型工程企业普遍使用这种方法，但在法国却并不常见。 欧瑞特雇佣了一家美国大型水资源处理公司的前任市场营销部门负责人蒂埃里·布利乍得担任副总经理。 欧瑞特依然是主席，监管战略发展，但他希望更多地参与产品开发。 因此，他将与蒂埃里先生合作，共同维持公司的发展。

　　欧瑞特先生认为，很多时候，科学家成立一家公司，然后拒绝

from Belgium and Galia Gestion to join them. "The ambition has always been high, so I was willing to bring in outside investors," says Auret. When he started out, he planned to sell portable test kits direct to users, vaunting① his advanced technology. But companies wanted continuous monitoring and were more interested in reliability than technical prowess.

In response, Auret reinvented the business model. Partnering with big chemical or water treatment companies enables Neosens to access big markets. Utilities such as Vé olia Environment or Suez Environment, and systems makers such as Alfa Laval have the potential to open doors to their customers worldwide. It is an approach that is common among small German engineering firms, but rare in France. Auret hired a deputy managing director, Thierry Brisard, a former marketing boss at a big US water treatment company. Auret will remain chairman, overseeing strategic development, but wants to be more involved in product development. So he will work in partnership with Mr Thierry to maintain the company's growth.

Too often, says Mr Auret, scientists found a company then restrict its growth by refusing to bring in outside investors or managers. "I find it rather sad if you don't want your baby to grow." But what will he do if he sells Neosens to a trade buyer? He is rather young to retire. "Creating a company is like a virus," he says. "Nothing stops you creating another."

(1,004 words)

---

① vaunting ['vɔːntiŋ] *adj.* 吹嘘的

引进外部投资者和管理人员，以致限制了公司的成长。"我觉得不让自己的孩子成长是很可悲的事情。"但是如果他将 Neosens 公司出售给一个商业买家，他会从事什么职业呢？他离退休还很远。他说"创办一个公司就像发明了一种病毒，没有什么东西可以阻止你继续去创办其他的公司"。

知识链接 🔍

Neosens Neosens 公司成立于 2001 年，总部设在法国的图卢兹市区外。它主要是针对环境和工业领域中液体的质量问题，开发并向市场推广新的探测器件，并最终实现工业过程的最优化、环境保护的最大化以及工业期间的最大寿命化。

Areva 阿海珐集团是一家法国核工业公司，在核能源建设领域全球首屈一指。阿海珐集团目前已成为拥有资产 120 亿欧元、6 万多名员工的知名跨国企业，凭借其遍布全球 40 多个国家的生产设施，以及在 100 多个国家的销售网络，为客户提供可靠的无二氧化碳气体排放的发电及输配电解决方案，其主要业务包括核燃料采矿、核燃料提炼和销售、核反应堆制造、废料回收。

Véolia Environment 威立雅环境是世界领先的环境服务公司，目前在五大洲有超过 31 万名员工，它为工业、市政和客户提供定制的解决方案，包括水资源管理、能源管理和运输管理。

Suez Environment 苏伊士环境集团是法国的公用事业公司，公司总部设在巴黎，主要经营污水处理和废物管理。

题 记

　　眼镜是百转千回的时尚界展现魅力的诱惑之一，也是潮流达人装饰自由生活必不可少的另类元素。玛丽·帕金斯夫人把握商机，创造了全球最大的私营眼镜集团，成为世界排名第三的眼镜零售商。帕金斯夫人敏锐独到的洞察力无处不在，简直无与伦比。作为消费者，正是价格昂贵的眼镜和买眼镜时被胁迫的过程给她留下的挫败感，促使她成立了Specavers眼镜店。撒切尔政府对行业管制的撤销，给了她东山再起的契机，通过合伙人的方式将公司规模扩大到一千多家。助听器价格昂贵、品种稀少的现状同样引起了她的关注，她利用公司拥有的庞大数据库和客户群成为英国最大的助听器供应商。也许，玛丽·帕金斯夫人本身就是一副时尚眼镜，给我们带来永久的回头率和关注度。

The Queen of Specsavers
— Dame Mary Perkins

Next time you are in a Specsavers store, trying on Jasper Conran or Missoni frames, pay attention to the lady in her sixties clutching shopping bags and chatting to a fellow customer. She just may be the founder of what is now the world's biggest privately owned optical retailer, whose turnover every year topped £1bn.

Dame Mary Perkins is obsessed with the customer experience. It was her frustration with the expensive and often intimidating process of buying glasses that led to Specsavers being established. It is the same drive that, at the age of 64, keeps her covertly① visiting the group's shops across the country, often in disguise. "We have professional mystery shoppers but I will go round on my own," she smiles. "I've got a couple of wigs and different glasses, and I'll go in with M&S carrier bags and people don't expect to see you. If it's a busy place you can sidle up to the customers and say: 'what do you think of these?' "

Dame Mary has always been confident of knowing what customers

---

① covertly ['cʌvətli] *adv.* 偷偷摸摸地

眼镜女王——
玛丽·帕金斯夫人

当你下次在一家 Specavers 店试戴贾斯帕·康兰或者米索尼眼镜时，请留意一位六十多岁、手挽购物袋与旁边的顾客闲谈的女士。她可能正是目前世界上最大的私人眼镜零售店的创始人，她的眼镜店每年营业额逾 10 亿英镑。

玛丽·帕金斯夫人对于她作为顾客的经历耿耿于怀。正是价格昂贵的眼镜和买眼镜时被胁迫的过程给她留下的挫败感，促使她成立了 Specavers 眼镜店。也正是同样的原因促使 64 岁的她常常乔装打扮，暗访她在全国各地的分店。她笑着说："我们有些职业化的神秘客户，但我喜欢自己四处看看。我有几个假发和各种款式的眼镜，我会拿着马莎百货公司的手提厚纸袋走进去，人们没想到会碰见你。如果店里人多繁忙的话，你可以侧身走到顾客身边问一句：'你觉得这些眼镜怎么样？'"

她和丈夫道格在接受作为眼镜商的培训时相遇，然后建立了贝兵顿（她的娘家姓）和帕金斯眼镜店公司，在英格兰西南部有"23个小型的连锁店"，自此以来，玛丽夫人一直自信地认为她了解顾客的需求。玛丽夫人 36 岁时，夫妻俩卖掉了连锁店。玛丽夫人说，

want since she and husband Doug, who had met while training as opticians, then set up Bebington (her maiden name) and Perkins, a "little chain of 23" opticians in the south-west of England. They sold it when she was 36. In many ways, she says, it was a forerunner of Specsavers: they tried to create a more welcoming experience for customers in spite of the then strict regulation of the profession that outlawed advertising, price labelling and generic names. "Even with the small chain I have always been as much retail-focused as possible. Shops then had venetian blinds and frames were kept in drawers. We had showrooms, although we were not allowed to price anything."

The couple moved to the Channel Island of Guernsey in 1980— because that was where Dame Mary's parents lived, rather than for its tax advantages — with little thought about what to do next. But within a few years the Thatcher government's deregulation① of the profession caught their eye. However, the experience of owning a chain of shops meant the couple knew it was not a model they wanted to revisit. "We didn't want a big chain and worrying about a head office and whether staff were working properly. You lost touch with people, " she says.

So they devised a strategy that would allow opticians to become joint venture partners in each Specsavers store. "We were very close to the opticians we employed in the last business and we knew that professional people were very much better working for themselves, " she says. "But if

---

① deregulation [diːregjuˈleiʃən] *n.* 违反规定

在很多方面，那家小型连锁店是 Specavers 的前身：尽管当时行业管制严格，广告、标价、使用通用名称均不合法，但他们尽力给顾客营造一种更为愉快的购物经历。"即使是小型连锁店，我也一直尽可能做到以零售为主。 商店当时装有软百叶窗帘，镜框存放在抽屉里。 尽管我们有样品陈列室，但仍然不能给出任何商品标价。"

1980 年，这对夫妇搬到了格恩西海峡群岛，并不是因为那儿的有利税率，而是因为玛丽夫人的父母生活在那里。 那个时候，他们根本没有考虑接下来要做什么。 但是几年后他们注意到撒切尔政府撤销了对行业的管制。 夫妇俩有过开连锁店的经历，他们可不想再按那样的模式发展。 玛丽夫人说："我们不想开大型连锁店，为总店操心，担忧员工们是否在好好工作。 你失去了跟顾客接触的机会。"

因此，他们制定了一项策略，每一家 Specavers 店都允许眼镜商成为合资伙伴。 玛丽夫人说："在以前的经营中，我们与雇佣的眼镜商关系非常紧密。 我们清楚，职业经理人为自己工作会做得更好。 但如果让他们独自经营的话，他们又不可能把业务做得非常出色，因为还有太多管理方面的事务需要处理。 所以我们认为，如果让他们只管自己的业务，而让另外的人员来做管理方面的服务，在这把保护伞下，他们就可以自由地从事自己最擅长的工作。"于是乎，Specavers 每家分店一般有两名合伙人，其中至少一名是眼镜商。 这些合伙人拥有"A"股，有权获得分店的利润；而 Specsavers 拥有"B"股，对分店如何运行具有决定权。

you leave them on their own they are not going to make a very good business of it because there is so much back office stuff that needs doing. So we thought if they could own their own business but shelter under an umbrella with somebody else doing all the management services, that would leave them free to do what they are good at." So Specsavers' partners— typically two per store, with at least one of them an optician— jointly own the individual stores with the group. The partners own "A" shares, which give them the right to a store's profits, while Specsavers owns the "B" shares which gives them the controlling vote in how the store is run.

The Specsavers group derives its income from the management fees paid by each store in return for services such as product development, advertising and marketing, financial operations, store design, human resources, training and so on. Specsavers controls buying and supplying frames to its stores at cost. Lenses are largely manufactured by laboratories in the UK that are also jointly owned by the group. Specsavers, which is still wholly owned by the couple, this year opened its 1,000th store. It plans to double the number of stores and turnover within four years, partly by expanding overseas — half the stores are in the UK — as well as by a move into hearing centres.

After the success of the Specsavers model, it is hardly surprising that the company is keen to drive into other areas, notably hearing aids. "That was a golden opportunity with the database we have got and the customers we have, " says co-founder Dame Mary Perkins. She sees

Specavers 公司的收入来源于每一家眼镜分店支付的管理费。 每家分店则相应地获得产品开发、广告营销、财政运行、店面设计、人力资源、培训等各种服务。 Specavers 公司负责购买镜架，并以成本价供应给每家分店。 镜片主要由英国的集团合资的实验室生产。这对夫妇仍然拥有对 Specavers 公司的所有权，今年，他们开了第1 000家分店。 他们计划四年内让分店的数量和销售额翻一番，包括部分海外扩张——公司一半的分店在英国——同时，部分分店将迁往听力中心。

Specavers 公司运行模式成功后，公司热衷于将业务扩展到其他领域，特别是助听器，这一点都不奇怪。 共同创始人玛丽·帕金斯夫人说："这是一个绝好的机会，因为我们拥有庞大的数据库及客户群。" 她看到助听器与几十年前的眼镜业一样，价格昂贵，品种稀少。 公司三年前创建第一家听力中心之后，现在已经成为英国最大的助听器供应商。 玛丽夫人还观察到牙科产业潜在的发展前景。大约10年前，公司在英国西南部买下了一家牙科诊所，经营了一年，"仅仅是为了感受一下"。 她认为，"由于目前不能将健康服务工作与私人牙科诊所业务结合起来，这样做行不通"。 但是很明显，玛丽夫人并不想放弃。"牙科医学中还有零售原则。 这种原则可能不会写在人的脸上，但他们正在出售产品。 它值得我们去实践，我们也只是花了一年的时间对它进行了再次探讨而已。"

不过，这样的投资不会转移 Specavers 公司的核心业务。"你可以关注其他的东西，但不能变得很分散，一定不能涉足太多行业。 我

parallels with the optical industry of a couple of decades ago with high prices and lack of choice. After opening its first hearing centre three years ago, the company is now the biggest supplier of hearing aids in the UK. Dame Mary also sees potential in dentistry. About 10 years ago the company bought a practice in the West Country and ran it for a year "just to get the feel of it". "At the present time, because you cannot mix health service work with private dentistry, it doesn't work," she says. But she is clearly reluctant to give up on it. "You still have retail disciplines in dentistry. It might not be on your face, but they are selling products. It needs doing, and we had a second look at it only one year."

Such ventures must not detract① from the core business, however. "You can look at other things but it can't become a distraction and there must not be too much spread. I'm not a Richard Branson."

(885 words)

---

① detract [di'trækt] *vi.* 减损

不是理查德·布兰森。"

知识链接

Specsavers 是世界排名第三的眼镜零售商，也是全球最大的私营眼镜集团。目前，Specsavers 集团在全球拥有 1 150 多家眼镜店，全球员工数量超出 25 000 人。集团提供欧洲顶级时尚风格的镜框、高品质的宾得镜片、最新的数字助听器以及值得信赖的眼保健服务。

M&S 马莎百货公司从一个市场上的货摊发展到现在，已经在英国生存了 125 年。它是目前英国最大的服装零售商，在全球拥有超过 800 个商店和 76 000 名职员。马莎百货所有的商品都采用自己的品牌，确保质量和款式。它们的品牌囊括女装（Autograph、per una、LIMITED COLLECTION、Portfolio、CLASSIC）、男装（Autograph、BLUE HARBOUR、Collezione）、内衣、鞋子和饰品，其式样适合各个年龄段的人群。

Richard Branson 理查德·布兰森。理查德·查尔斯·尼古拉斯·布兰森爵士（Sir Richard Charles Nicholas Branson，SRB，1950 年 7 月 18 日— ）是英国著名企业维珍集团总裁，1999 年，英国伊丽莎白女王册封布兰森为爵士。集团旗下包括：维珍航空（英国航空的主要竞争对手）、维珍铁路、维珍电讯、维珍可乐、维珍能源，连锁零售店维珍唱片行以及维珍金融服务。

题　记

　　拥有梦幻般传奇经历的苹果电脑公司创始人史蒂夫·保罗·乔布斯的成就和人格魅力影响了一代人和世界，改变了整个计算机硬件和软件产业。苹果Ⅰ型计算机问世即大获成功，苹果Ⅱ型计算机更是化腐朽为神奇，将图形界面带进了一个崭新的时空。乔布斯设计了麦金托什机与个人电脑的竞争，反过来使苹果电脑的新产品充满活力。乔布斯的苹果引爆了全世界拥趸心中持续的热情，将最佳的计算机使用体验带给全世界的学生、教育工作者、创意专家及普通消费者。而就在此时，公司管理层将这位个人电脑范畴的梦想家"请出"了苹果电脑公司。但乔布斯的一生，尽管跌宕起伏，却又总是峰回路转、柳暗花明。10年后，乔布斯又引领苹果转型为一个消费类电子、甚至是娱乐公司，它的产品光怪陆离，五花八门，风靡时尚，引领潮流：iPod, iTunes, iTouch, iPhone, iPad … Apple 从此涅槃。而史蒂夫·保罗·乔布斯也从出类拔萃、单纯执著的技术天才脱胎换骨，成为让无数人膜拜的商界艺术大师。

Ups and Downs of
Steve Paul Jobs

Early in 1974 Jobs took a job as a video game designer at Atari, Inc., a pioneer in electronic arcade recreation. In that autumn, Jobs returned to California and began attending meetings of Wozniak's "Homebrew Computer Club." Wozniak, like most of the club's members, was content with the joy of electronics creation. Jobs was not interested in creating electronics and was nowhere near as good an engineer as Woz. He had his eye on marketability of electronic products and persuaded Wozniak to work with him toward building a personal computer.

Wozniak and Jobs designed the Apple I computer in Jobs's bedroom and they built the prototype in the Jobs, garage. Jobs showed the machine to a local electronics equipment retailer, who ordered twenty-five. Jobs received marketing advice from a friend, who was a retired CEO from Intel, and he helped them with marketing strategies for selling their new product. Jobs and Wozniak had great inspiration in starting a computer company that would produce and sell computers. To start this company they sold their most valuable possessions. Jobs sold his Volkswagen micro-

史蒂夫·保罗·乔布斯
的跌宕人生

　　早在 1974 年，乔布斯就已经作为一名视频游戏设计师在雅达利有限公司工作，该公司是电子游戏娱乐的先锋。 当年秋季，乔布斯回到加州，并开始出席沃兹尼亚克的"自制电脑俱乐部"会议。 沃兹尼亚克及大多数俱乐部的成员，满足于电子创造带来的愉悦心情。 而乔布斯对创造电子产品不感兴趣，远不及工程师沃兹尼亚克的能力。 但他有良好的市场观察力，发现了电子产品的市场潜力，并说服沃兹尼亚克跟他合作，制作个人电脑。

　　乔布斯和沃兹尼亚克在乔布斯的卧室设计了苹果 I 型电脑，在乔布斯的车库里建造了电脑原型。 乔布斯向当地的电子设备零售商展示了他们的模型，对方当即订购了 25 台。 乔布斯接受了一位已退休的英特尔公司首席执行官朋友的营销建议，他帮忙制定了销售新产品的营销战略。 乔布斯和沃兹尼亚克拥有伟大的灵感，开办了一家生产和销售计算机的电脑公司。 为了成立这家公司，他们卖掉了各自最有价值的财产，乔布斯卖掉了他的大众微型客车，沃兹尼亚克卖掉了他的惠普科学计算器，用筹集到的 1 300 美元成立了新公司。 他们用那笔资金基数以及从地方电子产品供应商讨来的信贷，

bus and Wozniak sold his Hewlett-Packard scientific calculator, which raised $ 1,300 to start their new company. With that capital base and credit begged from local electronics suppliers, they set up their first production line. Jobs encouraged Wozniak quit his job at Hewlett-Packard to become the vice president in charge of research and development of the new enterprise. And he did quit his job to become vice president. Jobs came up with the name of their new company Apple in memory of a happy summer he had spent as an orchard worker in Oregon.

Jobs and Wozniak put together their first computer, called the Apple I. They marketed it at a price of $ 666. The Apple I was the first single-board computer with built-in video interface, and on-board ROM, which told the machine how to load other programs from an external source. Jobs was marketing the Apple I at hobbyists like members of the Homebrew Computer Club who could now perform their own operations on their personal computers. Jobs and Wozniak managed to earn $ 770,000 from the sales of the Apple I. The following year, Jobs and Wozniak developed the general purpose Apple II. The design of the Apple II did not depart from Apple I's simplistic and compactness design. The Apple II was the Volkswagon of computers. The Apple II had built-in circuitry allowing it to interface directly to a color video monitor. Jobs encouraged independent programmers to invent applications for Apple II. The result was a library of some 16,000 software programs.

For the Apple II computer to compete against IBM, Jobs needed better marketing skills. To increase his marketing edge he brought Regis

建立了第一条生产线。 乔布斯鼓励沃兹尼亚克辞去惠普公司的工作，出任新公司的副总裁，负责研发。 他也辞职担任副总裁。 乔布斯将新公司命名为苹果，以纪念他在俄勒冈州当果园工人时度过的那个愉快的夏天。

乔布斯和沃兹尼亚克把他们的第一台计算机称为苹果Ⅰ型计算机。 他们以 666 美元的价格将它投入市场。 苹果Ⅰ型计算机是首款单板计算机，具有内置视频接口和板上只读存储器，可以指示机器如何载入来自外源的其他程序。 乔布斯将苹果Ⅰ型计算机的营销定位在自制计算机俱乐部成员之类的爱好者，他们可以在个人电脑上运行自己的程序。 乔布斯和沃兹尼亚克设法从苹果Ⅰ型计算机的销售中赚取了 77 万美元。 接下来的一年，乔布斯和沃兹尼亚克开发了一般用途的苹果Ⅱ型计算机。 苹果Ⅱ型的设计并没有偏离苹果Ⅰ型简单和紧凑的传统设计思路。 苹果Ⅱ型计算机好比是德国大众汽车。 苹果Ⅱ型电脑具有内置电路，能够直接连接彩色视频监视器。 乔布斯鼓励独立程序员发明适用苹果Ⅱ型的应用软件，其结果是 16 000 左右的软件程序相继入库。

乔布斯需要更好的营销技巧，以应对苹果Ⅱ型电脑与美国国际商用机器公司的竞争。 为了扩大自己的销售范围，他为公司请来了瑞格斯·麦肯纳和诺兰·布什纳尔。 麦肯纳是硅谷最显赫的公共关系人，诺兰·布什纳尔是乔布斯在雅达利时的前主管。 布什纳尔敦促乔布斯与风险资本家唐·瓦伦坦取得联系，乔布斯于是告诉英特尔的前营销经理，请他对苹果予以关照。 据多方估计，苹果公司的

McKenna and Nolan Bushnell into the company. McKenna was the foremost public relations man in the Silicon Valley. Nolan Bushnell was Jobs's former supervisor at Atari. Bushnell put Jobs in touch with Don Valentine, a venture capitalist, who told Markkula, the former marketing manager at Intel, that Apple was worth looking into. Buying into Apple with an investment variously estimated between $ 91,000 and $ 250,000, Markkula became chairman of the company in 1977. The following month Michael Scott, who was director of manufacturing at Semi-Conductor Inc., became president of Apple. Through Markkula, Apple accumulated a line of credit with the Bank of America and $ 600,000 in venture capital from the Rockefellers and Arthur Roch.

Quickly setting the standard in personal computers, the Apple II had earnings of about $ 140,000,000 within three years, a growth of 700 percent. Impressed with that growth, and a trend indicating an additional worth of 35 to 40 percent, the cautious underwriting① firm in cooperation with Wall Street's prestigious② Morgan Stanley, Inc., took Apple public in 1980. The underwriters price of $ 22 per share went up to $ 29 the first day of trading, bringing the market value of Apple to $ 1.2 billion. In 1982 Apple had sales of $ 580,000,000 up 74 percent from 1981. Its net earnings were $ 1.06 a share, up 55 percent, and as of December 1982, the company's stock was selling for approximately

---

① underwriting [ˈʌndəraitiŋ] *n.* 保险业
② prestigious [presˈtiːdʒəs] *adj.* 享有声望的

前任董事长马库拉购买的苹果投资在 9.1 万美元和 25 万美元之间，并在 1977 年成为苹果公司的董事长。 随后的一个月中，一个半导体公司生产部前经理迈克尔·斯科特担任苹果总裁。 通过马库拉的努力，苹果公司获得了美国银行的信用贷款及洛克菲勒家族和亚瑟·洛克 60 万美元的风险资本投资。

苹果 Ⅱ 型电脑迅速设定了个人电脑的标准，其三年内的销售收入达到 1.4 亿美元左右，增长速度为 700%。 受这种增长趋势的影响以及显示出的 35%~40% 增长值，行事谨慎的保险公司与华尔街著名的摩根士丹利公司合作，1980 年完成了苹果公司的公开上市。首个交易日，股票价格就从每股 22 美元升到每股 29 美元，使苹果公司的市值达到 12 亿美元。 1982 年，苹果销售额达 5.8 亿美元，比 1981 年增长 74%。 其每股盈利 1.06 美元，增长 55%，公司的股票售价大约为每股 30 美元。

乔布斯设计了麦金托什机与个人电脑的竞争，反过来使苹果电脑的新产品获得成功。 为了使公司重新充满活力，阻止它成为公司官僚主义的牺牲品，乔布斯发起了一场运动，试图找回苹果当初在车库经营时的价值观念和企业精神。 在发展麦金托什机的过程中，他试图重新营造一种气氛，使计算机行业高度个性化和智能化，使行为怪异的软件和硬件设计师可以施展才华。 麦金托什机的内存为 128K，是个人计算机的两倍，其内存可以扩充到 192K。 麦金托什机的 32 位微处理器超越了个人计算机 16 位微处理器，能完成更多的任务。 管理层更关注的问题是麦金托什机不能与美国国际商用机

$ 30 a share.

Jobs designed the Macintosh to compete with the PC and, in turn, make Apple's new products a success. In an effort to revitalize① the company and prevent it from falling victim to corporate bureaucracy, Jobs launched a campaign to bring back the values and entrepreneurial spirit that characterized Apple in its garage shop days. In developing the Macintosh, he tried to re-create an atmosphere in which the computer industry's highly individualistic, talented, and often eccentric software and hardware designers could flourish. The Macintosh had 128K of memory, twice that of the PC, and the memory could be expandable up to192K. The Mac's 32-bit microprocessor did more things and out performed the PC's 16-bit microprocessor. The larger concern of management concerning the Macintosh was not IBM compatible. This caused an uphill fight for Apple in trying to sell Macintosh to big corporations that where IBM territory. "We have thought about this very hard and it could be easy for us to come out with an IBM look-alike product, and put the Apple logo on it, and sell a lot of Apples. Our earning per share would go up and our stock holders would be happy, but we think that would be the wrong thing to do, " says Jobs.

As the Macintosh took off in sales and became a big hit, John Sculley felt Jobs was hurting the company, and persuaded the board to strip him of power. John Sculley tried to change the discipline of the company by

---

① revitalize [ˌriːˈvaitəlaiz] vt. 使重新充满活力

器公司兼容。 苹果试图将麦金托什机出售给美国国际商用机器公司占据的大企业，这导致了一场艰难的斗争。 乔布斯说："我们已经想到这样的尝试非常困难，而推出与美国国际商用机器公司外观类似的产品，贴上苹果的标志，销售很多苹果电脑，对我们来说倒会容易一些。 我们的每股收益将会上扬，股票持有人也会很高兴，但我们认识到那样做是不对的。"

麦金托什机销售大增，成为畅销产品，苹果公司前总裁约翰·斯卡利认为乔布斯损害了公司利益，说服董事会剥夺了他的权力。约翰·斯卡利试图通过控制成本、减少管理费用和合理化产品线等方式建构一种机制，改变公司的准则。 斯卡利得出的结论是："撤销乔布斯的工作，我们会运营得很好。"他认为，乔布斯追求技术价值的"优雅"而不顾客户的需求，这在滞销期是一种昂贵的奢侈。乔布斯深陷麦金托什机项目，挫伤了苹果公司其他部门的士气。

乔布斯被放逐到一栋他戏称为"西伯利亚"的附属大楼办公室。 乔布斯说，公司没有给他安排任何任务，慢慢地，他还发现公司的重要文件不再放到他的办公桌上。 他告诉每一位行政人员，希望能够以任何方式帮助他们，并确信每个人都有他家的电话号码。可几乎没人给他打电话。 他说："情况非常清楚，我已无事可做。我需要一个让我走开的目标。"但他很快就认识到，在苹果他找不到任何目标。 斯卡利在一次会议上对安全分析师们说，不管"现在还是未来"，乔布斯对公司的运作都不会起到任何作用。 乔布斯听到这一消息时说道："也许已经有人重击了你的腹部，排除了肚子里的

controlling costs, reducing overhead, rationalizing product lines to an organization. Sculley came to the conclusion that "we could run a lot better with Steve out of operations." he says, Jobs tended to value technological "elegance" over customer needs which is a costly luxury at a time of slowing sales. And Jobs's intense involvement with the Macintosh project had a demoralizing effect on Apple's other divisions.

Jobs was exiled to an office in an auxiliary building that he nicknamed "Siberia." Jobs says he did not get any assignments and gradually found that important company documents no longer landed on his desk. He told every member of the executive staff that he wanted to be helpful in any way he could, and he made sure each had his home phone number. Few ever called back. "It was very clear there was nothing for me to do, " he says, "I need a purpose to make me go." He soon came to believe that he would find no purpose within Apple. Sculley had told security analysts in a meeting that Jobs would have no role in the operations of the company "now or in the future." When Jobs heard of the message he said, "You've probably had somebody punch you in the stomach and it knocks the wind out you and you cannot breathe. The harder you try to breathe, the more you cannot breathe. And you know that the only thing you can do is just relax so you can start breathing again."

(1,188 words)

空气，你不能呼吸。 您越用劲呼吸，越是无法呼吸。 然后你明白了，你唯一能做的是放松，那么你就又可以呼吸了。"

知识链接 🔍

Morgan Stanley*, *Inc. 摩根士丹利是一家全球领先的国际金融服务公司，财经界俗称"大摩"，总部位于美国纽约，业务范围涵盖投资银行、证券、资产管理、企业合并重组和信用卡等多种金融服务，目前在全球 37 个国家设有超过 1 200 家办事处，雇员总数达 5 万多人。

Hewlett-Packard 惠普是一家来自美国的资讯科技公司，主要专注于生产打印机、数码影像、软件、计算机与资讯服务等业务。

题 记

　　乔·吉拉德，这个创造了吉尼斯汽车销售世界纪录、名
耀汽车名人堂的"世界上最伟大的推销员"，在15年的汽车
推销生涯中总共卖出了13 001辆汽车，平均每天销售6辆，
而且全部是一对一销售给个人。他凭借坚忍不拔的信念，积
极地将自己的启发和想法传达给他人，在全世界竞争最激烈
的汽车工业重镇底特律杀出一条血路。乔笃信智慧地工作和
坚持不懈能够创造奇迹，从不放弃任何一个卖车机会，连跳
槽、升迁的机会也总是拒绝，持续每天在一线从事推销工
作，享受每一次成交所带来的快感与金钱奖赏。乔·吉拉德
创造了一个从出身于贫民窟的擦鞋童走进环境幽雅的迪尔伯
恩汽车名人堂的神话。

The Car Seller in Automotive Hall of Fame — Joe Girard

Joe Girard is one of those rare creatures: a highly motivated man who can communicate his inspiration and attitudes to others. Joe refers to it as "spark." In his own words, "sparks create fires." His first sparks would come painfully at an early age. He was born on the east side of Detroit, Michigan, in one of the city's most deplorable ghettos. He lived about one mile from one of his earliest heroes, Joe Louis, who escaped from poverty and became heavyweight champion boxer of the world while Joe was still a struggling adolescent.

The initial struggle began with his own father, Antonino Gerard, an extremely poor man of Sicilian birth who found no success in his new country and vented his bitterness, both physically and emotionally, upon his younger son. Joe often speculates as to whether his father's behavior was the carefully planned campaign of a man who desperately wished to challenge his son. Whatever the truth, the senior Gerard chose to constantly berate[1] his son with the message that Joe would never amount to anything worthwhile. This was Joe's first spark: the determination to prove that his father had been wrong. At the same time, Joe's mother fed

---

① berate [biˈreit] vt. 严责

汽车名人堂的销售员
——乔·吉拉德

　　乔·吉拉德属于罕见人物之一，他能将自己的灵感和态度传递给他人，并让这种激励发挥到极致。乔将其称之为"火花"。用他自己的话说，"火花创造火焰"。他的第一次火花来自痛苦的童年。他出生在密歇根州的底特律东部最肮脏的贫民窟里。住所离他早期崇拜的英雄乔·路易斯的出生地大约 1 英里，路易斯摆脱了贫困，成为重量级的世界拳击冠军，而那时乔还是一个在底层挣扎的青少年。

　　乔最初是与自己的父亲作斗争，安东尼亚·吉拉德是一名出生在西西里岛的极度穷困者，他在新国家没有获得成功，便将怨气发泄到小儿子身上，对他进行身体上和精神上的摧残。乔经常猜想父亲的行为是否出于男人精心策划的战役，企图不顾一切地挑战自己的儿子。无论真相如何，老吉拉德经常斥责儿子，预言乔决不会成就任何有价值的事业。这是激励乔的第一束火花：他决心证明父亲的错误。与此同时，乔的母亲赋予他源源不断的爱和信念，她认为乔能够在生活中取得成功。这是激励乔的第二束火花：他要向母亲证明，她的爱和判断不会寄托在错误的地方。这两束火花使乔获得了第一个启示：智慧地工作和坚持不懈能够创造奇迹。

him her constant love and belief that Joe was capable of succeeding in life. This was Joe's second spark: to show his mother that her love and judgment had not been misplaced. These two sparks led to Joe's first revelation: that smart work and persistence could work wonders.

The Detroit Free Press can probably be credited with the first insight given to Joe with regard to exceptional progress. A contest was proclaimed for the solicitation① of new readers. The grand prize was to be a new, sparkling two-wheeler bicycle. Now 12 years of age, this driven youngster had never possessed a bike. Joe knew the secret that could win the bike. He would spend every unused, waking moment knocking on doors and asking for business. This had always been his secret. He knew that it worked— what he could not comprehend was why the other newsboys did not see the obvious. Joe won more than the bicycle. He won the knowledge that if he planned his work and worked his plan, he could succeed. He learned that most people were not willing to make this sacrifice. As he once said, "any one of those kids could have beat me, but they weren't willing to work. They didn't want it badly enough."

Formal education for Joe ended during the eleventh grade. He was talking during a study period and was addressed by the school principal, but not by his name. Well aware of the existence of bigotry②, but not willing to bow to it, Joe advised the man that he would not respond until he was called by his proper name. The principal stated "you people don't seem to understand how society will be run" and then called Joe a derogatory name reflecting upon his Sicilian ancestry. Joe's heated reaction

---

① solicitation [səˌlisiˈteiʃən] *n.* 恳求;诱惑
② bigotry [ˈbigətri] *n.* 顽固

　　《底特律自由报》设立的杰出进步奖最先让乔有所顿悟，可以说这是该报的功劳。 该报为争取新读者宣布了一项竞赛，大奖是一辆崭新、闪闪发光的二轮自行车。 时年 12 岁、欲望十足的年轻人却从未有过自己的自行车。 乔知道能够赢取自行车的秘密。 他将花费每一个空闲、清醒时刻去敲门找生意做。 这一直以来就是他的秘密。 他知道这个方法很奏效，他无法理解的是为什么其他报童没有注意到这么明显的商机。 乔赢得的远不是一辆自行车，他弄懂了经商之道，即如果他给工作设定计划，并按计划工作，就能取得成功。 他认识到大多数人不愿意做出这样的牺牲。 正如他曾说过的："这些孩子谁都可以打败我，可他们不愿意工作。 他们想要这个奖项的愿望不是很强烈。"

　　乔只接受了 11 年的正规教育。 他在一次学习期间谈到，学校校长对他的行为提出批评，但没有指名道姓。 乔清楚地意识到这种偏执的存在，却不愿对其屈服。 他劝告校长说，除非他有礼貌地叫出自己的名字，否则他不会做出回应。 校长宣称："你们这种人看来连社会如何运转都不了解"，然后用反映西西里岛人血统的贬称侮辱乔。 乔对此强烈反抗，结果学校将他永远除名。

　　在接下来的两年里，乔换了一个又一个的工作，却始终不尽如人意，他一直都很沮丧，认为自己缺少教育，才不得不只能干体力活。 虽然经常感到泄气，但他从没有放弃过希望。 他感到世界上总有一个地方适合自己。 他有幸遇见了建筑承包商亚伯拉罕·塞伯斯坦先生。 塞伯斯坦先生为人热情、慷慨和善解人意，像父亲一样邀请乔进入他的建筑生意圈，承诺教给乔他所知道的一切。 乔终于找到了他在生活中的定位。 乔和塞伯斯坦先生之间的关系日益密

resulted in his permanent dismissal from school.

During the next two years, Joe would move from one unsatisfactory job to another, constantly frustrated with the belief that his lack of education kept him from all but manual labor. He was often discouraged, but never gave up hope. He felt that somewhere in the world there was a place for him. He had the good fortune to meet Mr. Abraham Saperstein, a building contractor. Mr. Saperstein, a warm, generous, and understanding man, became his father surrogate① when he invited Joe to enter the building business with the pledge that he would teach Joe everything he knew. He'd finally found his niche in life. The relationship between Joe and Mr. Saperstein grew over the years until his dear old friend retired and turned over the business to Joe. Joe contracted to build a number of private homes in a Detroit subdivision. He accepted the word of a real estate speculator that the area was to have a sewer system installed, but this was not true. Individual septic② tanks would have to be installed, greatly reducing the value of the homes. As a result, Joe lost his business. Joe Girard found himself without a job, without savings, and in debt to the tune of $ 60,000. It was the lowest moment in his life.

The next year Joe would find himself in an endless struggle trying to recover his losses and his ego. Things would finally hit rock bottom when June Girard tearfully told her husband that there was no food in the house and that their kids were begging for something to eat. Joe had been job hunting without success, but on that day he pleaded with the sales manager of a Chevrolet dealership to hire him as a salesman. The manager

---

① surrogate ['sʌrəgeit] *n.* 代理
② septic ['septik] *n.* 化粪池

切，直到他亲爱的老朋友退休，把生意转交给他。 乔签了合同，要在底特律分部建造一定数量的私人住宅。 他相信了一位房地产投机商的话，以为这个地方会安装污水排放系统，但这话不是真的。 必须安装单个的化粪池，而这大大降低了房产的价值。 结果，乔弄丢了生意。 乔·吉拉德发现自己没有工作，没有存款，负债达6万美元之多。 这是他生活中最低谷的时期。

在接下来的一年里，乔发现自己一直在不停地奋斗，设法弥补损失，恢复自我形象。 当妻子琼·吉拉德眼泪汪汪地告诉他家里已经断炊、孩子们乞讨度日时，事态最终陷入捉襟见肘的境地。 乔寻找工作总是无望而返，但那天他恳求一名雪佛兰汽车代理商的销售经理雇佣他做推销员。 由于他缺乏经验，而传统上一月份是销售淡季，这位销售经理不太愿意雇他。 可是乔向经理表明，他只是搬张桌子在代理商后面的某个地方待着，指望有人打电话过来，给他一线希望。 那天晚上乔卖掉了第一辆汽车，并从经理那里借了10美元，买了一袋食品带回家。 第二个月他卖出了18辆汽车和卡车，开始感到自己可以放心地喘口气了。 但令他惊愕不已的是，经销商因为他太有闯劲而将其解雇。 其他的一些推销员也对此怨声载道。

这时，乔知道自己会卖车。 他已经对自己证明了这一点，他准备向世界证明自己的能力，包括父亲安东尼亚·吉拉德。 乔很快在密执安东点的麦卢里斯雪佛兰汽车点找到了一份工作，在这里他成为了世界上最棒的汽车销售员。 乔连续12年稳居汽车和卡车销售量的榜首。 他一个人的销售量比大多数经销商销售的总和加起来还要多。 他是唯一将此纪录保持一年以上的销售员，而且是对汽车和卡车两项销售量的保持。 乔是唯一进入"汽车名人堂"的销售员，

237

was reluctant because of his lack of experience and traditionally slow sales in the month of January, but Joe stated that he would only take a desk somewhere in the rear of the dealership and count on the telephone to provide prospects. That evening he sold his first car and borrowed $ 10 from the manager to bring a bag of groceries home to his family. In his second month he would sell eighteen cars and trucks and was beginning to feel he had a secure breath. Much to his amazement, the owner of the dealership fired him for being too aggressive. Some of the other salesmen had complained.

At this point, Joe knew he could sell cars. He had proved it to himself, and was ready to prove it to the world— including Antonino Gerard. Joe quickly found employment at Merollis Chevrolet in Eastpointe, Michigan, working at what he did better than anyone else in the world, selling automobiles! For 12 straight years Joe sold more cars and trucks than any other salesperson. More as an individual than most dealers sell in total. No other salesperson has ever attained this title for more than one year, and not for both cars and trucks. Joe is the only salesperson ever inducted into the Automotive Hall of Fame, renowned for selling more cars than anyone else in the World. During his fifteen year selling career, he sold 13,001 cars, all at retail — no fleet, wholesale or used cars. Most of his time is now spent writing books, giving lectures, and sales rallies.

(1,058 words)

以汽车销量超过世界上的任何人而闻名。 在 15 年的职业生涯中，他以零售的方式售出 13,001 辆汽车，而不是团购、批发或卖旧车。乔·吉拉德现在用大部分时间写书、做演讲和出席销售会议。

知识链接

The Automotive Hall of Fame "汽车名人堂"于 1939 年 10 月 18 日在纽约市成立。当时，来自世界各地的汽车行业领导人拟建立一个组织，维持早期汽车先驱的记忆，这个组织最初起名"汽车老前辈"。1960 年，该组织转移到华盛顿。1971 年，落户离底特律约 120 英里处的密歇根州米德兰。1975 年，第一个永久性"汽车名人堂"的建设在米德兰开幕。进入"汽车名人堂"的名人均为汽车业界的先驱与灵魂人物，包括奔驰、布加迪、雪佛兰、克莱斯勒、雪铁龙、戴姆勒克莱斯勒、道奇、杜兰特、杜里埃、法拉利、福特、本田、迈巴赫、奥兹、标致、保时捷、雷诺、斯隆和丰田等创始者和领导人。乔·吉拉德是唯一进入汽车名人堂的销售员。

题 记

艾伦·G. 雷富礼在宝洁任职达 32 年，在其 9 年的首席执行官生涯中，宝洁从深陷危机一步步走向复兴之路，重塑了宝洁在日用消费品行业的霸主地位，而这一切不得不归功于雷富礼的"长袖善舞"、创新精神和温文尔雅的管理理念。他彻底改变了宝洁的固有模式和失败的前任过于激进的改革步伐，有的放矢，收缩战线，剔除非核心业务，将"消费者是老板"的概念深入到每一位员工的内心深处。雷富礼推崇的工作表达方式是简简单单的口号。当他发现宝洁过于注重技术而忽视消费者需求时，便提出"顾客至上"的理念；当他发现宝洁忽略零售商在销售环节对消费者的重要影响时，提出"零售商的感觉是检验企业营销真理的第一契机"的理念；当宝洁不够重视消费者使用产品的切身体验时，他提出"消费者的体验是检验营销真理的第二契机"的理念。雷富礼的创新精神，最终把宝洁从一家墨守成规、内向型的公司转变为一家更加开放、外向型的公司。

The Game Changer
— A.G.Lafley

How is Alan. G. Lafley revolutionizing a bastion of corporate conservatism? As CEO, Lafley hasn't made grand pronouncements on the future of P&G. Instead, he has spent an inordinate① amount of time patiently communicating how he wants P&G to change. In a company famed for requiring employees to describe every new course of action in a one-page memo, Lafley's preferred approach is the slogan. For example, he felt that P&G was letting technology rather than consumer needs dictate new products. Ergo: "The consumer is boss." P&G wasn't working closely enough with retailers, the place where consumers first see the product on the shelf: "The first moment of truth." P&G wasn't concerned enough with the consumer's experience at home: "The second moment of truth."

Lafley uses these phrases constantly, and they are echoed throughout the organization. At the end of a three-day leadership seminar, 30 young marketing managers from around the world present what they have learned to Lafley. First on the list: "We are the voice of the consumer within P&G, and they are the heart of all we do." Lafley, dressed in a suit, sits on a stool in front of the group and beams. "I love the first

---

① inordinate [i'nɔːdinət] *adj.* 过度的

游戏颠覆者——
艾伦·G.雷富礼

　　艾伦·G.雷富礼如何彻底变革了公司保守主义的堡垒？ 作为首席执行官，雷富礼从未就宝洁的未来发表过重大声明。 相反，他花费了过多的时间耐心与人沟通，以改变宝洁的经营方式。 宝洁公司以要求员工在单页备忘录记述每一项新的行动过程而著名，而雷富礼的首选方法就是广告语。 例如，他意识到宝洁公司过去靠出租技术、而不是根据消费者的需求开发新产品，便提出了"消费者是老板"的理念。 他意识到宝洁公司与零售商的合作不够密切，于是消费者初次考察货架上的产品就进入"真相的第一时刻"。 他意识到宝洁对消费者在家中的经历关注不够，又推出了"真相的第二时刻"。

　　雷富礼不断地使用这些警句，让它们回响在公司的各个角落。在一次为期三天的领导人员研讨会结束时，30 名来自世界各地的年轻营销经理总结了他们从雷富礼身上学到的经验。"我们是宝洁内部的消费者之音，消费者是我们为之服务的中心"这句话被列在首位。 身穿西装的雷富礼坐在团队前排的一张凳子上，面带微笑。随着会场爆发出的雷鸣般的掌声，他笑着说："我喜爱第一条经

243

one, " he laughs as the room erupts① in applause. When he talks about his choice of words later, Lafley is a tad self-conscious. "It's Sesame Street language — I admit that, " he says. "A lot of what we have done is make things simple because the difficulty is making sure everybody knows what the goal is and how to get there."

Lafley has also mastered the art of the symbolic gesture. The 11th floor at corporate headquarters had been the redoubt of senior executives since the 1950s. Lafley did away with it, moving all five division presidents to the same floors as their staff. Then he turned some of the space into a leadership training center. On the rest of the floor, he knocked down the walls so that the remaining executives, including himself, share open offices. Lafley sits next to the two people he talks to the most, which, in true P&G style, was officially established by a flow study: HR head Antoine and Vice-Chairman Bruce Byrnes. As if the Sunday night meetings with Antoine weren't proof enough of Lafley's determination to make sure the best people rise to the top. And Byrnes, whom Lafley refers to as "Yoda" — the sage-like Star Wars character — gets a lot of face time because of his marketing expertise. As Lafley says, "the assets at P&G are what? Our people and our brands."

Just as emblematic② of the Lafley era is the floor's new conference room, where he and P&G's 12 other top executives meet every Monday at 8 a.m. to review results, plan strategy, and set the drumbeat for the week. The table used to be rectangular; now it's round. The execs used to sit where they were told; now they sit where they like. At one of those meetings, an outsider might have trouble distinguishing the CEO: He occasionally joins in the discussion, but most of the time the executives

---

① erupt [i'rʌpt] *vi.* 突然发生
② emblematic [embli'mætik] *adj.* 象征的

验。"雷富礼后来谈到这些口号时，显得有点害羞。他说："我承认，这是芝麻街的语言。我们已经完成的很多工作让事情变得简单，因为困难使每个人都知道目标是什么以及如何实现目标。"

雷富礼也已经掌握了象征性姿态的艺术。自 20 世纪 50 年代以来，公司总部的第 11 层一直是高级管理人员的据点。雷富礼废除了这种办公模式，请五个部门的主管全部搬迁，与自己的员工在同一楼层办公。然后，他把一些空间改造成领导培训中心。他拆掉了其余楼层的墙壁，连同他本人在内的管理人员都在一起公开办公。雷富礼坐在和他联系最多的两个人旁边——人力资源负责人安托万和副主席布鲁斯·伯恩斯，而这恰是宝洁公司真正的风格：通过顺畅的交流确立正式的办公制。周日晚与安托万的会见似乎不足以证明雷富礼的决心，即确保最优秀的人才晋升到高层。雷富礼经常和伯恩斯见面，并称其为"尤达"——星球大战中圣贤般的人物，因为他具有市场营销方面的专业知识。正如雷富礼所说的："宝洁的资产是什么？我们的员工和我们的品牌。"

大楼的新会议室是雷富礼时期的象征性标志，每周一上午 8 时，雷富礼和宝洁的其他 12 位高层管理人员在这里开会、评估结果、规划策略和制订本周计划。会议桌以前是长方形，现在改成了圆形。高管们过去常常坐在规定的位置，而现在他们想坐哪就坐哪。局外人参加其中的一次会议，很难分辨出谁是首席执行官：他有时会参加讨论，但大部分时间，高管与雷富礼交谈的时间和其他人相同。雷富礼过后说道："我更像一个教练。我一直在寻找不同

talk as much to each other as to Lafley. "I am more like a coach," Lafley says afterward. "I am always looking for different combinations that will get better results." The execs describe him as "an excellent listener. He's a sponge."

And now, Lafley is carefully using this information to reshape the company's approach to just about everything it does. When Lafley describes the P&G of the future, he says: "We're in the business of creating and building brands." Notice, as P&Gers certainly have, that he makes no mention of manufacturing. While Lafley shies away from saying just how much of the company's factory and back-office operations he may hand over to someone else, he does admit that facing up to the realities of the marketplace "won't always be fun." Of P&G's 102,000 employees, nearly one-half work in its plants. So far, "Lafley has deftly① handled the outsourcing deals, which has lessened fear within P&G," says Roger Martin, a close adviser of Lafley's who is dean of the University of Toronto's Joseph L. Rotman School of Management. All 2,000 of the information-technology workers were moved over to HP. At the bar-soap operations, based entirely in Cincinnati, 200 of the 250 employees went to work for the Canadian contractor.

Lafley's approach to selling P&G products is unprecedented at the company, too: He argues that P&G doesn't have to produce just premium-priced goods. So now there's a cheaper formulation for Crest in China. The Clairol deal gave P&G bargain shampoos such as Daily Defense. And with Lafley's encouragement, managers have looked at their most expensive products to make sure they aren't too costly. In many cases, they've actually lowered the prices.

And Lafley is pushing P&G to approach its brands more creatively.

---

① deftly ['deftly] *adv.* 熟练地

的组合，以便得到更好的结果。"高管们将雷富礼描述为"一名出色的听众。他是一块海绵。"

现在，雷富礼正在谨慎地运用这些信息重塑公司在各方面的行事法则。雷富礼在描述宝洁公司的未来时说道："我们正在做创造和建设品牌的大事。"注意，正如宝洁人确信的那样，他从不提制造。尽管雷富礼回避提及宝洁的公司国外代理商和移交他人的企业后勤业务究竟占多少份额，但他仍然承认直面市场现实并"不总是好玩"。宝洁的 10.2 万名员工中，将近一半在宝洁自己的工厂工作。与雷富礼关系密切的一个顾问、多伦多大学约瑟夫·L.罗特曼管理学院院长罗杰·马丁认为，到目前为止，"雷富礼已经灵活地处理了外购交易，减轻了宝洁公司内部的恐惧"。2000 名信息技术工人全部被移交给惠普。固体肥皂的运营完全基于辛辛那提，250 名员工中有 200 名为加拿大承包商工作。

雷富礼销售宝洁产品的方法也是公司前所未有的。他认为宝洁公司没有必要生产溢价商品，于是就有了现在中国更便宜的佳洁士配方。宝洁公司开发了廉价香波，如"每日防护"牌香波等。在雷富礼的鼓励下，经理们已经开始关注那些价格最贵的产品，确保价格不至于太高。在许多情况下，他们实际上已经降低了价格。

雷富礼正在努力使宝洁品牌更富有创造性。拿佳洁士的例子来说，它不再只是一种牙膏，它还指宝洁公司收购的一种电动牙刷，即"旋转电动牙刷"。宝洁公司也愿意为自己的技术发放许可证，以便它们以更快的速度进入市场。它与制造佳能食物保鲜袋的高乐

Crest, for example, isn't just about toothpaste anymore: There's also an electric toothbrush, SpinBrush, which P&G acquired. P&G is also willing to license its own technologies to get them to the marketplace faster. It joined with Clorox Co., maker of Glad Bags, to share a food-wrap technology it had developed. It was unprecedented for P&G to work with a competitor, says licensing head Jeffrey Weedman. The overall effect is undeniable. "Lafley has made P&G far more flexible, " says Banc of America's Steele.

But Lafley still faces daunting challenges. Keeping up the earnings growth, for example, will get tougher as competitors fight back and as P&G winds down a large restructuring program — started under Jager but accelerated① under Lafley. Furthermore, some of the gains in profit have resulted from cuts in capital and R&D spending, which Lafley has pared back to the levels of the company's rivals. And already, P&G has missed a big opportunity: It passed up the chance to buy water-soluble strips that contain mouthwash. Now, Listerine is making a bundle on the product.

Still, Lafley may be uniquely suited to creating a new and improved P&G. Even Jager agrees that Lafley was just what the company needed. "He has calmed down the confusion that happened while I was there, " says the former CEO. Jager left a letter on Lafley's desk the day he resigned telling his successor not to feel responsible for his fall. "You earned it, " he recalls writing. "Don't start out with guilt." Lafley says he learned from Jager's biggest mistake. "I avoided saying P&G people were bad, " he says. Lafley, a company man through and through, just can't resist trying out a new slogan.

(1,089 words)

---

① accelerated [əkˈseləreitid] *adj.* 增加(数量)的

氏公司合作，分享一项已经开发的食品包装技术。发放许可证的部门主管杰弗瑞·魏德曼表示，与竞争对手合作是宝洁公司前所未有的举动。总体效果不置可否。美国银行的斯蒂尔认为"雷富礼使宝洁公司的运营更加灵活"。

但是雷富礼仍然面临令人畏惧的挑战。例如，保持盈利增长将随着竞争对手的反击和宝洁公司大型重组计划的滞怠变得越来越艰难。重组计划始于杰格，但雷富礼加速了它的发展。此外，公司利润的部分收益来自对资本和研究开发费用的削减，雷富礼已经把资金紧缩到公司竞争对手的水平。而宝洁公司已经错过了一次重要的机遇：购买含有漱口水的水溶性清除材料。现在，李斯特防腐液正在靠这种产品发大财。

尽管如此，雷富礼可能是革新宝洁公司的独一无二的合适人选。就连德克·雅格也认同，雷富礼正是宝洁所需要的管理者。前首席执行官说："他已经平息了我管理时的混乱情况。"雅格辞职的当天，在雷富礼的办公桌上留下一封信，告诉这位继任者不要因为他的离开而感到自责。他回忆了自己的留言："这是你应该得到的。上任时不要心存内疚。"雷富礼说，他从雅格最大的错误中学到了经验教训。他说："我会回避对宝洁人不好的指责。"雷富礼，一个完全彻底的宝洁人，无法抗拒尝试新的口号。

知识链接 🔍

P&G 宝洁公司(Procter & Gamble Co.)，简称 P&G，是一家美国消费日用

品生产商，也是目前全球最大的日用品公司之一。总部位于美国俄亥俄州辛辛那提，全球员工近 11 万人。

Crest　佳洁士是美国宝洁公司的品牌，诞生于 1955 年，一直在全球享有美誉。因为其独创的氟泰配方具有卓越的高效防蛀功能，所以成为第一支被世界权威牙防组织——美国牙医学会(ADA)认可的防蛀牙膏，这被视为世界牙膏技术发展史上的一大里程碑。

Clorox Co.　高乐氏公司总部位于加州奥克兰，是全球领先的消费产品生产和经销商。全球员工达 7 600 名，在全球 25 个国家设有生产基地并在 100 多个国家销售。

题　记

　　TrialPay 首席执行官亚历克斯·兰佩尔从10岁起就开始自己做生意，哈佛毕业后创立了一家支付机构——TrialPay公司：为消费者提供虚拟物品和货币，鼓励他们去 Gap、Netflix 等网站消费，TrialPay 从中抽取佣金。他是一位与众不同的企业家，给"人们的生活带来了不同"，使人们享受网络消费。兰佩尔表示，早期融资的最大智慧就是要选择合适的投资者，有些投资者会给你灌输错误观念，你得选择那些能提供支持、并帮助你向正确方向前进的投资者。兰佩尔在互联网淘到的第一桶金是他创造的"永远在线"软件。随着 TrialPay"刺激购买模式"(Purchase Incentives) 的诞生，通过一些额外的利诱来促成有购买意向的消费者，或者用一些有吸引力的出价来提高单笔订单的金额等营销手段目前已经风靡网络。年轻的 IT 企业家亚历克斯·兰佩尔向我们展示的不是一个噱头或一个游戏，而是超越模仿"一日一购"概念、对整个互联网产业起到的连锁反应——广告、支付和商务，因为越来越多的消费(数万亿规模)将从网络开始。

The Young IT Entrepreneur
— Alex Rampell

Alex Rampell sits with a Starbucks coffee in front of him and ponders the strange contradictions in what people are willing to pay for, and what they are not. "Here I am prepared to spend $3.50 on a cup of coffee. But somehow, I don't want to pay 99 cents for a music download ... People don't like paying for digital products." Mr. Rampell, a young entrepreneur, has built a business on this insight. He co-founded his company, TrialPay, two years ago on the suspicion that customers who do not want to pay for a product such as software might still be prepared to pay for something else — and get the software for free.

WinZip, for example, currently asks customers to pay $29.95 at its online store to download one of its file readers. But those who balk[1] at paying can get the software for free by using TrialPay's system to opt for over 150 alternative transactions from a range of companies. They might, for instance, spend $50 on clothes at Gap.com, or sign up for an American Express credit card. The successful advertiser then pays WinZip a fee for delivering a new customer, while TrialPay receives a small payment for its intermediary role along the way. Since the establishment of the company, more than 6,000 merchants have used TrialPay's online

---

① balk [bɔːk] *vi.* 犹豫不决

青年 IT 企业家——
亚历克斯·兰佩尔

亚历克斯·兰佩尔面前放着一杯星巴克咖啡，坐在那儿思考人们愿意把钱花在哪些方面，不愿意把钱花在哪些方面，这种矛盾突有些奇怪。"我会在这里花 3.50 美元买一杯咖啡。 但不知怎么的，我不愿意花 99 美分下载一首音乐……大家不喜欢为数字产品付款。"年轻的企业家亚历克斯·兰佩尔基于这一见解创立了一项业务。 据他推测，不想付钱购买软件之类产品的顾客，仍有可能购买其他商品——然后获得免费软件。 怀着这样的猜想，两年前他与人合伙创建了自己的公司——TrialPay。

例如，WinZip 压缩软件是通常要求消费者在其网上商店支付 29.95 美元后，才能下载其文件阅读器的一种。 但是，那些网上支付犹豫不决的顾客通过使用 TrialPay 系统，从一大批公司的 150 多种商品中选择交易，然后就可以免费下载该软件。 例如，他们可以在 Gap.com 上花 50 美元买衣服，或者注册美国运通信用卡。 成功的广告商而后支付 WinZip 一笔费用，因为 WinZip 带来了一位新顾客，而 TrialPay 公司因为在交易过程中的中介作用，也同时获得小额回报。 自公司成立以来，已有 6 000 多位商家使用 TrialPay 公司的在线消费者请求系统，1 000 多万人通过该系统购物。

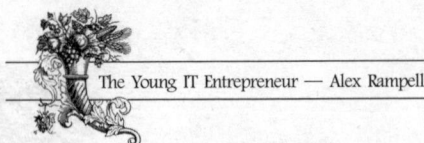

customer acquisition system and more than 10m people have made purchases through the system.

The idea for TrialPay originated from Mr. Rampell's own experiences as a software retailer, which began at an alarmingly① early age. When he was just 10 years old, he launched a screensaver product into the world of shareware (software that is freely available on the web, with suggested payments made to the originator under an honour code). "I uploaded it to CompuServe and AOL and I got a cheque in the mail a few days later for $5. I thought this was the best thing ever. And I kept doing that throughout high school and college," he says. His big early success came when he created his "Always Online" shareware— a program that allowed frustrated AOL subscribers to acquire and hold on to overloaded dial-in lines. He created the product for his own use in about four hours, but then decided to sell it initially for $8 a copy. "It sold about 100,000 copies in a very short period of time. I was only 15," he says. "Then AOL banned the product, and that was great for me. It was, like, big bad AOL is going after this little kid."

Since he was still at boarding school in Andover, Massachusetts, the need to attend a summer school programme forced Mr. Rampell to subcontract② handling of the payments. He also used the business as the basis for a school essay on price elasticity. At Harvard, aged 19, he was featured in a New York Times article on dorm-room internet business operators. After leaving college, Mr. Rampell continued his software business, now called Rampell Software and employing several college friends. Its main products were a site-security application called SiteAdvisor

---

① alarming [ə'lɑːmiŋ] *adj.* 扰乱人心的
② subcontract [sʌb'kɔntrækt] *vi.* 转包

TrialPay 公司的理念源于兰佩尔先生早期做软件零售商的经验。那真是个令人难以置信的年龄。当年他刚满 10 岁，就向共享软件（网上可以自由共享的软件，并附有通过荣誉代码给软件发起者的建议支付价）世界推出了一款屏幕保护产品。他说："我将该软件上传给 Compuseve 公司和美国在线服务公司，几天后在邮件中收到一张 5 美元的支票。我认为这是有史以来最好的事情。我在高中和大学里就一直做这种工作。"他早期最大的成功是创建"永远在线"共享软件，这款软件允许美国在线受挫用户占有，并能对拨入线超负荷持续使用。他做的这款产品自己只使用了大约 4 小时，便决定以每个副本 8 美元的起始价出售。他说："这款软件在很短的时间里就售出 10 万个副本。那时我才 15 岁。然后美国在线服务公司取缔了这款产品，但这对我来说，简直是太棒了。这就好像糟糕透顶的美国在线在我这个小男孩身后追赶。"

因为他当时还在马萨诸塞州安多佛的寄宿学校读书，需要参加学校的暑期班活动，这就迫使他分包处理支付款项。他还以这次业务经历为基础，完成了一篇学校布置的关于价格弹性的文章。在哈佛上学期间，年仅 19 岁的他登上了《纽约时报》，有篇文章特别介绍了这位宿舍里的网络交易操盘手。大学毕业之后，兰佩尔先生继续从事软件事业，即现名为瑞蒙佩尔的软件公司，雇佣了几位大学的朋友。公司主要生产一种键盘快捷键产品，即 SiteAdvisor 和 SureType 网站安全应用软件。

然而，随着互联网的蓬勃发展，共享市场开始出现停滞，因为越来越少的用户愿意主动付款。兰佩尔认为："很多人不喜欢花钱购买数码商品，这是我发现的第一手资料。现在的问题是你如何改

and SureType, a keyboard shortcuts product.

However, as the internet boomed the shareware market began to stagnate①, since fewer and fewer users were willing to make the voluntary payments. "A lot of people don't like paying for digital goods, and I found this out first-hand," Mr. Rampell says. "The question is how do you convert that 99.7 per cent who try but don't buy, or browse but don't buy? That's where the initial concept of TrialPay came from."

TrialPay's "pay in lieu②" product was originally developed as a way of dealing with the equally annoying problem of users being unwilling to pay for shareware. At college Mr. Rampell's company developed software aimed at making typing easier on small mobile devices and defending computers from the irritating threat of viruses. And his successful Always Online product, which he created as a teenager, was designed to cope with the problem of overloaded phonaccess lines e at AOL.

Rampell Software formed its first relationship with NetFlix, the online DVD-rental service, offering customers SiteAdvisor for free if they signed up with NetFlix, and making his money from NetFlix rather than his customer. Other deals followed. "We made a lot more mone on a unit basis by referring our customers to third-party, blue-chip advertisers like Discover, and Experian, Gap and NetFlix than we did from selling our products directly," he says. The experience convinced him that the future of his business lay in the system, rather than the site software.

TrialPay's range of products is now extending into other "transactional advertising" such as online coupons③, or cross-selling

---

① stagnate ['stægneit] vi. 停滞
② lieu [lju:] n. 代替
③ coupon ['ku:pɔn] n. 优惠券

变这 99.7% 的人：只试用不购买；或者是只浏览，但不掏钱。TrialPay 最初的概念就来自这一点。"

最初，开发 TrialPay 的"薪酬代替"产品是为了处理同样令人烦恼的问题，即用户不愿支付共享软件费用。 在大学里，兰佩尔的公司开发的软件旨在使小型移动设备上打字更加容易，抵御电脑不受病毒的刺激威胁。 他在青少年时期成功开发的"永远在线"产品，被用于处理美国在线 e 线上超负荷的电话接入。

兰佩尔软件首先与在线 DVD 租赁服务 NetFlix 建立了联系，如果顾客登录注册 Netflix，就可以享用公司为他们免费提供的 SiteAdvisor。公司利用 NetFlix 赚钱，而不是直接从顾客处收费。 其他交易也采取了相应的手段。 他说："把顾客推荐给第三方，Discover，Experian，Gap 和 Netflix 等蓝筹股广告商，比我们直接销售产品更赚钱。"经验使他相信，公司的未来在于系统，而不是网站软件。

TrialPay 的一系列产品现已延伸到其他的"交易广告"，如网上优惠券，或交叉销售折扣优惠。 这些优惠可以包括如下情况：如果顾客在其他零售店购买商品超过目标金额，可以享受特别折扣价；无论顾客在其他零售店购买任何商品，他们都可以享受赠送优惠。最新开发的一项服务是顾客决定购买商品之后，其他在线商人提供的一系列有时间限制的优惠。 它部分地承认了这样一个事实，虽然 TrialPay 的"薪酬代替"解决方案适用于成本较低的产品，但要找到那些准备支付赠送大件物品（如电视机）成本的人却较为不易。 兰佩尔说："如果考虑交易广告，它几乎无所不能。 比如说你要购买软件，你得输入信用卡的具体信息，这样我们才知道你住在哪里，你是否需要一张楼下饭馆 10 美元的优惠券。"

discount offers. These can include offers of special discounts at other retailers if a customer spends above a target amount, or offers of deals at other retailers if he or she spends anything at all. Its latest development is a series of time-limited offers from other online merchants after the conclusion of a purchase. It is partly a recognition of the fact that, while TrialPay's "pay in lieu" solution works well with lower-cost products, it is harder to find someone prepared to cover the costs of giving away bigger-ticket items, such as television sets. "If you think about transactional advertising, it works for pretty much anything, " he says. "Say you are buying software. You have entered you credit card details so we know where you live. Do you want a $ 10 coupon off the restaurant downstairs?"

Mr. Rampell argues that TrialPay is driving inefficiencies out of the web to the benefit of the consumer. He says his service is a way of turning some of the money that a retailer is willing to pay to acquire a customer into savings for that customer — unlike paid search, where the money goes to the search engine company. He warmly cites the example of Amazon, which boosts the value of transactions by promoting cross-selling between categories and offering free delivery to those who spend more than $ 25. Mr. Rampell argues that TrialPay can do the same, with products such as post-transaction coupons and a multitude of cross-selling opportunities between smaller online retailers. "There are hundreds of thousands of small sellers out there, what we're trying to do is turn anybody into Amazon."

(1,051 words)

兰佩尔先生主张，TrialPay 公司把效率低下的网页逐出网络对消费者有利。他认为，公司的服务是把零售商愿意支付给顾客的钱转化为顾客的储蓄，这不像付费搜索，钱都进了搜索引擎公司的口袋。他热情地列举了亚马逊模式。亚马逊为那些多支付 25 美元的顾客提供免费寄送所购商品服务，通过促进交叉销售提升了交易价值。兰佩尔坚持认为，TrialPay 公司也可以做同样的事情，因为它有交易后优惠券之类的产品和大量小型在线零售商之间的交叉销售机会。"成千上万的小卖家就在那儿，我们正在尝试把所有人都招到亚马逊来。"

知识链接

AOL 美国在线公司是美国在线—时代华纳公司的子公司。在互动服务、网络品牌经营、互联网技术以及电子商务领域，美国在线都居于全球领先地位。美国在线国际部在 16 个国家经营着本地化的美国在线网络服务，提供 8 种语言。

CompuServe 美国在线的网络服务公司，提供留言板、新闻和信息、电子商务以及其他类似网络功能的服务，拥有 280 万名用户。CompuServe 创建于 1979 年，曾是首家提供"网络服务"、全球规模最大的信息和网络服务公司之一。然而，当 CompuServe 开始与新的竞争对手如 AOL 竞争的时候，受到重创。AOL 通过密集的市场推广活动，并为用户提供包月而不是 CompuServe 的按小时收费方式，迅速获得了市场份额。1997 年，AOL 收购了 CompuServe。2011 年 7 月 1 日，CompuServe 被其母公司 AOL 关闭，意味着 CompuServe 公司结束了其 30 年的运作。

题　记

　　加特摩尔投资管理公司的首席执行官杰夫·迈耶身居要职却异乎寻常地谦逊。早年丰富的投行经历让他对投资有着独到的见解。没有哪个行业像投资一样，天天需要做出决策，而且效果很快就可以得到检验。他转身投行的第一件事就是组建优秀的管理团队，重塑公司的核心竞争力和公司文化。他意识到优秀的对冲基金必须具备出色的风险控制能力，以品牌革新为契机提升加特摩尔公司在英国和欧洲其他地区零售市场上的形象。他选择不断拓宽投资领域，猎取系统性风险可控情况下获取超额收益的机会，在融资入口的次货点拦截金融机构投资者利用对冲基金的大量套利。市场每一阶段都会有流行的投资"时尚"，代表了明显跑赢大盘的行业和板块。这就需要私募模式采取多元化投资，注重资产的配置。杰夫·迈耶就是多元化投资人中的佼佼者。他注重投资基础的多元化，建立广泛的投资策略，专注利润更高的产品，在一个相对长的时间维度内，寻找那些能够持续超预期成长的对冲基金，将真正的超额收益定位于"经典"。

The Diversifying Investor
— Jeff Meyer

Jeff Meyer is unusually modest for a man in his position. He may be chief executive of Gartmore Investment Management, but he does not want to be seen to be taking sole credit for the reinvention of the business. It is a team effort, he says.

Mr. Meyer was an investment banker earlier in his career — not a profession renowned for humility — whose previous employers included Bear Stearns and Lehman Brothers. So the move to the buy-side was a good one both temperamentally and tactically. He has been familiar with Gartmore when he was one of the bankers advising Nationwide Mutual on its acquisition. He subsequently became its chief financial officer and president, before moving into the chief executive role, a year before a management buy-out.

In partnership with private equity group Hellman & Friedman, an in-house team acquired the company from Nationwide Mutual and proceeded to shake it up. "We closed a lot of capabilities we didn't have confidence in, " says Mr.Meyer, offering as an example Gartmore's fixed income teams. "We closed them down and refocused on our core strengths, " which he identifies as all equity classes bar the US, and

多元化投资者——
杰夫·迈耶

　　杰夫·迈耶身居要职却异乎寻常地谦逊，他是加特摩尔投资管理公司的首席执行官，但他不想独揽重建业务的所有荣誉，他认为那是团队努力合作的成果。

　　迈耶先生职业生涯的早些时候是一位投资银行家，这种职业不以谦逊出名，他先前的雇主包括贝尔·斯特恩斯和雷曼兄弟。 所以向买方靠近的举动从性情和策略上来说都不失为一记良策。 在他还是建议全美互助保险公司采取收购行动的银行家之一时，就与加特摩尔一直保持着密切联系。 全面收购管理层一年后，他进入主要职能部门，随后成为加特摩尔公司的首席财政官和主席。

　　与私募基金公司海尔曼·弗里德曼合作时，全美互助保险公司的一个内部团队收购了公司，并着手重组。 迈耶先生认为："没有信心做好的事情，我们就不做。"他举了加特摩尔公司固定收入团队的例子加以说明："我们结束了他们的任务，重新专注于我们的核心竞争力。"他把这看成是除了美国和信贷之外的所有股本的教训。

　　物流部也来了个大"翻新"：先前物流部有四个领导，但现在只剩下菲尔·瓦格斯达夫一人，他从新星资产管理公司加盟物流部。

credit.

Distribution has been revamped① too: where there were previously four heads of distribution, there is now just Phil Wagstaff, who joined from New Star Asset Management. This reflects both a belief that different distribution channels are converging② and a desire to build a more efficient process. The streamlining③ included cutting the headcount by a fifth to 400. Those remaining have seen their remuneration reorganised to "standardise and align their compensation". The new scheme includes equity in the company — the management team reserved some of its half of the equity in the buy-out deal to use as incentives — and has a strong performance element. This is key to the reinvention of Gartmore, says Mr. Meyer. "It aligns everyone's interests and produces better risk-adjusted returns," he says. "It really refocused the firm." This refocusing did not happen overnight, however. "It takes two to three years to get into the culture of the firm." Whether it is due to a changed culture or to other factors, Mr. Meyer can now point proudly to a doubled profit margin. The ebitda, earnings before interest, tax, depreciation and amortisation, margin has climbed "from the high teens to the low forties", he says. "This gives you greater profitability to pay your people and to invest in growth."

And despite the hostile environment for financial services, Mr. Meyer

---

① revamp [ri'væmp] *v.* 修补,改造
② converging [kən'vɜːdʒiŋ] *adj.* 收缩的
③ streamlining ['striːm'lainiŋ] *n.* 流线型,使简化

这反映了人们相信不同的销售渠道正在进行整合以及渴望建立更加高效的销售过程。 精简包括裁员人头总数的五分之一，剩下 400 名。 留下来的人员工资待遇得到重新安排，"达到标准，与补偿数额持平"。 新计划包括公司股本的变动，管理团队保留了大约一半的买断股本，用作奖励，这种做法具有强烈的绩效因素。 迈耶先生表示，这是重建加特摩尔公司的关键。 他认为："这使每个人的利益捆绑在一起，产生更好的风险调整回报，它真的使公司重塑了核心竞争力。"然而，这种转变的发生不是一朝一夕的事情，"花了 2 年到 3 年的时间才了解了公司的文化"。 无论是因为改变了的文化还是其他因素，迈耶先生现在都可以自豪地指出，公司的利润已经翻番。 他认为，息税折旧摊销前利润，即利息、税、折旧、摊销前的盈利收入已经从"20 左右的高点攀升到 40 左右的低点。 这样一来，支付员工的工资和投资发展便有了更大的可能性。"

尽管金融服务业所处的环境非常恶劣，但迈耶先生确实拟定了发展计划。 目前，加特摩尔公司管理下的 240 亿英镑（折合 300 亿欧元，445 亿美元）分为三块：四分之一投资对冲基金（折合 60 亿英镑，100 亿美元），四分之一存入公司投资者相分离的账户，还有一半用于零售基金。 迈耶认为这还不够。 他说："对冲基金业务应该投资 200 亿英镑，公司业务应该投资 200 亿英镑。 零售基金就较难认定了。"虽然很难准确地推测他是如何计算加特摩尔公司每部分业务应投入的资金数目，但迈耶制定了如何实现增长的明确计划。

对品牌的革新还没有透露细节。 下个月将迎来一场大型的营销

does have plans for growth. Currently, Gartmore's £24bn (€ 30bn, $ 44.5bn) under management is split three ways: one quarter in hedge funds (£6bn, $ 10bn), one quarter in segregated accounts from institutional investors and half in retail funds. This is not enough, according to Mr. Meyer: "The hedge fund business should be $ 20bn and the institutional business should be $ 20bn. In retail, it's tougher to call, " he says. Although it is difficult to figure out exactly how he is calculating the rightful size of each of Gartmore's business lines, Mr. Meyer has definite plans on how to achieve this growth.

A revamp of the brand (details not revealed) will merit a big marketing campaign next month, attempting to raise Gartmore's profile in the retail markets in the UK and the rest of Europe. This, Mr. Meyer says, is the hardest market to crack, but it does not seem to daunt him. The strategy does not include competing on cost, despite the increasing number of index products available, such as exchange traded funds, that offer market returns for low fees. "If you have strong risk-adjusted returns, there isn't that much pricing pressure, " he says.

A range of absolute return funds is in the pipeline, aimed at offering low correlation to equity markets in exchange for active fees. Recruitment and an extension of capabilities are also on the agenda. Mr. Meyer views the current difficulties in the markets as "a great opportunity to acquire new talent" . He is even "spending time thinking about consolidation" , given that he expects some smaller asset management businesses to struggle over the next couple of years. On his shopping list are an Asia Pacific team, some additional expertise in the UK large-cap sector and,

活动，此举是要提升加特摩尔公司在英国和欧洲其他地区零售市场上的形象。 迈耶先生认为，这是最难攻克的市场，但困难似乎并不会令他沮丧。 尽管可用指标产品的数量呈上升趋势，如以低费用换取市场收益的产品交易基金，但营销策略里并不包括成本竞争。 他说："如果你具备强大的风险调整回报，定价压力并没有那么大。"

一系列绝对收益基金已经在筹备当中，旨在为产权投资市场提供低度相关，从而换取交易频繁的费用。 人才招聘和业务能力延伸的工作也被提上议事日程。 迈耶认为，当前市场面临的困境恰好是"猎取新人才的大好机会"。 他预期一些较小型的资产管理企业在未来几年的发展会举步维艰，有鉴于此，他甚至"花时间考虑合并的问题"。 他的购买单上有亚洲太平洋团队的专家们对英国大盘股组合的一些补充意见，在选择性方面更具备做多策略的能力。 他希望，这最终将使对冲基金和隔离委托交易陷入困境："金融机构投资者利用对冲基金大量套利。 他们的挂港首选对冲基金，其次采取做多策略。 我们可以在入口的次货点拦截他们。"而引进更多的养老基金作为投资者对实现这一重要的策略性目标很有帮助，这种做法能够使投资者的基础多元化。 目前，绝大多数的客户选择了对冲基金和私营银行的基金。 迈耶认为，未来几年全方位的多元化发展对中型公司非常重要。

他表示："我最担心的事情是，作为一种产业，我们将面临越来越多的收益波动。"这种波动性来自三个方面：市场，运作费用中收入比例不断扩大和非居间化造成的更多浮躁的零散投资者。 投资基

on the alternatives side, more multi-strategy capabilities. This last, he hopes, will build both the hedge funds and the segregated mandate business strands: "There's a large amount of interest from institutional investors in hedge funds. Their first port of call is hedge funds, but their second is multi-strategy. We can catch them at their second point of entry." Bringing in more pension funds as investors would help achieve an important strategic goal: diversifying the investor base. Currently funds of hedge funds and private banks make up most of the alternatives division's clients. Diversification in every possible way is going to be important for mid-sized players in the next few years, says Mr. Meyer.

"The thing that worries me most," he says, "is that as an industry we're going to be faced with increasing earnings volatility." This volatility① will come from three sources: the markets, an increasing proportion of earnings coming from performance fees and a more fickle retail investor as a result of disintermediation②. Diversifying the investor base, building a wider range of investment strategies, focusing on higher margin products such as alternatives and absolute return funds; these are all ways to provide the company with ballast in the coming storm.

(903 words)

---

① volatility [ˌvɔləˈtiləti] n. 挥发度,易变,反复无常
② disintermediation [disˈintəmiːdiˈeiʃən] n. 非居间化(指由储蓄银行存款转为直接的证券投资)

础多元化，建立更加广泛的投资策略，专注利润更高的产品，如替代品和绝对报酬基金，这些都是公司在未来激烈竞争中压舱的各种路径。

知识链接 🔍

Gartmore Investment Management　加特摩尔投资管理公司是一家令人尊敬的独立基金管理公司，主要经营资产管理。公司提供广泛的投资产品和服务，满足零散客户和机构客户的各种需求。

Nationwide Mutual　全美互助保险公司全称为 Nationwide Mutual Insurance Company & Affiliated Companies。它是美国最大的保险和金融服务机构，位于美国俄亥俄州首府哥伦布。公司在美国爱荷华州、得克萨斯州、佛罗里达州和弗吉尼亚州等地均设立了分部。

Hellman & Friedman　海尔曼·弗里德曼私募产权投资公司位于旧金山、伦敦和纽约。1987 年募集首笔机构私募产权基金。多年来管理了 160 亿美元的投资资产，项目涉及 50 多家公司。公司的目标是投资长期股票，从战略上和财政上支持杰出的管理团队在竞争激烈的市场处于可防御的地位掌控公司交易。

题　记

　　智必星诞生于美国科罗拉多州的一个地下室。一名普通的家庭主妇在和她的三个孩子们一起装饰自家的12双卡骆驰鞋子时突发灵感，设计出一系列好玩且有趣的智必星小扣子。这家的男主人敏锐地预见到自己的妻子和孩子们创造出的这些看似不起眼的小扣子的商业价值，于是，家庭式经营公司——智必星应运而生。卡骆驰正式收购智必星品牌后，两个同样充满奇思妙想的品牌强强联手，用富有创意的设计和多变的颜色为顾客提供多系列舒适、多功能性和休闲生活方式的鞋类。"让顾客用个性化的鞋饰充满创意地表达自我个性"是智必星赋予人们的时尚生活体验，智必星的成功意在传达产品设计上的突破与变革。卡骆驰和智必星用它们无穷的创意为人们打造新的惊喜，谱写一章又一章充满传奇色彩的美国梦。

A Woman of Great Originality — Sheri Schmelzer

When an upstart company called Jibbitz agreed to be acquired by Crocs, it had a chance to double its $10 million price tag if its quirky shoe ornaments met certain sales targets. The bet appears to be paying off, especially for Sheri Schmelzer, the mother of three young children who co-founded the company in her basement with her husband, Rich.

With 1,100 variations of the Crocs accessories on the market and many more on the drawing boards, fans keep snapping up new Jibbitz. And the more Jibbitz they buy, the more pairs of Crocs they seem to need. Even people who've shunned① the much-mocked Crocs in the past have become willing wearers now that they can personalize them with Jibbitz charms that celebrate their favorite sports team or other obsession. "We probably design 20 new ones a day," said Sheri Schmelzer, who had been a stay-at-home mom in Boulder until she started churning out so many Jibbitz she now works full time at company headquarters. "It's just endless, the possibilities."

Schmelzer sparked the idea one afternoon when she and her kids began decorating their Crocs with small items they found around their Boulder home. When her husband walked in, Schmelzer exclaimed:

---

① shun [ʃʌn] vt. 避开

谢里·施梅尔策的
创意人生

　　被称为暴发户的智必星公司同意被卡骆驰收购之时，获得了一次机会：如果其独特新奇的鞋饰品能达到特定的销售目标，它1 000万美元的收入将会翻番。 尤其是对三个孩子的母亲谢里·施梅尔策来说，这场赌博似乎得到了回报：是她与丈夫里奇在自家的地下室里一起创建了智必星公司。

　　市场上已有1 100种各式各样的卡骆驰配件，更多的尚在设计之中，粉丝们还在疯狂抢购新款的智必星。 他们购买的智必星越多，卡骆驰的需要量似乎越大。 甚至那些过去不愿意穿广受嘲笑的卡骆驰品牌的人，也成了心甘情愿的消费者，因为智必星的魅力使他们在为其最喜爱的球队助威或其他狂欢的场合彰显自己的个性。 谢里·施梅尔策说："我们一天大概可以设计20种新款的智必星。"在绞尽脑汁制出如此多的智必星之前，她一直是博尔德市的一名家庭主妇，但她目前在公司总部担任专职工作。"设计没有穷尽，一切皆有可能！"

　　一天下午，施梅尔策和孩子们用他们在博尔德的家中找到的小件物品开始装饰卡骆驰鞋时，突然萌生了设计智必星这一想法。 当丈夫进门的时候，施梅尔策兴奋地尖叫："看！ 我们正在装饰卡骆

"Look! We're accessorizing our Crocs." The former software entrepreneur said he immediately knew the family had hit on something big. "Coming from a patent background, I knew we needed to keep a lid on it, " said Rich Schmelzer. "I'm an inventor, so I know exactly what not to do."

The couple met when Sheri Schmelzer needed to find a roommate while studying for a psychology degree at the University of Colorado. She put an advertisement in the paper and Rich responded to it. Now married for years, they have two daughters and one son. Each member of the family has at least several pairs of Crocs, many of which get left en masse at the family's back door. Before the birth of Jibbitz, Sheri Schmelzer devoted most of her time to "raising babies and carpooling." The tall, lean blonde insists little has changed about her life now that she's flat-out busy expanding the company. "I'm still working; I'm just not working at home, " she said.

To celebrate their wedding anniversary, they launched the Jibbitz Web site, jibbitz. com. The orders began rolling in. In the first year, the company sold 8 million of the snap-on charms. "Once it started to take off, which was pretty much immediately, that's all I was doing, " she said. At first, she did most of the work herself and would comb through bead stores and fabric stores for the doodads① she needed to make the shoe ornaments. "I would call my mom in Parker and say, 'I need footballs, ' " she said.

One day when she was busy gluing Jibbitz by hand in her basement, her kids went to the pool with their grandfather. As they were handing out Jibbitz to other kids there, they unwittingly bumped into Lyndon "Duke" Hanson. Intrigued by the reaction children had to the

---

① doodad [ˈduːdæd] *n.* 小玩意儿

驰。"前软件企业家说，他马上认识到家人偶然之间完成了一件大事。里奇·施梅尔策说："我了解专利，意识到我们需要对其保护。我是一位发明家，因此我确实知道哪些是不能做的。"

夫妇俩在科罗拉多大学相遇，当时谢里·施梅尔策正在攻读心理学学位，需要找一位室友。她在报纸上投放了一则广告，里奇对此做出了回应。现在他们已经结婚多年，有两个女儿，一个儿子。每位家庭成员至少有好几双卡骆驰，后门口就扔着好多双。创建智必星之前，谢里·施梅尔策绝大部分时间在"带孩子和拼车"。即使她为扩展公司忙得天昏地暗，这位高挑、瘦削、金发碧眼的女性仍然坚持认为她的生活并没有发生多大改变。她说："我仍然在工作，只是不在家工作而已。"

为了庆祝结婚纪念日，这对夫妇创建了智必星网站：**jibbitz. com**。订单开始如雪片般向施梅尔策夫妇涌来。公司在第一年售出 800 万人扣入式配饰。她说："一旦项目启动，我所做的一切就是要让它尽快上市。"最初，她承担了大量的工作，亲自到卖珠子和面料的商店去搜寻装饰鞋子的小玩意。她说："我会给住在帕克的妈妈打电话，跟她说，'我需要一些足球'。"

一天，她在地下室手工黏合智必星，孩子们跟祖父一块去游泳。当他们给那儿的其他孩子分发智必星时，无意中撞见林登"公爵"汉森。孩子们对智必星的反应引起了卡骆驰的合伙创办人汉森的兴趣，他给施梅尔策的孩子们一张名片，叫他们请妈妈给他打电话。当时，总部设在里沃特的卡骆驰并不具备收购其他公司的资本。卡骆驰自己干这一行也只有几年，上市也还不到两年。但公司主管会见了施梅尔策夫妇，建议他们继续努力，进一步证明

Jibbitz, the co-founder of Crocs gave the Schmelzer kids a business card and asked them to have their mom call him. At the time, Niwot-based Crocs lacked the wherewithal① to be buying companies. Crocs itself has been in business for only a few years and went public less than two years ago. But executives met with the Schmelzers and advised them to go out and prove themselves some more.

About a year after the launch of the Jibbitz Web site, Crocs bought the company for $10 million and promised the Schmelzers another $10 million if the company could deliver more results. "I think they're well on their way to making that," Hanson said. "They've certainly exceeded our expectations." Jibbitz got a different sort of payout recently when it collected $1.8 million, plus attorney fees and other costs, after winning a patent infringement battle against Joinworld Industrial & Trading Limited and its principals. The U.S. District Court in Nevada ruled Jibbitz owns all rights to the shoe charm designs copied by the defendant.

The company now has roughly 80 employees, including a team of staff designers who work out of its brightly hued② headquarters in an office park east of Boulder's Foothills Parkway. A round rug in Sheri Schmelzer's office reads, "All you need is love." The name Jibbitz is shorthand for flibbertygibbit, a nickname given to Sheri because of her tendency to talk a lot.

Jibbitz recently moved to the new space when it outgrew its former offices on the Pearl Street Mall. Some of the walls in its new building are painted lime green, orange and other striking colors — some of the same ones found in the Schmelzers' family home. The couple apparently has

---

① wherewithal [ˈhweəwiˈðɔːl] *n.* 钱财
② hued [hjuːd] *adj.* 有某种色调的

276

自己。

智必星网站推出约一年之后，卡骆驰以 1 000 万美元的价格买下了这家公司，并承诺，如果该公司能够交付更多的成果，将会另外支付 1 000 万美元。 汉森说："我认为他们正在以自己的方式实现目标。 他们的确已经超出我们的预想了。"智必星最近获利 180 万美元之后，付了一笔多少有点不同的支出，包括律师费和其他费用。他们打赢了与联合世界工贸有限公司之间的专利侵权官司。 美国内华达州的地方法院裁定，智必星对被告仿制的鞋样装饰设计拥有所有权。

公司目前拥有大约 80 名员工，包括设计团队的工作人员，他们在色调明亮的总部办公，这是一个位于博尔德山麓大道以东的办公场所。 谢里的办公室里有一张圆形地毯，上面写着："爱是你需要的全部。"智必星这一名字是 flibbertygibbit 的缩写，是谢里的昵称，源于她健谈的性格。

智必星最近搬到了新的办公地点，因为公司规模已经超出其之前位于珍珠街购物中心的办事处。 新公司的一些墙壁被刷成酸橙绿、橙色和其他鲜艳的颜色，其中有些颜色可以在施梅尔策家里找到。 这对夫妇显然无意离开公司。 即使他们全家收拾东西去东海岸度假，也随身带着各种小饰物，以便能够远程工作，绞尽脑汁，不断创造新产品。 虽然里奇·施梅尔策在休假期间不像平常那样工作成性，但他说妻子现在却一如既往。 他说："我只是坐在一旁，看她不停地工作。 我认为她不知道如何度假。"

谢里·施梅尔策担任公司的首席设计师，里奇则担任总裁。 她说："我对创意比较在行，但对业务运营一窍不通。"尽管她梦想赋

no intention of moving on from the company. Even if they packed up for a family vacation on the East Coast, they still took their various gadgets with them so that they can work remotely and keep churning out new product ideas. While Rich Schmelzer no longer compulsively works while he is supposed to be on vacation, he says his wife now plays that role. "I just sit and watch her work away," he said. "I don't think she knows how to take one."

Sheri Schmelzer holds the title of chief design officer, and Rich serves as president. "I'm certainly more on the creative side," she says. "I didn't know how to run a business." Although she dreams up new themes for Jibbitz, she also works with various big-name concerns to initiate licensing deals that allow the company to attract new markets for its accessories. Harry Potter fanatics will soon be able to wear Jibbitz emblazoned① with the Hogwarts sorting hat and the crests② from the various houses. Then there are the deals with comics superheroes, including Batman, Superman and Wonder Woman. Similar agreements with Disney, the NFL and the NHL also have expanded Jibbitz's appeal. For at least $ 2.49 a pop, it's easy to spend way more on Jibbitz than the pair of Crocs that hold them.

The Schmelzers also have begun to cater to those who want Jibbitz but don't wear Crocs. A line of bags, hats and other products come with openings made expressly for snapping on Jibbitz. "I've been having a blast," Sheri Schmelzer said. "I don't want it to stop."

(1,055 words)

---

① emblazon [im'bleizən] vt. 用纹章装饰
② crest [krest] n. (鸟类的)羽冠

予智必星新的主题，但她也选择和各种各样的大品牌合作，启动营业执照交易，允许公司为其配件吸引新的市场。 哈利·波特的狂热追捧者很快能穿上印有智必星标志的霍格沃茨等级魔帽和来自不同家庭的羽毛装饰，还有漫画超级英雄，包括蝙蝠侠、超人和神奇女侠。 公司与迪士尼、国家橄榄球大联盟和国家冰球联盟也签订了同样的协议，这些都增强了智必星的吸引力。 如果每次至少花费 2.49 美元，那么购买智必星比购买有智必星装饰的卡骆驰更划算。

施梅尔策夫妇也开始迎合那些想拥有智必星、但又不穿卡骆驰的顾客。 一系列的提包、帽子和其他配套产品显然引发了对智必星的抢购热潮。 谢里·施梅尔策说："我一直处于爆发状态。 我不希望这种状态停下来。"

知识链接

Crocs 卡骆驰是一家总部位于美国科罗拉多州的鞋履设计、生产及零售商，以卡骆驰品牌在市场上推出舒适、愉悦和色彩丰富的男女休闲品牌鞋款。卡骆驰创立于 2002 年，最初的产品市场定位是帆船运动和户外运动者。2003年，融入时尚和趣味的多功能卡骆驰风靡全球。2010 年，亚洲市场推出"感受愉快革命"的卡洛驰营销主题，受到不同消费者的青睐。

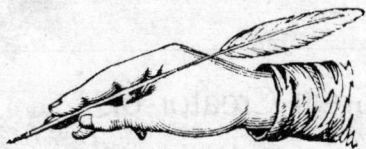

题　记

　　在世界航空业的史册上，最伟大的创业者无疑是出身名门的耶鲁大学毕业生、泛美航空的创始人胡安·特里普。他既是一位目光远大的航空运输业设计师，也是该公司的掌舵人。特里普利用能在水上起飞和降落的船身式螺旋桨飞机，率先进行跨太平洋和大西洋的定期航班运营。在他充满传奇的一生中，胡安·特里普一直受到强大的美国式本能的驱动，在行情发生之前洞察市场，然后促使其成为现实。他利用自己的创造力、善于说服人的本领以及巨大的人格魅力，缔造了自己的航空王国，令他的同辈人相形见绌，同时也改变了整个世纪的进程。他在职业生涯的鼎盛期，曾经控制了美国所有的海外航空线路，拥有覆盖太平洋、大西洋以及整个南美洲地区的专营权，从而使空中旅行延伸到了先前曾被认为无法到达的地方，刺激了大规模国际航空的腾飞，让进行国际飞行的美国人数量大增。从实际的意义上说，他称得上是国际航空业务的奠基人。

The Great Creator of Airways — Juan Trippe

By business school standards, Juan Trippe was not a model chief executive. He didn't delegate well. He made big deals without telling his top managers. He almost single-handedly built a world airline, Pan American, but often acted as if he owned the world. He also had a vision that would change it, at least as regards airline travel. While his Pan Am does not survive today, his vision does.

He graduated from Yale and worked briefly on Wall Street but got thoroughly bored. Planes fascinated him, though. Trippe was convinced that the future of travel was in the air. With an inheritance, Trippe began a business with Long Island Airways in New York, a taxi service for the well-heeled. When that failed, he raised money from some wealthy Yale pals and joined Colonial Air Transport, which won the first U.S. airmail contract, between New York City and Boston. That same crowd liked to play in the Caribbean (excellent choice), where he created Pan American Airways Inc. from a merger of three groups. Trippe began service with a flight from Key West, Fla., to Havana, Cuba.

What characterized Trippe thereafter was an uncanny① ability to pace his airline's growth with the range of the airliner as it slowly evolved:

---

① uncanny [ʌnˈkæni] *adj.* 不寻常的

航空业的伟大创业者
——胡安·特里普

按照商学院的标准，胡安·特里普并不是一位模范的首席执行官。 他没有完成好委托任务。 他没有告诉高层管理人员，就做成了数桩大笔生意。 他几乎是单枪匹马地建立了一个世界航空公司——泛美航空公司，但他经常表现出一副模样，好像自己是整个世界的主宰者。 他还有改变世界的幻想，至少在航空旅行方面改变这个世界。 虽然今天他的泛美航空公司已不复存在，但他的先见之明依然大放异彩。

特里普毕业于耶鲁大学，在华尔街有过短暂的工作经历，但很快便对工作彻底失去兴趣。 然而，他却对飞机着迷，特里普确信，未来的旅行一定是在空中。 特里普用继承的一份遗产开始与纽约长岛航空公司合伙做生意，为富人提供出租车服务。 生意失败后，他从一些耶鲁大学的富人朋友那里筹集资金，加入殖民地航空运输，赢得了纽约市和波士顿市之间的第一份美国航空邮件合同。 这群合作伙伴喜欢在加勒比（最佳选择）地区飞行，他在该地区合并了三家公司，并创建了泛美航空公司。 特里普开始了从佛罗里达州的基

first crawling from island to island across the Caribbean and into Mexico, then extending to Central and South America. Finally, it was Trippe's backing of the flying boat, the first Pan Am Flying Clippers, that pioneered global routes: across the Pacific and, in the late 1930s, across the Atlantic. By the end of World War II, Trippe had in place a route system that was truly global.

Before anyone else, he believed in airline travel as something to be enjoyed by ordinary mortals, not just a globe-trotting elite. Other airlines didn't think or act that way. Trippe decided to introduce a "tourist class" fare from New York to London. He cut the round-trip fare more than half, to $275, $1,684 in today's dollars, which makes current pricing a bargain. This went over like a lead balloon in the industry, where airfares were fixed by a cartel, the International Air Transport Association; it didn't want to hear about the tourist class. Incredibly, Britain closed its airports to Pan Am flights that had tourist seats. Pan Am was forced to switch to remote Shannon, Ireland. The industry's aversion① to competition. The first 707s were flying with five-abreast seating, two on one side of the aisle, three on the other. Trippe switched to six abreast and cut fares, and the Pan Am jet clippers made flying "the pond" far more accessible. By 1965 the company was predicting that 35 million people would be flying international routes and that there would be a 200% increase by 1980.

The relentless Trippe had the big idea: he reasoned that mass air travel could come to the international routes only with a larger airplane — a much larger airplane. Trippe put the notion to his old friend Bill Allen, the boss of Boeing, saying he wanted a jet two-and-a-half times the size of

---

① aversion [ə'vəːʃən] *n.* 厌恶

韦斯特到古巴的哈瓦那的航班服务。

此后，特里普形成了自己的特点，随着航空公司的缓慢发展，他以一种神奇的本领使公司的增长速度与大型客机的飞行范围保持一致：首先穿越加勒比地区的不同岛屿进入墨西哥，然后延伸到中、南美洲。最后，正是特里普的后补飞行船，即第一批泛美飞行船，开创了全球路线：横跨太平洋，并在 20 世纪 30 年代后期，穿越大西洋彼岸。到第二次世界大战结束时，特里普开发的航线形成了真正的全球性系统。

他最早认为，航空旅行不仅要为穿梭于全球的精英们服务，也应该让普通人得到享受。其他的航空公司尚未形成这种意识，也没有采取相应的行动。特里普决定在从纽约到伦敦的航班上引入"经济舱"票价。他把往返票价削减了一大半，降到 275 美元，相当于今天的 1 684 美元，使得现行定价非常划算。这一举措对航空业毫无作用，该行业中的飞机票价由国际航空运输协会这个卡特尔寡头垄断组织规定，它可不想听到有什么"经济舱"。令人难以置信的是，英国关闭了拥有经济舱位的泛美航空航班的机场。泛美航空被迫将航线切换到遥远的爱尔兰香农机场。这个行业厌恶竞争。首批 707 型飞机有五个并列的座位，两个在过道的一边，其余三个在另一边。特里普将之换为六个并排座位，并降低了票价，因此泛美客机更容易吸引旅客。到 1965 年，该公司预测，将有 3 500 万人乘坐国际航线，到 1980 年将有 200% 的增幅。

the 707. It was a staggering① request given the development cost of the 707. And Trippe didn't stop with size. Trippe set for Boeing the goal of reducing that 30%. By pure chance, it was Trippe himself who gave the jumbo its signature bulge. In a rare lapse of vision, Trippe thought the 747 would be superseded② by a big supersonic jet, as cheap to run as a subsonic③ jet. Some hope. And so as co-creator of the 747, Trippe gave us the world's traveling machine. Virgin Atlantic was launched in June 1984 with 747s at the point when it was really shrinking the world and air travel was truly democratized, as Trippe intended.

Sadly, the 747 also sank Pan Am. Trippe bought too many 747s in the early 1970s. A world oil crisis hit airline travel hard, and his business never recovered. Boeing itself almost went belly-up because of the cost of launching the 747. Trippe had been a continuous innovator, but the sad irony is that he failed to re-invent his company for the leaner, far more competitive age he had done so much to shape: the age of travel for Everyman. A decade after his death, his airline, substantially dismembered, finally expired in 1991.

Throughout his career, Juan Trippe had been driven by the great American instinct for seeing a market before it happened and then making it happen. In a real sense, he fathered the international airline business. To do so, he took on the entire airline industry, and risked his company to see his vision through. You've just got to admire a guy like that.

(794 words)

---

① staggering [ˈstæɡəriŋ] *adj.* 令人震惊的
② supersede [ˌsjuːpəˈsiːd] *vt.* 取代
③ subsonic [ˌsʌbˈsɔnik] *adj.* 次音速的

　　冷酷无情的特里普雄心勃勃：他判断出大规模空中旅行要向国际航线发展，只能跟较大的飞机——大得多的飞机合作。特里普把他的想法告诉了老朋友、波音公司的老板比尔·艾伦，说他需要一架相当于707两倍半的飞机。考虑到707型飞机的造价成本，这个要求实在令人大为吃惊。然而特里普没有在飞机大小上做出让步，他为波音公司制定了降低30%成本的目标。正是特里普本人让这个庞然大物身价大涨，这真是纯属偶然。特里普的洞察力很少出现偏差，他认为大型超音速喷气机将取代747型飞机，运行成本却与亚音速喷气式飞机一样低。因此，特里普作为747型飞机的共同创造者，给我们的世界带来了旅行机器。1984年6月，特里普携747型飞机成立维尔京大西洋航空公司之时，它从真正意义上缩小了世界，空中旅行真实地实现了民主化，特里普就是这么打算的。

　　可悲的是，747型飞机又毁了泛美航空。20世纪70年代初，特里普购买了太多的747型飞机。世界石油危机严重打击了航空旅行业，从那时起，他的生意再也没有恢复。由于启动747型飞机耗费了过高的成本，波音公司也几乎破产。特里普从来没有停止过创新，但是，他没能做到在收益较差、更具竞争力的时代，即普通人旅行的时代中重整公司，尽管他为此付出了许多努力。他去世10年后，其航空公司的财产被瓜分，最终在1991年倒闭。

　　在他的整个职业生涯中，胡安·特里普一直受到强大的美国式本能的驱动，在行情发生之前洞察市场，然后促使其成为现实。从

实际意义上来说，他称得上是国际航空业务的奠基人。 为了扮演好这一角色，他接管了整个航空业，并拿自己的公司冒险，以证实他的远见卓识。 你不得不钦佩像他这样的人物。

知识链接

Pan American 泛美航空公司是泛美世界航空公司（Pan American World Airways）的简称。泛美航空公司自 1930 年成立至 1991 年倒闭前，一直是美国的主要航空公司之一。其母公司为 Pan Am Corp。泛美为航空业带来很多革新，包括大量使用喷射客机、珍宝客机和电脑化订位系统等。这些渐行渐远的传奇已成为 20 世纪的文化象征。

题 记

现代人谈到 NBA，就会联想起迈克尔·乔丹；谈到高尔夫，就会提及老虎泰格·伍兹；谈到 F-1，就会仰慕迈克尔·舒马赫；当人们谈到首席执行官时，就不能不对杰克·韦尔奇佩服得五体投地。这位通用电气历史上最年轻的董事长和首席执行官，在短短 20 年间，将一个弥漫着官僚主义气息的公司，打造成一个充满朝气、富有生机的企业巨头。他启动的"解决方案"的计划，鼓励通用所有的员工参与解决问题和发明创新。他推行的"六个西格玛"质量标准、全球化和电子商务，几乎重新定义了现代企业。他实施的无边界公司行动，摆脱了角落办公室、官僚作风、"无法就地创造"的综合症。他倾尽全力打造公司文化和培植人力资源，通过增强实力来提升公司的长期竞争优势。今天的世界对他教授的价值观和行为准则仍然感激不尽：建立在绝对公正基础上的相互信任，对世界最先进的理念和最优秀的人才永无止境、"无边界"的求贤若渴。

The CEO's Legend
— Jack Welch

When he was selected as the new CEO of General Electric, Jack Welch was certainly not everyone's top pick. Many folks thought he was too young. At 45 he was youngest GE CEO ever. Others thought he was a bit of a playboy, not right for the GE culture. Some said he was too aggressive.

Welch succeeded Reg Jones as CEO of General Electric. He had big shoes to fill. Jones had been CEO of the Year and the Most Admired Business Leader in America. He'd gotten results, leading GE to 26 consecutive quarters of improved earnings through two recessions. He inaugurated several management innovations. Welch knew things looked good, but he also thought that big changes were needed. He started out by ripping apart the company he inherited. He took layers out of management. He laid off over 100,000 people. That earned him the nickname, "Neutron Jack," after the neutron bomb that kills the people but leaves the buildings intact. In fact, a lot of buildings disappeared too. Welch divested GE of billions of dollars in businesses. He told the company that every GE business unit should be number one or number two in its market. Or else what? "Fix it, sell it or close it."

Under Fred Borch and Reg Jones, GE had been one of the inventers of many practices of corporate strategic planning. They'd been developers

首席执行官的传奇
——杰克·韦尔奇

　　杰克·韦尔奇当选为新一任通用电气首席执行官，但他并不是每个人的首选。 很多人认为他太年轻了。 45 岁的他是通用电气公司有史以来最年轻的首席执行官。 另外一些人认为他有点玩世不恭，不符合通用电气公司的文化。 还有一些人说他太喜欢寻衅找岔子。

　　韦尔奇继雷吉·琼斯后出任通用电气公司的首席执行官。 他面临的任务艰巨，责任重大。 琼斯曾获得年度首席执行官和美国最受尊敬的商界领袖两项殊荣。 在两次经济衰退期间，他领导公司连续 26 个季度提高了盈利，成绩显著。 而且他还开创了几项管理革新。尽管韦尔奇清楚公司状况良好，但他仍然认为有必要对公司进行重大变革。 他从彻底整顿继任的公司开始着手，削减管理层，裁减 10 万多名员工。 为此他赢得了一个绰号"中子杰克"，这名字和中子弹有关，中子弹杀人但对建筑却毫无损坏。 事实上，许多建筑物也随之消失。 韦尔奇出让了通用电气数十亿美元的业务。 他对公司职员说，通用的每个业务单元都应该在市场排名第一或第二。 否则会怎么样呢？"处理、出售或关闭。"

of concepts like the business unit and the Attractiveness/Position Matrix. Businesses that wanted to do better strategic planning sent folks on a pilgrimage to Fairfield, Connecticut to learn from General Electric's full time strategic planners. Welch zapped the planners, but kept the concepts. He moved strategic planning into the business units and made it a line function. That wasn't uncommon behavior for him. Lots of corporate, bureaucratic functions wound up in business units, or being eliminated all together. Then there was the Great Research Department icon. After all this company was originally founded by Thomas Edison, the inventor of the modern concept of research and development. GE's Research and Development Center, supplemented by over 100 product-oriented labs was one of the most respected operations in the world. It boasted two Nobel Laureates[1].

After the slashing, severing and selling, Welch started making his own, more positive mark. He started a program called Work-Out whose purpose was to get all GE employees involved in problem solving and innovation. He said that, "We want to make our quality so special, so valuable to our customers, so important to their success, that our products become their only real value choice." One way to do that was Welch's Six Sigma Quality program to reduce defects to 3.4 per million operations. There were acquisitions, too. They've averaged about one hundred a year. In that mix are success like RCA and failures, like Kidder Peabody.

And what was the biggest change from Welch's perspective? Here's the answer from an interview in Business Week. "The biggest change we

---

① Nobel Laureate [ˈlɔːriət] *n.* 诺贝尔奖得主

　　弗雷德·博尔奇和雷吉·琼斯任职期间，通用电气公司一直是公司战略规划的很多条例的发起者之一。　他们已经开创了诸如业务单元和市场吸引力/业务地位矩阵的理念。　希望制定更出色的战略规划的企业将员工送到康涅狄格州的费尔菲尔德，向通用电气公司的全职战略规划者学习。　韦尔奇不赞成战略规划，但保留了他们的理念。　他把战略规划应用到业务单位，发挥它的部门职能作用。对他而言，这种做法再平常不过了。　许多公司、官僚机构职能在业务单位不再奏效，或者完全被消除。　大型研究部的偶像作用也发挥到了极致。　毕竟，这家公司最初是由提出现代研发概念的托马斯·爱迪生创立的。　通用电气公司的研发中心，有超过 100 个以上以产品为导向的实验室作为补充，是世界上最受尊敬的研究机构之一。该中心以拥有两位诺贝尔奖桂冠获得者引以为豪。

　　在降价、分解、抛售之后，韦尔奇开始以自己更加正面的形象出现在人们的视野中。　他启动了一项名为"解决方案"的计划，目的在于让通用所有的员工参与解决问题和发明创新。　他说："我们希望产品的质量对顾客来说如此特别，如此有价值，对他们的成功如此重要，以至于我们的产品成为他们唯一货真价实的选择。"要做到此，一种方法是实施韦尔奇的"六西格玛质量"计划，在每百万笔交易中把次品降低到 3.4 的比率。　公司还有收购项目，年平均约达一百次。　收购中有成功有失败，前者如对美国无线电公司的收购，后者如对基德皮博迪公司的收购。

　　在韦尔奇看来，公司最大的变革是什么呢？　从《商业周刊》的

made, without question, was the move to a boundaryless company. We got rid of the corner offices, the bureaucracy, the 'not-invented-here' syndrome. Instead, we got every mind in the game, got the best out of all our people."

How can we assess his performance after twenty years as head of the largest corporation in the world? We could just listen to the business press. That evaluation would be loud, laudatory and include multiple mentions of the word legendary. There would be lots of references to "The House that Jack Built." But the business press has fed itself on the Cult of the Celebrity CEO for so long now, that we're more likely to get gushing[①] admiration rather than good analysis. And Welch is a major celebrity. He gets as much press coverage as many movie stars. And, recently he got a $ 7.1 million book advance. That was the largest advance ever for a nonfiction book, until Bill Clinton came along.

We could compare the performance of Welch's GE with other large corporations over the same period of time. In this company, Welch looks pretty good. During his tenure, GE outperformed 93% of the Fortune 500 in total return on investment. There are several problems with this method, though. First, most of those companies haven't had the same CEO for the whole period. American companies have gotten into the habit of firing CEOs if the quarterly numbers don't soar and soar quickly. Beyond that, this method also compares companies with very different challenges and starting points.

We could always compare Welch to his predecessors among GE CEOS. That's really tough competition, because GE has had a succession of great

---

① gushing ['gʌʃiŋ] *adj.* 过分热情的

一次采访中可以找到答案。"毫无疑问，我们做出的最大变革是推行无边界公司行动。 我们摆脱了角落办公室、官僚作风、'无法就地创造'的综合症。 取而代之的是，我们让每一个人都参与到游戏中来，使他们发挥出自己的最佳状态。"

杰克·韦尔奇20年来一直担任世界上最大公司的总裁，我们应当如何评价他的成就呢？ 我们可以听一下商业报刊的评价。 它们的评价高调且不吝赞美，多次提到传奇这个词。 很多评价涉及"杰克建造的房子"。 但是很长时间以来，商业报刊助长了自身对名人首席执行官的崇拜，我们看到的更可能是装腔作势的赞赏而不是实事求是的分析。 韦尔奇是一位大名人，他就像许多电影明星一样，关于他的新闻报道颇多。 最近，他得到了一份710万美元的预付稿酬。 在比尔·克林顿的书问世之前，他的稿酬是迄今为止非小说类文学作品中最高的。

我们可以把韦尔奇在通用电气公司的成就与同时期的其他大公司进行对比。 在通用电气公司，韦尔奇看起来相当令人满意。 在他任职期间，通用电气公司在投资总收益上超过财富500强93%。 当然，用这种方法做比较存在一些问题。 首先，从整体上看，这些公司中的大多数在这段时期更换过不同的首席执行官。 如果季度销售额没有上升或上升不快，美国公司有解雇首席执行官的习惯。 除此之外，这种方法便于公司对比不同的挑战和起点。

我们也总是把韦尔奇与通用的前任首席执行官们做比较，这实在是很苛刻的竞争，因为通用电气公司的历届首席执行官都很了不

ones. In fact, based on average annual return on equity, Welch comes out number five among the seven CEOs that GE has had since 1892. The best way to measure Welch or any other CEO is based on how they do CEO work. CEO work is strategic. Strategy is what you do consistently to increase long term profitability and long term competitive advantage. It's not about increasing stock price or even shareholder value, though those may be by products of good strategy.

Let's drill down further. You build profitability by delivering value. For a CEO, that means that you put programs and processes and portfolios in place that are designed to deliver value over the long term. Welch's Work Out and Six Sigma programs certainly meet this criterion. You increase long term competitive advantage by building on your strengths. The best strengths to build on are those that involve culture and people. That's because those are the strengths that it's hardest for the competition to duplicate. Welch spent a lot of time on people stuff. He taught each month at GE's management training center. He personally reviewed the yearly appraisals of GE's top 3,000 managers. He wrote lots of personal notes to lots of people.

Welch retired after 40 years with General Electric more than 20 as Chairman of the Board of Directors of CEO. The world today is enormously grateful for the values and behaviors he taught: mutual trust based on absolute integrity, and the unending, insatiable, "boundaryless" thirst for the world's best ideas and best people.

(1,029 words)

起。 事实上，基于平均年度股本回报率，自 1892 年以来，韦尔奇在通用电气公司八名首席执行官中排名第五。 衡量韦尔奇或其他七位首席执行官中的任何一位的业绩，最好的方式要看他们如何执行首席执行官的工作。 首席执行官的工作具有战略性意义。 策略就是为增加长期收益和长期竞争优势而始终如一地工作。 它不是增加股票价格，甚至提升股东价值，尽管从产品角度来看这些可能是锦囊妙计。

让我们做进一步的探讨。 你通过传递价值来创造收益。 作为首席执行官，这意味着你将计划、流程和投资组合放在合适的位置，用于长久地传递价值。 韦尔奇的"解决方案"和"六个西格玛"两项计划显然符合这个标准。 你通过增强实力来提升长期的竞争优势。 增强最大的实力涉及公司文化和人力资源，因为这两种实力对于竞争而言最难复制。 韦尔奇花费了大量的时间培训员工。他每月在通用电气公司的管理培训中心授课。 他亲自审查通用电气公司 3 000 名高管的年度评估。 他给许多人写过大量的私人信函。

杰克·韦尔奇在通用公司工作 40 年后退休，其间有 20 多年一直担任首席执行官董事会主席。 今天的世界对他教授的价值观和行为准则仍然感激不尽：建立在绝对公正基础上的相互信任，对世界最先进的理念和最优秀的人才永无止境、"无边界"的求贤若渴。

知识链接

RCA 美国无线电公司（Radio Corporation of America，简称 RCA）于 1919

年由美国联邦政府创建，1985 年由美国通用电气公司并购，1988 年转至汤姆逊麾下。历史上曾生产电视机、显像管、录放影机、音响及通讯产品，雇用员工约 5.5 万人，分布全球 45 个国家，产品广销一百多个国家。RCA 现在已全面进入中国存储市场，凭其高新技术产品给中国的存储市场带来了强撼冲击。

GE 通用电气公司(General Electric Company)是世界上最大的多元化服务性公司，从飞机发动机、发电设备到金融服务，从医疗造影、电视节目到塑料，GE 公司致力于通过多项技术和服务创造更美好的生活。目前，公司业务遍及世界 100 多个国家，拥有员工 31.5 万人。